YOUR GRANNY'S COOK BOOK

Old Family Favourites from all over the country,
contributed by *Daily Express* readers, and
compiled and edited with footnotes and recipes

by Sheila Hutchins

Illustrated by Don Roberts

A DAILY EXPRESS PUBLICATION

CONTENTS

and space for your own Family Favourites

Printed by Ben Johnson & Co. Ltd., York YO2 5SS
and published by Beaverbrook Newspapers Ltd.,
Fleet Street, London EC4A 2WJ

HOW IT ALL HAPPENED

In a small country like ours with transport what it is and nowhere very far from anywhere else it is amazing to find that there is still any regional cooking. But there is, even if one seldom sees it in hotels and restaurants. This book proves it.

The whole thing began when I said in the *Daily Express* two years ago that there were hundreds of marvellous old dishes in Britain that were gradually being forgotten, wonderful things that your granny and my granny used to cook. and that if we were going to save these things we would have to do it quickly before they died out and disappeared. For Britain is changing and our eating habits are becoming international and Americanised, and it will be a great pity, not least for the tourist trade, if everywhere becomes exactly like everywhere else. So I asked you to send me recipes for things just like your granny cooked. It had to be granny, I thought, for it is she who remembers the really good cooking.

I got thousands and thousands of recipes from all over the country. I have had letters from retired cooks, from former kitchen maids at great country houses, from farmers' wives, from aunts, great-aunts and grandmothers, some in spidery copperplate handwriting. From men as well as women, sailors, Chelsea pensioners, eel jelliers, and salmon smokers. They speak in many different voices with many different accents and most of the recipes have their own regional flavour.

Even I have been amazed at the excellence of the dishes. There is nothing quaint or gimmicky about them. These are real family favourites. People have fished round and hunted out the old well-loved recipes from behind the kitchen clock, some of which have been enjoyed in their family for more than a hundred years.

Some readers sent me whole hand-written cookery books, and there are memories of hot dinners from long distant childhoods, of old brick ovens and black leaded coal ranges. *Daily Express* colleagues have chipped in with their own family favourites. And if you think the traditional cooking of this country is just a lot of stodge which takes ages to prepare you have a pleasant surprise coming. Forget the granny image if you wish, you will get a lot of flavour from just eating your way through them. For this is real food, it opens up a whole new concept of British cooking.

There are recipes for beef stewed in beer with cheddar cheese dumplings, devilled pheasants, legs of lamb in pastry, duck pie and Cornish under-roast, for red flannel hash and Liverpool scouse. There are all kinds of half-forgotten lovely things which some people always eat for Christmas, and I have given details of some of the often neglected gastronomic delicacies, the Dorset knobs, white truffles, Welsh salted duckling, fresh water prawns, elvers, malt whiskies, Scottish venison and Manx kippers which we don't always appreciate as we should. Our foreign tourists would love these but how often do they find any in British hotels?

I should like to see some of the good old British vulgarity brought back into the kitchen. British cooking took a turn for the worse when it began to be thought vulgar to dip your bread in your gravy. I should like to see more people with napkins tied round their necks and hunks of bread to mop up the thick brown gravy and even for salvaging the last vestiges of it from the ends of their moustaches.

Our beef and lamb and salmon are still the best in the world but it is astonishing how seldom our national dishes are now really properly cooked. When did you last savour the pleasure of hot home made steak and kidney pudding, smelling deliciously of onions, with second helpings hot enough to mist up your spectacles? There is something extremely comforting and heart warming about old fashioned British food, the mere thought of boiled beef and carrots, warm and pink and trembling with soggy onions and suet dumplings in thin clear gravy boggles the mind and enhances the appetite whether or not you have it with large black pickled walnuts or just a modicum of English mustard and a pint of mild and bitter.

Much of the food that granny cooked, though cheap, is still as delicious as ever and many of her slow simmered stews and sausage pots and things would be worth making in double quantity so that half may be stored in the deep freezer.

You will find dishes for high teas and harvest suppers, recipes from English vicarages, huge country houses and the back streets of some of our gloomier cities as well as from the Shetlands, Guernsey, Skye and Lewis. Open this book and you can almost hear the whole country chewing. There are recipes for Breakfast Railway cakes, Aunt Emma's biscuits and Poachers' soup. Then there are some absolutely superb and very surprising rabbit recipes which I have neither seen nor tasted anywhere else. Many of them would be equally suitable for the now cheaper chicken. There are Edwardian party dishes, mouth watering farm dinners, hand-raised pork pies, Lincolnshire Whitsuntide cakes, partan bree and Cornish pasties, saddle of Devon lamb stuffed with pâte de foie gras and topped with toasted cheese, as well as hairy willies, potted hough, clapshot and clootie dumplings. It will be a pity if these things are forgotten and become museum pieces.

It was impossible, of course, to include everything and difficult when there were many similar recipes to decide which to print. For faggots, for instance. Judging by the number of recipes I got these must be one of the best loved, if least eaten dishes in the country, though they are very easy to make. Some people will disagree with me and say that things left out are the very ones that ought to have been in. Yorkshire pudding is made differently, for example, in Barnsley, Leeds and Bradford. But which way is right and how many recipes do you want? There are lots of things like that. In the end I abandoned any kind of system and just put in what I liked best which is the only honest way to do it. Sometimes I have had to explain the method in greater detail or perhaps more clearly than granny but I have never added anything to the recipe. The notes and things with no name on are, I'm afraid, my own work. If your particular recipe didn't get in please forgive me for I have done my best.

I do want to thank my *Daily Express* readers very much for all their wonderful letters and I now feel that I have thousands of charming friends all over the country. I am also very grateful for the enthusiasm of my secretary Miss Jill Walker who has been tireless at deciphering frail and faded hand-writing and in collating your letters, reminding me of the most delicious dishes as well as much else and sometimes merely preventing your letters, when the window was open, from fluttering up like a cloud of fantail pigeons and settling somewhere else.

1971   **Sheila Hutchins**

East Anglia

Cambridgeshire. Parts of Essex (round Colchester). Huntingdon-shire. Lincolnshire (Lindsey, Holland and Kesteven). Norfolk. Suffolk. The Broads. The Fens. The Wash. Sandringham. Cambridge.

Agricultural Products

Norfolk Ducklings, Norfolk Turkeys, Malting Barley, Peas, Wheat, Potatoes, Onions. Lincolnshire rainbow trout farms. There are also huge oven-ready duckling farms in Lincolnshire where one can see thousands and thousands of ducks white against the hillside. Norfolk Biffins — dried red cheeked apples sold in Norwich.

Gastronomic Specialities

Colchester Steak, Kidney and Oyster Pie; West Mersea, Colchester, Oysters; Norfolk Partridge, Pheasant and Wild Duck; Yarmouth Bloaters; Suffolk Sweet Cured Hams; Norfolk Hog's Head "Cheese"; Lincolnshire Hand Raised Pies; Trinity College Cambridge Burnt Cream. Maldon Salt, Stuffed Chine, Epping Sausages, Cambridge Sauce, Pig's Fry and Norfolk Dumplings, Samphire. Cambridge Sausages, Whelks, King's Lynn Shrimps, Leigh-on-Sea Cockles, Norwich Roast Cygnet. Suffolk Rusks, Grantham Gingerbread.

FISH

COCKLES AND WHELKS

At Brancaster Staithe, Norfolk, the boatmen go out six to seven miles for the whelk fishing, boiling their catch in big coppers in sheds on the edge of the marshes and sending them off by motor lorry to Birmingham and London. They often have a glut of whelks but though the fishermen like them hot in Norfolk nobody seems to have thought of a good way of serving them. When I was in the local pub there, everyone seemed to be drinking keg mild and talking about bird watching, and when one of the fishermen produced a hot boiled whelk from a paper in his pocket, began slicing it with a penknife and offered it to me as a sort of *aperitivos*, I nearly screamed. Without the shell they look like nothing in particular, though in fact when not too tough they are very good. Unlike the French who are ready to tackle anything *gastronomique*, I think

1

English people are put off whelks because they think they are rather common.

The Jolly Sailors, at Brancaster Staithe, is a tiny pub miles from anywhere, it specialises in roast Breckland duckling, pineapple fritters, lemon pancakes, roast chicken with hot cockle sauce, and also hot buttered Brancaster cockles with brown bread and butter. I thought they were delicious, the kind of thing you might expect in some remote Spanish village. They bring you a great heaped up blue and white soup plate of hot cockles, and a brown Nottingham jar for the empty shells, a plate of bread and butter, a sauceboat full of melted butter. You pour this onto a tilted side plate and dip the cockles in it as you eat them. "If the cockles are not absolutely fresh they are no good" *Mrs. Cox*, the licensee, told me. "These only have to be carried across the road really. They take a nice long time to eat and you can sit in the sun and drink your wine and enjoy them."

This part of Norfolk is the kind of place where you can spend ages and ages doing nothing in particular without getting fidgets. Nothing seems to happen, and you can just listen to the wind and watch the tide coming in across the marshes. I don't think the cockles would taste the same in a big city. "There seems always to have been a sort of hostelry here" said *Mrs. Cox*, "for the Roman camp opposite. People keep digging up bits òf Roman pot lids and things in the shifting sands. I often think I hear them tramping over the hills at night." The Romans were very fond of shellfish, they founded the Colchester oyster beds and archaeologists even dig up heaps of cockle shells in places where there are Roman remains.

LOWESTOFT HERRINGS WITH MUSTARD SAUCE

Wash, clean and scale the herrings, put them in clean boiling sea water or salt water, simmer 10 minutes, drain, put on a hot dish with boiled potatoes and mustard sauce (see page 64 North of England).

English Mustard, a classic with roast beef and ham, comes from Norwich. It is made correctly from a fine dry powder mixed with cold water and allowed to develop for about 10 minutes (and is stirred into the sauce served, for instance, with herrings).

Early English mustard used to be grown and milled to a powder at Tewkesbury, then in about 1710 a Mrs. Clements from Durham found a way of making finer and better looking mustard powder than had been done before. It became famous, won the approval of King George I, was known as Durham mustard and the city remained the great mustard centre for over 100 years, until a young Norwich miller named Jeremiah Coleman became interested in it at the beginning of the 19th century.

DABS

Dabs or Flounders are caught outside estuaries on the sandy bottom of the shore from a boat and you can sometimes pull them

2

in as fast as you can re-bait and lower your line again. They are flat fish of course, usually sand coloured and should never be filleted but dipped whole in seasoned flour and shallow fried in butter, then served with a jug of melted butter.

Michael Leigh,
Brightlingsea, Essex.

BUTTERED BLOATERS

Cut the heads and tails off the bloaters and split them open and take out the backbone. Sprinkle the inside of each bloater with ½ teaspoon dry mustard powder, a little chopped onion, 1 tablespoon soft white breadcrumbs, a little chopped parsley and a dash of Yorkshire relish.

Put three or four knobs of butter on each bloater, bake them in the oven or cook them under the grill, lining the pan with foil.

Mrs. L. Smith,
Great Yarmouth.

Great Yarmouth is an important herring port, like Lowestoft, and famous for its bloaters. The herring season is mainly November when Scots "girls" from Banffshire come down for the herring gutting and packing. A bloater is a whole unsplit herring which after light salting is smoked without the gut being removed, this gives it a rather gamey flavour.

Years ago herring were only available fresh to the people who lived in seaports and, inland, people had to be content with salted (pickled) herrings or heavily smoked (red) herrings. The Great Yarmouth Herring Fair, which lasted 40 days, was first held in 1270 and went on until well into the 18th century.

BAKED BLOATERS AND BLOATER PASTE

One each makes a good quick breakfast. Wipe and trim them and put them in a pie dish, pour hot water over them. Cover them with foil or a paper. Bake in a moderate oven (350 F., Mark 4) for 10 minutes, while making the breakfast toast. Serve piping hot.

Bloater Paste

Having baked three nice bloaters about 20 minutes, dry, in a moderate oven (350 F., Mark 4) bone, skin and mash them with their own weight in butter. This is nice for tea and keeps well in the refrigerator if you press it into little pots. Some people add a little red pepper. Bloaters done in hot water and left over from breakfast can be made into paste, but are not so tasty.

Mrs. J. Millington,
Lowestoft.

3

BAKED STUFFED HADDOCK AND PARSLEY SAUCE

Wash and clean 1 fresh haddock about 1½ lbs. in weight, take out the eyes and gills, remove the inside, fill with parsley and thyme forcemeat. Sew up, put the tail through the eye socket and fasten with a skewer, brush over with milk and sprinkle with brown breadcrumbs. Put a few pieces of dripping on the top and bake in a moderate oven (350 F., Mark 4) for 30 minutes. Baste once or twice. Serve parsley sauce with it.

Mrs. R. Carratt,
Heckington, Sleaford, Lincolnshire.

HADDOCK AND BACON

Fry 2 rashers of streaky bacon gently in 2 tablespoons of lard and afterwards place 1 golden haddock fillet in the pan, skin downwards, and baste it with the fat. Place a lid on and fry it slowly for about 10 minutes. Serve with bread or toast and mustard.

Mrs. N. Burgess,
Ipswich, Suffolk.

NORFOLK SHRIMPS

One can buy quantities of local cooked, fresh peeled shrimps tasting deliciously of the seaside in the market in King's Lynn on Tuesdays. The stalls are piled high with them, as well as with local sole and fresh Cromer crabs. King's Lynn is an old port on the River Ouse about six miles from Sandringham. "The ladies here won't peel shrimps if they are cooked in salt water", one fisherman told me, "as the shells don't come off easily enough, so we salt ours after cooking." Sometimes they overdo it.

Peeled, cooked shrimps — whether fresh, frozen or tinned — are very good heated in a little white wine, or dry sherry, with a sprinkling of nutmeg and pepper, and then stirred into scrambled eggs. I use the wine from heating the shrimps, and, adding a lump of butter, just stir it all till it thickens.

This old English dish is good for "starters", whether hot or cold, and a pleasant change from shrimp cocktails.

LOBSTER OR CRAB WITH BECHAMEL SAUCE

Mix 1 cup of breadcrumbs with an equal amount of hot milk and leave to cool. Add 1 tablespoon of chopped fried parsley, together with a pinch of nutmeg, 1 saltspoon of fresh milled black pepper and salt to taste. Then mix well with 2 eggs. Chop up some lobster or crab (if tinned, save the liquid for the sauce below). Mix well with the breadcrumb mixture. Butter a mould and coat the same with more breadcrumbs. Add the mixture and top it with breadcrumbs, plus a few small knobs of butter. Bake in a hot oven (400 F., Mark 6) for between 20 to 40 minutes according to the size. Dress

4

with the lobster coral plus crumbled hard-boiled egg and fresh parsley sprigs. Serve it with thin Bechamel sauce to which has been added a half teaspoon of tarragon vinegar and a half teaspoon of lemon juice. If tinned fish has been used, add the liquid to the sauce with the milk. This is really delicious, and most suitable for parties when made in individual moulds.

Mrs. M. E. Williams,
Swinderby, Lincolnshire

OYSTERS

East Anglia has always been ideal for breeding oysters, as they need a great deal of plankton and a tidal estuary without so much water that it washes the young oysters out to sea. Those of Pyefleet and Colchester in Essex are perhaps the most famous of our native oysters, the Colne Backwater and the estuaries of the Roach and the Crouch are where they are found, but there are other less famous oyster beds along the East Coast. The idea that one cannot eat oysters unless there is an "R" in the month is a mistaken one. English native oysters spawn during the summer and are therefore protected during the breeding season, like a pheasant or other game bird. The regulation is for the protection of the oysters, not because they are in some way unwholesome during the warmer weather. Portuguese oysters laid in English beds to fatten — and known to the trade as Re-lay Ports are not so protected and can be eaten all the year round.

There are little seaside cafes along the East Coast where you can get oyster fritters, chips and tea with a bottle of sauce. Before the war a lot of Suffolk and Essex people habitually had oysters and bacon for breakfast. Steak, kidney and oyster pie is a popular dish in the Colchester area as well as Sea pie — for this the meat, vegetables etc. are stewed in a large pan, a lid of suet crust is laid on top, and the oysters can be slipped under this at the last moment, so there is little risk of their becoming tough through prolonged cooking.

POULTRY AND GAME

JUGGED PHEASANT OR HARE WITH JACKET POTATOES AND TURNIPS IN BUTTER

I can still recall the delicious smells of the cooking which went on when I was a child in this fruit growing area of East Anglia. Our house boasted a large bakers' oven at the side, where dinners were baked for a small charge. Cakes, bread and also special dishes could be placed in the huge oven when the fire died down to a gentler heat which lasted for hours.

The pheasant, or hare, after being cleaned and sometimes jointed, was placed in a huge brown earthenware jar and partly covered with water. Parsley, thyme and cloves were used for flavouring. The jar was covered and placed in the huge oven for several hours where it simmered gently, sending out a delicious aroma. During the cooking more liquid was added, and a wineglass of port at the last with a gravy thickener, to complete the dish fit for a gourmet.

At the present time a pheasant can be cooked in a casserole and left in the bottom of a modern cooker whilst other dishes or pastry and cakes are being cooked in the hotter part of the oven. It was served with baked jacket potatoes and turnips mashed with butter.

Mrs. E. Denson,
Willingham, near Cambridge.

JUGGED HARE WITH FRIED FORCEMEAT BALLS

Cut a hare up into convenient pieces and dredge with flour. Melt 2 ozs. butter in a frying pan and fry the hare until a nice brown. Lay some thin slices of streaky bacon on the bottom of a large stewpan, then place the hare on top. Sprinkle with salt and a little cayenne pepper. Now put in the herbs, a bay leaf, marjoram, parsley and a strip of the peel of a lemon, 1 onion stuck with 3 cloves, 6 peppercorns. Add $\frac{1}{2}$ pint of claret and $\frac{1}{2}$ pint good beef gravy (stock). Cover tightly and simmer gently for $1\frac{1}{2}$–2 hours.

Take out the hare and keep it hot. Strain the gravy and thicken it with about 1 large tablespoonful of flour mixed smooth with a little claret and add 1 tablespoon redcurrant jelly. Boil the gravy, stir in the thickening and a wineglass of port wine. Put the hare back to get very hot then dish up and serve with forcemeat balls and fried croutons of bread.

For the forcemeat balls you need 1 oz. suet, 1 egg, 2 ozs. breadcrumbs, 1 teaspoon chopped parsley, 1 teaspoon grated lemon peel, $\frac{1}{4}$ teaspoon mixed herbs, salt and pepper, the liver of the hare. Chop the suet, put it in a basin with the parsley, breadcrumbs, lemon peel and seasoning and the chopped, cooked liver. Add enough beaten egg to bind. Form into balls and fry a golden brown in butter. The forcemeat balls however are better if made fresh at the time of serving.

Miss G. Barnatt,
Northgate, Sleaford, Lincolnshire.

ROAST PARTRIDGE

Cover the breast with bacon. Roast the bird in a fairly hot oven (373 F., Mark 5) for about 30-35 minutes, basting with butter. Allow half a bird per person, split them in two and serve garnished with watercress and game chips. Stir a little port into the pan juices to make the gravy.

Cold partridge and salad makes a good supper with cheese and plum cake. They are in season 1st September - 1st February.

Mrs. E. M. Winters,
Castle Rising, Norfolk.

WILD DUCK (MALLARD, SHOVELLERS AND POCHARDS)

To roast, stuff the birds with butter. Pour orange juice over them. Roast the birds in a quick oven (375 F., Mark 5) for about 30 minutes. Baste with the orange juice. Mix 1 dessertspoon lemon juice, 1 dessertspoon sugar, with a good pinch of salt and cayenne pepper, 1½ tablespoons port, 1 tablespoon mushroom ketchup. Pour this over the birds. Do not serve any other gravy. They are in season from the beginning of September to the end of February.

Mrs. Robert Ware,
Northwold, Norfolk.

In Norfolk the amount of grain farming breeds partridges in vast numbers and pheasant, too, where there are woods to give them cover. Near the big Suffolk estates they are almost as domesticated as chickens. The Broads are also full of wild duck and grey lag geese and in East Anglia there are thousands of acres of widgeon haunted saltings.

ROAST RABBIT WITH MILK

I can remember my mother using this recipe as far back as 1908. It was delicious *roast rabbit*. In those days a rabbit cost about eight pence or a shilling. It was skinned at home, and the skin sold for twopence. Sometimes it was so stiff after keeping for a week or two it would stand on end. The rabbit was cleaned and left whole in salted water for about 2 hours, it was then dried in a cloth and stuffed with sage and onions. The stuffing was made by boiling 1 or 2 onions, according to size, until nearly cooked. These were then chopped and mixed with breadcrumbs, adding plenty of salt, pepper and chopped sage.

After stuffing the rabbit was stitched up, sprinkled with seasoned flour and put into a baking tin with blobs of dripping on top. Skimmed milk was poured into the tin. During the cooking the milk was frequently basted over the rabbit, until it was nicely browned.

This also made delicious gravy. It was served with mashed potatoes and sprouts and sometimes a Yorkshire pudding. Result: a very appetizing meal.

Miss E. M. Richardson,
Somersham, Huntingdon.

RABBIT OR CHICKEN HOT POT

Mix 1 oz. flour with a little salt, pepper and grated nutmeg. Roll a rabbit in it, fry it in 1 oz. butter for 5 minutes. Place half a cup of breadcrumbs in a greased pie dish then half of the rabbit and 2 rashers of bacon. Add another half cup of crumbs and the grated rind of a lemon. Finish with another layer of rabbit then lay more breadcrumbs. Half fill the dish with water, cover it with greaseproof paper and bake in a fairly slow oven (325 F., Mark 3) for one hour.

Mrs. F. Brown,
Cringleford, Norwich.

A CHICKEN SUPPER

Mince up some cooked chicken and a small onion, add the same amount of breadcrumbs, the yolk of one egg, pepper and salt to taste. Whip up the whites of an egg, stir it into the mixture. Place into a pie dish and spread mashed potato on the top. Bake for 20 minutes in a moderate oven (350 F., Mark 4) or until the potatoes are a nice golden brown. It makes a nice supper dish.

Mrs. S. L. Curtis,
Scunthorpe, Lincolnshire.

POTTED BOSTON TURKEY

Use turkey that has been left over. Cut the meat into small pieces and put them through the mincer twice, using a fine cutter. Place in a basin, add salt and pepper to taste, a little stock or gravy and a little melted butter. Work the mixture with a wooden spoon until a fine paste is obtained. Serve on rolls etc.

This recipe is useful after Christmas, for using up the left over turkey. It is greatly enjoyed by guests at an after-Christmas party. It can also be prepared with left over chicken or ham.

Mrs. M. P. Sheffield,
Buddewick, Boston, Lincolnshire.

VARIOUS

PEA SOUP WITH NORFOLK DUMPLINGS — A NORFOLK RECIPE.   Serves two

Soak ½ lb. split peas in cold water overnight. Put a smoked hock in a saucepan and cover it with cold water. Bring it to the boil, take out the hock and throw the water away. Put the hock in the saucepan and cover with water again, bring to the boil, simmer for about an hour. Remove the hock and add the soaked split peas to the water then bring to the boil and skim. Simmer, stirring occasionally, add a chopped onion, 2 sliced carrots and 2 sticks of chopped celery. Remove the skin from the hock, cut the meat from the bone, chop it up and add it to the soup. Cook for about 1 hour to 1½ hours (stirring occasionally). Serve with Norfolk dumplings.

Mrs. P. Marjoram,
Bradwell, Norfolk.

POACHER'S SOUP

Any game you can poach or failing a moonlit night buy, or otherwise use a young rabbit cut up small, add a piece of diced bacon. Boil it in about 3 pints of water with 2 potatoes, an onion, 2 sticks celery, parsley and peppercorns, adding when well boiling, a small cabbage cut in four. Season the soup and let it simmer until the game is tender. If liked, add suet dumplings.

A large plateful of this and you can sing "The Lincolnshire Poacher" oblivious of gamekeepers, cold, and the cost of living!

Mr. Owen McConnell,
Lough, Lincolnshire.

BOILED NORFOLK DUMPLINGS (to serve 8 - 10 people)

½ oz. yeast or ½ sachet of dried yeast   2 teaspoons salt
1¼ lbs. plain flour   ¾ oz. of lard (optional)
¾ pint of warm water

Cream the fresh yeast with part of the warm water or reconstitute the dried yeast with ⅛ pint of recipe warm water. Mix the flour and salt in a warm bowl. Rub in the lard (optional). Make a small well in the flour and add the yeast and the remainder of the water to the flour. Mix until the dough leaves the bowl. Knead thoroughly. Divide into 12-16 dumplings. Leave to prove in a warm place for 30-40 minutes. Allow the dumplings 20 minutes cooking time, cooking for 10 minutes on one side and then turning and cooking 10 minutes on the other, in with the stew.

Dumplings must not be cut with a knife as they compress and go "doughy", but they must be torn apart with two forks.

Dumplings can also be cooked in plain boiling water and served as a sweet course with golden syrup, butter and sugar or jam. Very filling.

Mrs. Barbara Cook,
Hunstanton, Norfolk.

BAKED NORFOLK DUMPLING
— to be served with a roast joint, casserole or partridge stew and so on.

Mix 8 ozs. self raising flour, 6 ozs. shredded suet and a pinch of salt together. Make into a soft dough with milk, knead to a flat round with your hands, place on a well greased tray or dish. Mark criss cross on top with a knife, brush the top with milk. Bake in a moderate to hot oven (350 F., Mark 4).

Mrs. P. E. Chandler,
Northchapel, Near Petworth, Sussex.

BREAKFAST RAILWAY CAKES

Mix 4 tablespoons plain flour with some salt, pepper and 2 teaspoons of baking powder with cold water to a stiff paste. Roll into flat cakes about ½ inch thick with floured hands. Fry some bacon in lard and put it away to keep hot, drop the cakes in the hot fat and fry them slowly until the centre is cooked, turning them, so *each* side is golden brown, adding more lard if needed.

Serve them with bacon and at the last moment cut the cakes in half (like scones) and add a small knob of butter.

Phyllis Ladds,
Cambridge.

NEW POTATOES, GREEN PEAS AND BACON

Cook the required amount of small new potatoes, young broad beans and green peas (flavoured with mint), separately, when done, place in soup tureen, meanwhile cook small dices of ham or bacon in frying pan, carefully. Then pour this over the vegetables and mix carefully. Season with pepper and allow to stand in warm place for thirty minutes.

Mrs. F. M. Thomson,
Worlington, Bury St. Edmunds.

SAMPHIRE: PETER'S CRESS OR ROCK SAMPHIRE

This is a plant that grows wild in the sandhills round Snettisham, a Norfolk delicacy which is seasonal in July. It is eaten hot, boiled, and served with melted butter, something like asparagus. It used to be commonly pickled in England and is still sold fresh at some country markets. At the Jolly Sailors at Brancaster Staithe they also make it into a sauce for the sea trout which is caught about a mile along the beach. It is also served occasionally as a vegetable at hotels in King's Lynn. Samphire also grows round the Mediterranean and pickled samphire is sometimes sold with olives in the markets there. It is also found at the Welsh seaside in summer and used to be pickled in Wales with nasturtium seeds and horseradish, but is now almost forgotten there.

MEAT

LINCOLNSHIRE PORK, HAM, SAUSAGES

November 11th is the feast of Martinmas, the medieval Feast of Sausages and Gut Puddings. It was widely celebrated throughout the Middle Ages and is still remembered in some parts of Europe.

Long, long ago when there was no winter grazing, most farm stock was killed off in autumn and salted down for the cold weather, or made into sausages. Farms and cottages would be full of all kinds of delicacies, hot trotters and potted pork, grilled kidneys, fresh shining black puddings and all the things that epicurean old gentlemen smack their lips over in delight. Some readers still remember the country feasts at the time of the autumn pig-killing. In Lincolnshire even 20 years ago what they called the Pig's Cheer — the bits not suitable for preserving — were always given away to friends. It is a part of England where they know good food, expect it to be right and where many of the old customs linger.

I remember once arriving in Lincoln, one night in November in a thick fog, to find the gargoyles on Lincoln Cathedral peering down at me in the gloom. As Thursday night is bell-ringing practice, the Company of the Ringers of the Blessed Virgin Mary of Lincoln were making what I suppose could properly be described as the welkin ring. I felt as though the Middle Ages were upon me. In Lincolnshire, like nowhere else in England, even the pork butchers' shops have, or at any rate had, an almost fairy-tale strangeness and opulence. I saw rows and rows of hand-raised pork pies — the Lincolnshire ones are round and made of leg of pork — great glistening bowls of brawn, savoury ducks, and mounds of haslet made from minced pork. At one little shop near the cathedral — I think it was called Inkley's — they were selling roast pork chaps or cheeks. And there were those small hocks of cold boiled salted pork which are so nice to take home and eat cold with pickled walnuts.

In Boston, the pork butchers' shops have a little of the miraculous too. They mostly have beautiful pieces of Lincolnshire stuffed chine, proudly displayed in the middle of the window. This is a most unusual and decorative cut, which would look well on any buffet or supper table. It comes out of the boiling water in pink and white stripes, and has a fine sharp, prickly-parsley flavour.

But it is useless to ask for a chine in, say, London, as any of the local people will tell you. This is a purely regional cut of meat which is virtually unknown outside East Anglia, and parts of Wales, though it was fashionable in London in the 18th century.

"A chine" as *Mrs. Hanson* of Gainsborough, Lincolnshire, writes, "is part of the pig's backbone with meat each side. We always killed a pig before Christmas, and the chines, four or five of them, were salted down and kept, apart from one which we roasted. Then in late April a chine would be soaked in water, cut down into the bone and each cut stuffed with finely chopped parsley. It was then baked in the oven in a pastry case made of plain flour and water — today we would use foil. It was baked for 3 or 4 hours until cooked, then the case was broken open and discarded. The Stuffed Chine was the Traditional Dish for May Day (as my father-in-law called it), the first week in May, to be eaten and some given to special friends."

NORTH LINCOLNSHIRE BAKED STUFFED CHINE (another way), FORMERLY A DAINTY FOR MAY DAY WEEK

You will need 1 neck chine of bacon, as well as herbs, chiefly parsley, a quantity will be required. Also thyme and marjoram, a small amount. A few nice raspberry and black currant leaves, and a small quantity of lettuce as well as a few spring onions.

Soak the chine overnight (24 hours). Pick and wash all the herbs. Score both sides of the chine. Put all the herbs through a mincing machine then mix them and stuff them into all the scorings tightly until all are filled. Make a paste of flour and water, cover the chine entirely with it and bake in a moderate oven (350 F., Mark 4) 20 minutes a lb. and 20 minutes over. When cooked, place on a dish strainer.

Mrs. Gladys Martin,
Lincoln.

BOILED STUFFED CHINE

Take a chine of bacon, soak it overnight in cold water, dry, and score it very thinly with a sharp knife, taking care not to cut the rind. Pick and wash thoroughly a large bowl of parsley, chop and stuff it firmly in the scored chine. Wrap in a cloth, fasten securely and boil until done in a large pan. Lift out and drain, remove cloth when cold. Most people add a little vinegar when it is served.

Mrs. E. Bailey,
Newport Pagnell, Buckinghamshire.

HAND RAISED PORK PIES — LINCOLNSHIRE
Pork Pie Crust

1 Stone plain flour (14 lbs.)   2½ pints water
5 lbs. lard (home rendered preferred)   Salt to taste.
Save a little flour for working. Boil lard and water 2 minutes and pour on the flour and work it at least half an hour. Let it stand for half an hour or a little longer if necessary, until it is fit to work.

Then mould it round a 5- or 6-inch jar (suggest a glass sweet jar) to the depth required. Fill with cut seasoned pork in alternate layers of lean and fat pressed well down until full. Add a little water.

Cut out round for the lids, damp the edges and seal. Nick the top to let out steam. Decorate with pastry rolled out and then cut into flower or leaf shapes. Damp and stick on. Makes 13 pies.

This recipe for pork pies was used by my sister, our mother and grandmother. I visit my 80 year old sister two or three times a year at Sleaford, still hale and hearty, and during our stay she takes her pick from the several pork butchers and gives us a real treat cooked in the old traditional style.

I remember for years as a boy and young man taking these pies to the village bakery to be baked in a large brick oven after the bread had been baked. The charge was one penny per pie and cooked to perfection.

Mr. A. H. Musson,
Ilkley, Yorkshire.

PIG'S FRY

In Lincolnshire and Norfolk everyone buys pig's fry, another luscious local delicacy not nearly well enough known outside East Anglia. Unfortunately it is often difficult to buy all the bits and pieces for a genuine pig's fry in other parts of the country though this is an excellent dish quite as full of flavour as the better known steak and kidney pudding. The recipes and methods of cooking it vary. "Some slice it up and cook it in a frying pan" as one Norfolk butcher told me, "but the older ladies cut it up, put it in a tin with onions and bake it about $1\frac{1}{2}$ hours in a moderate oven". It is often served with mashed potatoes, vegetables and Lincolnshire sage and onions. These are big onions, peeled and left whole, and boiled in salted water until tender in about 35 minutes. They are then served well drained with a lump of butter and lots of chopped sage on top. Norfolk dumplings are sometimes served with pig's fry, too.

LINCOLNSHIRE PIG'S FRY

My father was a butcher who came from an old Grantham family and so this was his way of doing pig's fry. My mother died when I was 3 so it was a good thing he was such a good cook having to bring up a family of 4 children and run a business in 1914.

The fry consisted of pig's kidney, liver, heart, pork belly, melt all cut up into small pieces. This was cooked slowly with sliced onion rings, salt and pepper and a little pork dripping in the oven. When tender take some of the fat out and add $\frac{1}{4}$ pint of stock, then add $\frac{1}{4}$ pint of milk and thicken with 1 heaped dessertspoon of cornflour mixed in milk and serve with mashed potato, sprouts or any green vegetable.

Mrs. Irene Smith,
Ashby, Scunthorpe, Lincolnshire.

SUFFOLK SWEET CURED HAMS

Fifty or sixty years ago most Suffolk villagers kept their own pigs and nearly all the meat eaten in cottages was bacon or pork, mutton and beef were for special occasions such as harvest time. Suffolk people made a fine art of curing the bacon, steeping it in old ale and smoking it over sawdust. Most families owned a complete pig killing equipment which included a large earthenware ham pot, glazed on the inside, in which the pork was cured, first in salt, then in the local sweet pickle. After dry salting the fresh ham (in other words rubbing it with salt and saltpetre and leaving it in the ham pot for about a week) they wiped the ham, rinsed out the pot and put it in a pickle, for example 2 lbs. black treacle, 2 lbs. dark brown sugar and a quart of hot stout or porter which was poured over it. The ham was put back in the pot well rubbed with stout and treacle, and left in the pickle weighted down with a stone for about six weeks. Smaller pieces of meat were ready sooner. It used then to be sent off to be dried in the "Smokey House", which often belonged to the local joiner and undertaker, or perhaps a cooper or wheelwright, who thus had a way of using up all his sawdust, oak chips and wood shavings. The sawdust was damped to make it smoke a lot and the bacon and hams usually hung there for about three weeks. These Suffolk Sweet Cured Hams which once hung in every farmhouse kitchen are now a luxury. The longer they were kept the better they tasted, anything from one to two years.

At Christmas or sheep shearing or harvest time they used often to be boiled in the kitchen copper usually with a bunch of hay in the bottom to stop them sticking to it. The brick ovens commonly used for baking bread were also used for baking hams on special occasions, the ham being covered with a thick layer of dough or huff paste which kept it moist during baking, a method still used for baking a haunch of venison, a notoriously dry meat. The pastry covering was not eaten but went into the hen bucket.

One of our older readers, *Mrs. H. J. H. Bobbins*, of Harris Avenue, Lowestoft, who was 80 last February, has been writing to me about how her mother prepared the family pig in the Norfolk village where she was a child 70 years ago.

She clearly remembers the sides of bacon for their breakfast hanging to smoke from the rafters in the kitchen.

"The hams were also smoked in a home-made smokehouse made from a huge barrel turned up on a smouldering fire for about 3 days.

They were those delicious sweet cured hams, pickled in black treacle and hot stout, which you found in every Norfolk and Suffolk farmhouse a few years ago.

The little weakling of the litter used to be brought up by us children in a shed near the house.

We used to call it the little peppermint, why that name I have never found out but in little country villages you can always find strange names which only the villagers would understand.

The little pig would be brought indoors, put in a little box in which my mother would put an old wool shawl or vest or some old wool garment.

We fed it on strained milk in a little blue and white jug which was very much like in shape to the feeding cup used in hospitals today.

All the rough parts of the pig are made into something" *Mrs. Bobbins writes*, "there's nothing wasted on a pig."

The pig's chitterlings — or runners as *Mrs. Bobbins* calls them — were cut up and baked with apples and currants on a deep plate between two pastry crusts.

14

"Some of the fat was kept to cover the pig's fry, baked in the oven and eaten with huge Norfolk dumplings, making a really tasty dinner.

As we couldn't eat all the meat ourselves, we sold various small joints to our neighbours; and always a jolly good weight was given, the scales always went down with a bang.

We children were set to cut up the parts to make into sausages. No meal or anything was added except spice. We only let or sold a few sausages, as it took so long to put them through the mincer.

I think they were 9d. a lb., but most families would buy ½ lb. of pork cheese at 4d. and 2 lb. of pork in the joint. That was a lot to spend in those days as most men's farm wages amounted to 10s. a week."

Mrs. Bobbins wants me to tell you that she thoroughly enjoys life in spite of her arthritis. "I think it must be my very cheerful, happy disposition," she said, "I used to be flaming redhead you see, years ago."

MRS. BOBBINS BACON AND TOMATO PIE

Make a bacon and tomato pie by laying the fat bacon over the lean in a fireproof dish with layers of sliced tomatoes between, then a little batter on top.

This is made with 1 egg, about 2 tablespoons of milk, and just enough plain flour to make a smooth batter which drops easily off the spoon. It must not be too thin a paste.

It takes about 15 minutes to bake in a fairly hot oven (375 F., Mark 5) and makes a really delicious lunch served with runner beans and potatoes.

No need for gravy as the bacon fat and the juice from the tomatoes make a form of gravy, which holds the flavour on its own.

MRS. LIQUORICE'S BOILED BACON

Soak 3 or 4 lbs. bacon (gammon or collar or forehock) two hours in cold water. Put it in a pan of fresh cold water and boil till tender, strip off the skin and cover the fat with browned breadcrumbs. Serve it hot with broad beans and parsley sauce, mashed potatoes and home made crusty bread.

This is a traditional Fenland recipe, served at village feasts.

Mrs. Liquorice,
Peterborough, Northants.

HOME MADE SAUSAGES

The sausages are worth the effort of making them, having much more flavour than many commercial sausages. Some electric mixers have an attachment for filling sausage skins.

To each pound of pork shoulder (lean and fat mixed) take 4 ozs. dry bread (crusts may be included if not too dark), soak in cold water then squeeze as dry as possible. Put both through the mincer. To each pound of this mixture add 1 level teaspoon salt, $\frac{1}{4}$ level teaspoon white pepper, $\frac{1}{4}$ level teaspoon black pepper, one large pinch of cayenne pepper, one large pinch of ground mace, and one large pinch of ground nutmeg, eight large sage leaves. Mix well and fill into runners which have been cleaned. Or the butcher will oblige with some sausage skins.

Mrs. D. P. Ruff,
Warboys, Huntingdon.

FAGGOTS

Breadcrumbs (fresh), sage, salt, pepper, 1 lb. proper pig's fry with a little extra liver and veiling or kell.

Cut up fry into smallish pieces and put into saucepan with 4 ozs. medium peeled onions. Put the veiling into a basin for use later. Cover the fry with cold water and bring to simmering point very slowly. When partly cooked take off heat and allow to cool. When cool enough to handle put through the mincer leaving the liquid in the saucepan for gravy. Add sufficient breadcrumbs to make a nice consistency and not too wet. Add salt, pepper and sage to taste. Mix very thoroughly, put the veiling into warm water for a few minutes then pull out into small pieces to wrap each faggot in. Make the faggots small and top each one with veiling. Put into greased dishes and cook in a moderately hot oven for half to three quarters of an hour (375 F., Mark 5). Thicken and colour the gravy a little. Serve hot with creamed potatoes.

Mrs. G. Green,
Ramsey, Huntingdon.

FAGGOTS — Another way

Soak 1 lb. bread in water, drain well, then beat it up with a fork. Wash and dry 8 ozs. pig's liver and put it through a mincer, with 2 onions and 2 rashers of bacon. Mix this with the soaked bread, 1 tablespoon fresh sage, some salt and pepper. With floured hands form mixture into cakes. Cover with caul from the pig, as it is the caul covering that makes all the difference to the flavour of the faggot. Bake for about 45 minutes in a moderate oven (350 F., Mark 4).

Mrs. K. Biggadike,
Holbeach, Spalding, Lincolnshire.

Faggots, Haslet and Savoury Duck are all very similar and I have had many excellent recipes for them from all over the country. Some scholars say they are of Roman origin although the use of the caul suggests an even earlier date, a similar dish known as *crepinettes* is widely sold by French pork butchers.

16

FRITTER PIE

Being a Suffolk "born and bred of farming stock" woman, I remember so well the autumn pig killing, and what a riotous time we had! What with the succulent hams being cured in the butter kiln presumably for the space required, and the sides of bacon being slung up the big open chimney. The villagers used to line up for the pig's fry, and there was always masses of lovely pork cheeses (which took care of the head and trotters) and then, finally, there was the delicious Fritter Pie.

Just the surplus pig fat used to be cut into small pieces and "done down" slowly over a low heat. As it melted the fat was poured off until it ceased to give. This resulted in a pure delicious lard. Then the resulting "fritters" which remained from melting down the lard were mixed with sultanas, apples, some brown sugar and spice.

We used to line a tin with short pastry, fill it with the mixture and put pastry on top, then brush it over with dissolved sugar and bake it. This was served hot with or without custard or cream — it's lovely (the children adore it). I might add that many butchers sell this surplus fat reasonably.
Mrs. Adeline Gilby,
Stamford Hill, London N.16.

FAMILY WARMER-UPPER

Put enough water in a saucepan — about 2 pints — to cover 4 large peeled onions, and salt it well. When the water is boiling put in the onions, cover tightly and simmer until soft (about one hour). About 30 minutes before meal-time put in 1 lb. pork sausages, bring back to the boil and simmer until just before needed. Then strain off about half the liquid and replace it with 1 pint milk. Reheat, but do not let it boil as the milk will curdle. Serve the sausages and onions with lots of lovely mashed potatoes to sop up the oniony milk. Enough for three–four people. Good eating.
Mrs. Mollie Hudson,
Drayton, Norwich.

The strained off liquid will make a good basis for soup stock.

To be really good, however, it must be made with coarse-cut country sausages. This is an excellent regional dish virtually unknown outside East Anglia for which I have received numerous recipes from Norfolk and Lincolnshire.

BAKED MARROW AND SAUSAGES

Peel and seed a thick ring of marrow, then parboil or steam. Put the ring into a large baking tin, larded with haslet dripping and fill with home made, well seasoned onion and sage stuffing. Roast and well baste until half cooked. Then fat, thick pork sausages should be draped over and around the ring of marrow and all basted and cooked till cripsy brown.

This should be served staight from the tin with a rich brown gravy and either mashed or jacket potatoes.

This was sometimes known as Poor Man's Duck.

Miss E. M. Broughton,
Holbeach, Spalding, Lincolnshire.

THE DUNMOW FLITCH

At the Essex town of Dunmow there's an ancient ceremony of awarding a Flitch of Bacon to a married couple who can convince the Manorial Court that they have been happily married for a year and a day and have not quarrelled. It is believed that this ceremony was instituted more than 600 years ago though firm records only go back to 1701.

The twentieth century proceedings are rather more light-hearted than the medieval ones but great care is taken to see that the winners are really happily married. Most of the candidates have been married for about 12 years and are tried by two judges and a committee of six maidens and six bachelors at the Foakes Memorial Hall, Great Dunmow.

PORK "CHEESE"

Put a hock or knuckle of pork in a pan with salt, pepper and herbs to your taste. Add just enough water to cover and boil for 2 hours or more until dropping from the bone. Then cut up all the meat, fat and everything, and place it in basins with the liquor, and let it set.

Mrs. B. Hamit,
Ely, Cambridgeshire.

POOR MAN'S PORK "CHEESE" — Another way

Purchase two or more pig's feet according to the size of your family. Wash thoroughly, place them in a saucepan and cover with water, simmer for 1½ hours. Remove the feet from the saucepan, remove all the bones, then cut the meat as finely as possible, return it to the saucepan adding a few finely chopped sage leaves, salt and pepper. Boil for 15 minutes, turn into moulds putting an equal share of meat in each mould and leave until set, turn out onto a plate as needed.

E. Feast,
Waterbeach, Cambridgeshire.

In Victorian England the cooks in bigger houses referred to pig's feet not as trotters but *pig's pettitoes.*

18

PORK AND VEGETABLE PIE

6 pig's trotters or 3 lbs. belly pork, 2 chopped celery sticks, leaves as well, 1 tablespoon chopped parsley, 1 bay leaf, 1 cup lentils, 1 tablespoon grated onion, 1 teaspoon salt, 1 saltspoon black pepper, 1 chopped onion, 8 ozs. plain flour, 4 ozs. suet.

Put all the filling ingredients (all except chopped onion and suet) into a heavy saucepan with 2 pints of water. Bring to the boil and then simmer gently for 2 hours. Remove the bones and bay leaf, leave to cool. For the pie crust mix the flour, suet and onion into a pliable paste, line a pie dish, fill it with the meat and vegetable mixture and bake until the pastry is well browned.

This recipe is over fifty years old and comes from Clare, Suffolk.

Mrs. E. Moore,
Horton, Kirby, Kent.

HUNTINGDON "HEDGEHOG"

My grandmother used to make this recipe in the late 1800's, it was a real favourite.

Make the pastry in the usual way with 8 ozs. self raising flour, 4 ozs. lard and 1 oz. butter and a little water to mix. Divide it into two, roll out half and spread it with 12 ozs. sausage meat. Cut 3 shelled hard boiled eggs into slices (not too thin, each egg into four) and put them on top of the sausage meat. Cover it with the remaining pastry, moisten the edges and pinch them together, brush the top with milk, place the "hedgehog" in a greased baking tin and bake in a moderate oven (350 F., Mark 4) for about one hour. Serve with mashed potatoes and grilled tomatoes or fried onions, it is sufficient for three to four servings.

Mrs. M. Burgess,
Bell Lane, Fenstanton, Huntingdonshire.

RIPE MARROW AND PORK PIE

Some sixty to seventy years ago, every year we had a pig killing for the house. I can remember all the meals derived from it, great dishes of pig's fry with onions and Norfolk dumplings as light as sponges. Then there was this pie which was a great favourite.

It was made from marrow in the ripe yellow state, potatoes, onions and chunks of pork, all cooked together and seasoned. They were then placed in a pie dish and covered with delicious short pastry and baked till the pastry was cooked.

Mrs. M. Royall,
Cromer, Norfolk.

LEG OF LAMB OR MUTTON IN A SUET CRUST

Boiled Mutton and Caper Sauce is an old-fashioned delicacy perhaps more frequently seen in pubs nowadays than in private houses, though it is much liked and often found in East Anglia. A Leg of Lamb boiled in a Suet Crust is, however, a purely local speciality which seems to be peculiar to Norfolk. An excellent recipe for this follows from a Norwich reader.

Wipe a leg of lamb or mutton with a clean cloth and sprinkle it with salt. Make a suet crust, using half quantities of suet to self-raising flour. Wrap the leg completely in the crust so as to enclose it like a parcel, tie it in a floured cloth and simmer it in a pan of water for 4 hours, depending on size. When cooked, take the crust off and you have the meat with all the natural juices.

This is a method my mother used 70 years ago to cook a leg of mutton (nowadays lamb).

Mrs. J. Ryall,
Trivetshall St. Mary, Norwich.

LAMB DUMPLING FROM SUFFOLK

Cut some cold cooked lamb into very small pieces. Make a suet crust, preferably with the fat from the kidneys. Place the meat in the crust and form into dumplings. Cook them in boiling stock or water for 30 minutes. Serve with a thick gravy and vegetables.

V. Wilcox,
Brighton, Sussex.

BREAST OF LAMB IN PASTRY

Take a boned and skinned breast of lamb. Spread 1 oz. chopped stoned sultanas over it, seasoned with salt and pepper. Roll and tie it up with string Swiss roll fashion. Put it in a roasting tin, bake in a hot oven (400 F., Mark 6) for 20 minutes. Remove and cool the meat, discarding the string. Then completely encase this meat roll in pastry. Roll it once in fat and surround it with sliced onions. Bake for 40 minutes in a moderate oven (350 F., Mark 4). Very tasty and economical.

Mrs. J. Rayner,
Saffron Waldon, Essex.

MALDON SALT

A kind of natural sea salt from a small town in Essex, it comes in crisp flaky crystals and is very good with steaks and chops.

HARICOT OXTAIL

Wash 4 ozs. haricot beans and soak overnight. Wash 1 oxtail in cold water and cut it in pieces where jointed. If available, cut up 8 ozs. bullock's cheek, not too small. (If unobtainable, shin beef or Chuck steak might be substituted. S.H.). Put the meat in a saucepan, cover with water, add 1 or 2 peeled sliced onions, salt to taste. Simmer for 2½ hours. When cold skim all the fat from the top. And 1 lb. scraped sliced carrots, the soaked haricot beans and cook till tender in about 2 or 3 hours. Add suet dumplings 15 minutes before serving. (It is a good idea to partly cook the oxtails etc. the day before they are required).

Mrs. R. Lipsham,
Rocklands, Attleborough, Norfolk.

LINCOLNSHIRE STUFFED STEAK

My grandmother died before I was born in 1909, but I still remember with relish a recipe of hers that I have never heard of anywhere else. It was for Stuffed Steak.

You need best steak, cut thick, a quantity of stale bread and suet, pepper, salt and thyme for seasoning. Soak the bread in boiling water, squeeze out the surplus, add suet and seasonings. Melt some dripping in a baking tin, put a layer of stuffing in the bottom, add the steak, then cover with stuffing. Dot with dripping and bake in a hot oven (400 F., Mark 6) until the outside is all brown and crisp and the inside soft and juicy. Serve with creamed potatoes and brussels sprouts.

Mrs. Norah Peel,
Fleetwood.

STUFFED OX HEART WITH DUMPLINGS

This is an old East Anglian recipe made by farmworkers' wives during the winter months. It is at least a hundred years old, for my great grandmother cooked it for her family. As well as being tasty it is nourishing and economical — as it had to be to support the low paid, hard working farm labourers of a hundred years ago.

Ask the butcher to clean a whole ox heart thoroughly, removing tubes and sinews. Prepare the stuffing:—

Push 6 cloves into 1 large peeled onion, place in a saucepan of cold water, bring to the boil and cook till soft, drain, but keep the water to one side. Remove the cloves and chop the onion finely mixing it thoroughly with 8 ozs. soft, white breadcrumbs, salt, pepper and 1 teaspoon chopped sage. Bind it with 1 beaten egg. Fill the heart with it and stitch or skewer firmly to close.

Fry 2 to 3 peeled, sliced onions and 1 lb. peeled, sliced root vegetables in dripping, put them in a casserole with a close fitting lid, on top place 4 ozs. lightly fried mushrooms or a small stick of celery chopped. Season, place the heart on top of the vegetables and cover. Put the casserole in a moderate oven (350 F., Mark 4), after 15 minutes cover the vegetables with boiling water. Replace the lid and cook for about 2½ hours or until the meat is tender.

Mix the dumplings in the usual way using 8 ozs. plain flour and 1 teaspoon baking powder, 4 ozs. suet, seasoning to your taste and water to mix. Use the onion water to make the gravy and 20 minutes before cooking is complete add it to the casserole. When it boils add the dumplings and continue cooking. Serve with boiled or mashed potatoes. When cold, the heart is delicious in sandwiches.

Note: The stuffed cooked heart may be frozen, but the dumplings are best made fresh and added after reheating and 20 minutes before serving.

Mrs. A. G. Whitbread,
Leavesden, Watford, Hertfordshire.

STEAK AND KIDNEY PUDDING

Cut 1½ lbs. steak and 8 ozs. kidney into neat strips and dip each piece into flour seasoned with salt and pepper. Make a rather stiff paste by mixing 6 ozs. flour, 2 ozs. suet, a small teaspoon salt and baking powder thoroughly with a little water. Roll it out and place in a greased basin. Fill it with prepared meat, ½ pint stock and a small piece of onion. Trim the pastry round the edge of the basin. Roll these out and cover the top, cover with a cloth or with foil and place in a pan of boiling water. Boil for 4 hours. Serve hot.

Mrs. E. Archer,
Lincoln.

TWO-WAY SUET PUDDING

I shall always remember my mother's two-way suet pudding that used to fascinate us as children. It came to the table steaming in its cloth cover, one end was opened and delicious slices of steak and kidney and suet crust were served onto our plates, then it was quickly wrapped up again and dropped back into the boiling pot. It came out again for our sweet, but this time the slices were filled with apples, apricots or any available fruit or even sultanas or currants. We never knew what it was going to be. It was great fun, especially trying to discover how mother knew which end to cut first. She was always right.

Sift 1 lb. flour, ½ teaspoon baking powder and a little salt into a bowl. Rub in 8 ozs. beef suet and mix it to a stiff paste with cold water; knead slightly and roll out after pulling off a small roll to use as a divider between savoury and sweet fillings. Spread savoury and sweet fillings over the suet pastry and wet the edges before rolling it up, sealing the ends. Wrap it in a scalded and floured cloth and tie firmly. Steam or boil for 1½ hours. Serve the savoury side with gravy, and the sweet side with sauce or custard.

Fillings:—Steak and kidney, pre-boiled to tenderise the meat (using a sliced onion if liked) or any meaty pieces can be used. Keep back the stock for making the delicious gravy.

Fillings for the sweet side:— Apples and sultanas, mincemeat, apricots, dates. Any type of jam can be used, and we have had it just as steamed pudding in slices, with lovely, sticky syrup run over the top.

Mrs. M. I. Rogers,
Canwick, Lincoln.

PUDDING

CAMBRIDGE BURNT CREAM

The Burnt Cream of Trinity College, Cambridge, is simply a very rich and extravagant, but delicious, English cold custard pudding with an impeccable pedigree. Known variously as Crème Brûlée, Burnt Cream or Cambridge Cream it really does seem to have originated at the University. They base their claim on a recipe left them in manuscript by a nineteenth-century pastry cook at Trinity. "It seems easy," says Mr. Eden, Trinity College's catering manager, "but people are always startled when they see how good it is when we serve it".

You will need a pint of single cream and the yolks of six fresh eggs with 8 ozs. of caster sugar. Beat up the egg yolks with ½ oz. of sugar. Bring the cream to the boil and pour it gradually over the beaten yolks, stirring all the time. Heat the mixture gently, stirring all the time, until it is thick enough to coat the back of a spoon. If it boils it will curdle and be quite spoiled, so it is safest to heat it, either in the top of a double saucepan standing in another pan of hot, but not boiling, water.

When it has thickened, strain it into the shallow fireproof serving dish and place in a very slow oven till the cream is set. When cold sprinkle it evenly all over with the remaining sugar to form a thick layer. Get the grill really hot. Stand the dish in another with chunks of ice round it. Put it under the grill until the sugar forms a kind of caramel top. The ice stops the heat curdling the cream while you are toasting the top.

Serve it very cold, perhaps with an orange salad or some very good sweet biscuits, or some large fluffy, absolutely perfect hot baked apples.

The Catering Manager,
Trinity College, Cambridge.

STEWED DAMSONS OR PEARS

In my childhood the pears were a hard cooking variety which required long gentle cooking and lemon juice and cloves to flavour them. The gentle heat of the old brick bread oven was ideal for this, and they were placed in a large earthenware jar, covered with water and dark brown sugar, tied down with greaseproof paper and left until nearly soft.

The damsons were cooked in the same way, with plenty of sugar, always brown, and were served with a jug of rich cream.

After this a huge wedge of cheese of a local variety would be placed on the table, chiefly for the men of the party to enjoy with their wine in days when coffee was rarely served at a meal of this sort.

Mrs. E. Denson,
Willingham, Cambs.

SUFFOLK LEMON SOLID

It was a lady on the Ipswich bus who gave me the recipe for Lemon Solid, one of those old fashioned country set creams which used to be popular for farmhouse tea with the first of the soft fruit.

Warm 1 pint of milk with the grated rind of 2 lemons, 6 ozs. sugar and ½ oz. of powdered gelatine. Heat it, stirring until the sugar and gelatine have really melted, then add the juice of 2 lemons and stir for a moment until the curd separates. Pour it into a basin and turn it out when set. This is really very good and not half as odd as it may sound.

"The Suffolk people like their food separately" my friend added, "suet pudding and gravy first, then the meat and vegetables. Of course, it has got to be good gravy, then it's always beautiful. My husband likes batter pudding with gravy first on a plate. Suet dumplings are another favourite with stew; it makes the dinner start off very nice".

BOILED BATTER PUDDING

Mix 6 ozs. flour and a good pinch of salt together and make a well in the centre of the flour. Beat 4 eggs thoroughly, strain them into the flour and stir gently so that the flour becomes gradually incorporated. Add ¾ pint to 1 pint milk, a little at a time, until the batter has the consistency of thick cream, then cover and let it stand for 1 hour. When ready, pour it into a well buttered basin, cover with a scalded, well floured cloth and boil for 1¼ hours.

Boiled batter puddings may be varied by the addition of either fresh or dried fruits. They should be placed in the basin and the batter poured over them.

Mrs. M. P. Wignall,
Burwell, Cambridge.

MYSTERY PUDDING (AND PANAGI)

When I was a child our sweet on a Monday was mother's "Mystery Pudding". Any cakes, pies or buns left over from Sunday were all cut up, put in a pie dish, covered with a pint of custard and baked in the oven for about thirty minutes, it was delicious.

Friday was hard-up day, because everyone got paid on Saturday, so it was "Panagi" *for dinner*.

Peel potatoes required for size of family, two large onions, slice into dish, alternate layers, pepper, salt to taste, knob of dripping, cup of water, cook in oven for about forty-five minutes, serve with fried bacon, sausage, or corned beef, this is very tasty.

Mrs. E. Best,
Grimsby, Lincolnshire.

A LARGE BOILED APPLE DUMPLING

Make some pastry with 8 ozs. plain flour, 4 ozs. lard, a pinch of salt and 1½ teaspoons baking powder, adding water to mix.

Roll out the pastry on a floured board; peel, core and slice the apples. Cover with sugar to taste. Place the apples on the pastry and make one large dumpling. Tie it in a clean, floured cloth. Have ready a pan of boiling water. Place the dumpling in it and boil for 1½ hours. Take out and serve immediately.

G. Mawer,
Lincoln.

FURMENTY OR FRUMENTY OR FIRMITY

1 teacup of prepared wheat grains
1 quart milk
2 ozs. stoned raisins
2 ozs. cleaned currants
2 eggs
2 ozs. loaf sugar
nutmeg to flavour
little brandy

Boil milk in a large saucepan. In another pan put the currants and raisins with enough boiling water to cover them. Cook these about five minutes. Drain off water and add milk to fruit. Put in the wheat, sugar and nutmeg. Boil slowly for twenty minutes. Take it off the heat, let it cool a little, beat up and strain in the eggs. Stir it over heat until it thickens — but it must not boil. Add brandy, pour into a bowl and serve.

Mrs. D. F. Manning,
St. Ives, Huntingdonshire.

This was an old Lincolnshire dish which was served either hot or cold at sheep clipping time, harvest suppers and so on. There are also Yorkshire recipes for this dish.

A CHOCOLATE SWEET

Steam 4 ozs. of plain chocolate in a basin over hot water for 30 minutes to melt it. Then mix in the beaten yolks of 4 eggs. Whip the whites to a stiff froth and fold into the mixture. Pour the mixture into a dish and leave it in a cool place for 12 hours. Decorate with chopped almonds and whipped cream. It may be served with sponge fingers if wished.

Mrs. Thurston,
Revesby Vicarage.

25

THE BLACKBERRY SHAPE

Cook 1 lb. blackberries, 1 lb. apples, 4 ozs. sugar and 2 cloves till the fruit is soft. Press through a sieve and add $\frac{1}{2}$ oz. of gelatine dissolved in a little hot water. Set in a mould. Serve with cream.

Mrs. E. M. Edwin,
New Bolingbroke Rectory.

From "'Food for Thought', a Book of Parsonage Recipes" compiled by Mrs. Shirley M. Hanson, published in 1961 by the Lincolnshire Old Churches Trust, The Subdeanery, Lincoln.

MANCHESTER PUDDING WITH CREAM

Boil $1\frac{1}{2}$ pints of milk and pour over 1 cup of breadcrumbs, add a teaspoon of sugar, the grated rind of a lemon. When cool, add the beaten yolks of 2 eggs. Put a layer of jam in a pie dish, pour the mixture over. Bake half an hour in a moderate oven (350 F., Mark 4). Whip the egg whites with sufficient cream. Spread over the pudding when quite cold.

Mrs. S. J. Godfrey,
Ramsey, Huntingdon.

PRESERVES

DAMSON PICKLE

The same recipe can also be used for blackcurrants. I made the blackcurrant pickle (my own concoction) last year and it's so thick and delicious I use it on pancakes or any plain pudding — but like the damson it's really to eat with cold beef etc.

Boil $\frac{1}{4}$ pint vinegar and 1 lb. sugar together. Pour it over 1 lb. of cleaned damsons, and leave overnight. Boil gently for a short time. Bottle when cold.

M. M. Gray,
Ruskington, Sleaford, Lincolnshire.

PICKLED ONIONS OR SHALLOTS

Peel and wash the onions in the usual way. Take a large oval jar and fill it as follows:—a deep layer of onions, a layer of pickling spice (loose), and a good layer of sugar. Continue until the jar is full. Cover the onions completely with ordinary cold vinegar, straight from the barrel. Screw down the top and leave it for several weeks. Onions done in this way will be found to be sweet and really crisp.

Mrs. M. P. Sheffield,
Buddewick, Boston, Lincolnshire.

APPLE JAM

Peel and core 3 lbs. Russet apples. Cut into half inch cubes. Wet cut apples and cover with 3 lbs. granulated sugar. Leave for forty-eight hours. Pour off syrup into a preserving pan and bring to the boil. Add apple chips and boil slowly without stirring until transparent. Put into pots.

Mrs. Barbara Cook,
Hunstanton, Norfolk.

GOOSEBERRY CHUTNEY

2 lbs. gooseberries, 1 lb. raisins, 2 lbs. sugar, ground ginger $\frac{1}{2}$ oz. – 1 oz. according to taste, a few chillies, onion or garlic, 2 oz. salt. Boil the fruit in enough vinegar to cover and when soft add the other ingredients. Boil together for about twenty minutes. Then bottle.

Mrs. A. G. Ingram,
Louth, Lincs.

BAKING

The old Suffolk brick ovens, rather like huge boxes, were heated by burning the fuel inside them and the door was the only outlet. The fuel was mostly whin — faggots or dry gorse bound with elm withies. There were usually two bakes a week, the brick oven took about an hour to heat up, and when a handful of flour thrown against the sides burned up with a blaze of sparks, it was ready. The fire was then scraped out, the dough was "set in" the hot oven and the door quickly shut. The bread took about an hour, but often the weekly joint, which took almost two hours, was baked at the same time in the back of the oven behind the bread. In front of this there would sometimes be Suffolk Rusks which were ready, and taken out, in about ten minutes. Bits of charcoal and embers of the fire often stuck to the bread and gave it extra flavour.

Old people who remember these ovens say the bread had a better taste than anything you get now.

SUFFOLK RUSKS

Jonathan Wright and John Tester, the Woodbridge bakers, are famous for their hand-made bread and Suffolk rusks. These are eaten buttered for breakfast and the drier they are the better people like them.

Mix 1½ lbs. of plain flour with ¾ oz. of baking powder, rub in 4 ozs. of lard and 4 ozs. of butter, stir in just over ¼ pint of milk, a beaten egg, ½ oz. of sugar and ¼ oz. of salt. Mix to bind. Roll out the dough half an inch thick, cut it in rounds with a 2-inch cutter, leave it about 30 minutes then bake them in a pre-heated hot oven (400 F., Mark 6) for 20 minutes. When cool enough to handle split them in two and bake them again about 10 minutes in the hot oven until golden brown.

Jonathan Wright and John Tester,
Woodbridge, Suffolk.

BREAD

Now I shall tell you how I make *my* bread; my first loaf was made when I was twelve years old, and my mother used to make lots of loaves, and I was always around to see her do it.

Take 3 lbs. of plain flour, 3 teaspoons of dry yeast, 1 teaspoonful of salt. Now put the flour and salt in a warm basin, then mix the dry yeast with a good teaspoonful of sugar and warm water. When this has started to rise (bubble), put it in the flour and mix with nice warm water. Knead it well and stand it in a warm place to rise to twice its size. Then take and break it up to put in tins to bake, but let it stand in the tins for 20 minutes in a warm place then bake.

A piece taken off the dough for a dumpling was always used when mother did her baking and they were lovely with gravy or stew. Another thing to do for tea, when baking, was hot suet cake, made with sweet spice and cake fruits.

Mother would also buy a large marrow bone, boil it for tea time and all the trimmings would be eaten with vinegar and the liquid used for Pea Soup next day. Of course wages were small in those days. Engine drivers and Firemen only got 15s. and 14s. per week, but the food was good.

Mrs. E. Marjoram,
Lowestoft, Suffolk.

PIG KILLING: Apple Tart made with Pig Lard

I lived in Boston, Lincolnshire, as a child, and my grandparents lived in the country near Swineshead; they had a small farm cottage with a soft water pump in the yard and apple trees and raspberries in the garden.

Once a year they killed a pig and Grandma made all sorts of lovely things, haslets and a mincemeat using some part of the pig, I remember it well but don't know her recipe; someone once said it would be the puck or pluck. Grandma's pastry was delicious, too, she would make a plate tart — with pastry at the bottom of the plate then a good layer of mincemeat, which she topped with pastry. Another tart she would make would be a pastry bottom, then a layer of thinly sliced apple, then a layer of mincemeat, then a layer of apple again, topped with pastry, brushed with milk, and sprinkled with sugar. This would be served with the top off the milk, or with custard. She made delicious milk puddings, too, all thick and creamy.

Another pudding using apple was:— slice the apples thinly into a pie dish, add sugar and about 3 or 4 cloves and top with pastry again. Brush with milk and sprinkle with sugar. Grandma 'picked out the cloves as she cut the pie. Cloves add a delicous flavour to apples.

Mrs. Nora Cook,
Donington, Near Spalding, Lincolnshire.

LINCOLNSHIRE WHITSUNTIDE CAKE

Rub 6 ozs. butter and a little salt into $1\frac{1}{2}$ lbs. flour, mix 1 oz. yeast with a little water and then add it to another 6 ozs. of butter and $\frac{1}{2}$ pint milk after warming them together. Pour this mixture into the flour and knead it to a nice soft dough, while it is growing light mix the filling and that is 1 lb. of currants, 1 lb. of moist sugar, 2 ozs. butter and a little nutmeg and allspice and the yolk of an egg. Increase the butter and sugar if you like the internal layers of pastry decidedly moist. Put all these in a saucepan and warm up over the heat till the currants are soft and will be thoroughly cooked after the ensuing baking. When the dough is quite light and has not risen too much, roll out a layer to the size you require and put on a layer of filling, above this place another layer of dough and another layer of filling until you have 4 layers of dough and 3 of currants. Fasten the edges well together with the white of egg left over when the yolk was put in the filling. Bake in a fairly sharp oven (375 F., Mark 5) for about an hour. When half baked, brush over the top of the cake with white of egg, adding a little sugar to make it browner if preferred, or sugar and milk, but the sugar may give a slight taste of caramel. The above makes two cakes the size of pudding plates, it is better to divide the dough and filling exactly before beginning to roll out the first cake. The cakes should be kept several days in a tightly closed tin for the filling to flavour the layers of pastry.

Miss A. Birkitt,
Tewkesbury, Gloucester.

AUNT EMMA'S BISCUITS

Mix 1 lb. flour, 8 ozs. white sugar, a little grated lemon rind and 6 ozs. butter. Add 2 well beaten eggs and mix together. Form it into a roll on a pastry board, cut into slices $\frac{1}{4}$ inch thick. Lay them on a greased baking sheet and bake in a moderately hot oven (350 F., Mark 4) until a light brown.

Mrs. S. J. Godfrey,
Ramsey, Huntingdon.

LINCOLNSHIRE APPLE TART

Line a 7–9 inch tart tin with pastry then fill it with the following mixture:—

Cream 4 ozs. sugar and 2 ozs. butter, beat in an egg, add 8 ozs. grated raw apple. This can be grated on the coarse grater. Cook in a medium to hot oven (400 F., Mark 6) for about 20 minutes. When cooked it will be a nice golden brown.

Mrs. Watkinson,
New York, Lincoln.

GRANTHAM WHITE GINGERBREAD (LINCOLNSHIRE)

Cream 4 ozs. butter, 4 ozs. sugar, beat in 1 egg yolk, add 8 ozs. flour sifted with a little baking powder and 1 oz. ground ginger. Whip the egg white so stiff that the basin may be turned upside down without it falling out, and fold in. Bake in a moderate oven (350 F., Mark 4) on a greased paper for 30—40 minutes but keep it pale in colour.

ALMOND PASTE FOR CHRISTMAS PUDDING

Beat 4 ozs. butter to a cream, add 8 ozs. caster sugar, 4 ozs. ground almonds and a few drops of almond essence. Mix well. Put in a dish and it is ready to serve when firm.

Mrs. C. Gimbert,
Ely, Cambridgeshire.

Midlands

Derbyshire, Gloucestershire, Leicestershire, Northamptonshire, Nottinghamshire, Oxfordshire, Rutland, Shropshire, Staffordshire, Warwickshire.

Dairy

Stilton Cheese, Leicester Red Cheese, Sage Derby, Double Gloucester, Single Gloucester Cheese, Nottingham Colwick Cheese (now rare), Shropshire Butter.

Agricultural Products

Hereford Beef Cattle (red and white like the famous Staffordshire pottery cows), Fat Leicestershire Sheep, Vale of Evesham Asparagus, Strawberries, Pershore Plums, Hereford Cider Apples.

Gastronomic Specialities

Raised Leicester and Melton Mowbray Pork Pies, Hough and Dough, Pheasants, Worcester Sauce, Derbyshire and Staffordshire Oatcakes, Bakewell Pudding, Oxford Marmalade, Fitchett Pie, Malvern Water, Burton-on-Trent Pale Ale.

Pastries

Banbury Cakes, Ashbourne Gingerbread, Scratching Cake, Mint Pastry, Oldbury Tarts.

PIES

PIES

We have had almost enough interesting and sometimes half forgotten recipes for pies from Daily Express readers to make a book in itself. They are a great English speciality, usually particularly well made in the Midlands.

Leicestershire is noted for its raised pork pies, the kind made with hot water crust pastry and no pie dish. Those of Melton Mowbray, made originally for hunting people, are coloured a delicate pink with anchovy essence which also gives them a delicious, if elusive, flavour. Excellent raised pork pies are also made in Leicester but without the anchovy. Until 1836, when the custom was discontinued because of the cost, the City of Gloucester was required to send a lamprey pie to the sovereign every year. Lampreys were considered a delicacy at Court for centuries and the pie is still sent for coronations.

Among the more curious traditional English pies is one which comes from Witney in Oxfordshire which is made with lamb's tails. "Thoroughly clean half a dozen lamb's tails, singe with a candle to remove the wool" it tells us, going on to explain how they should be simmered with onions before being put in the pie dish. The pie used to be served cold. Nowadays, however, lambs no longer have their tails docked. The shepherd instead fixes an elastic band round the

31

tail which eventually causes it to drop off — it would make a poor pie.

The famous Shropshire Fidget or Fitchett Pie is usually made with apples, onions, potatoes and bacon and ham, it is not unlike the squab pie so popular in the West Country. Medley Pies are evidently peculiar to the Midlands and Sea Pie (which has suet crust pastry on top and is cooked in a saucepan, not in the oven) is one which used to be made on the narrow boats on inland waterways, such as the Grand Union Canal, as well as on fishing boats. It was convenient as the whole dinner was prepared in one saucepan. Crokky Pie was another name for it.

COUNTRY STYLE PORK PIE

For Pastry:—

8 ozs. plain flour   ½ teaspoon salt
3 ozs. home rendered lard or best cooking fat

Meat:—

½ lb. fresh minced pork or the same quantity of left-over cooked pork, chopped fine and mixed in a small cup of water, salt and pepper to taste.

Rub the fat in the flour, mix with a knife. Add enough boiling water to make a firm ball. Cut off about a third and mould the rest into a loose-bottomed round tin 6 inches across by 4 inches deep. Fill in the meat and mould the rest of the pastry on top to form a lid. Pierce a small hole in the top to let out the steam. Bake in a moderate oven (350 F., Mark 4) for 1 hour.

My grannie used to make this pie and we had it for breakfast every Sunday morning when we lived in a cottage at Trowell.

Mrs. Frances Martin,
Babbington via Eastwood, Notts.

RAISED CHICKEN PIE

The Cotswold village of Broadway in Worcestershire is one of those picture postcard places where every second house does teas or antiques and in summer is full of motor coaches.

H. H. Collins's bow-fronted pie shop in the main street has been there for the past 70 years. They cure their own Wiltshire bacon and do Bath chaps, black puddings and sausages. Lately their fame has spread as far as London and they have been selling some of their more luxurious pies to famous shops in the West End. They have had a startling success, for instance, with the chicken and ham pies, Cardinal Heenan, they told me, is very fond of them. "They are the sort of pies" they added, "which we expect will be eaten at Ascot."

They have also had a great trade lately in game pies and stuffed, decorated boar's head for hunt balls. Many of the pies are hand raised, by this I mean that the hot-water crust pastry of which pork and other pies are made is moulded by hand into the shape of pastry cases by Mrs. Beryl Watts and three other traditional craftswomen who shape and model the soft dough rather as if they were making pottery. It looks and tastes much nicer than when the pie is moulded in a tin.

They say the chicken and ham pie would not be too difficult to make at home if you know how to do a hot-water crust pastry. Melt 8 ozs. of lard in $\frac{1}{3}$ pint water. Bring to the boil. Stir in 1 lb. plain flour, a pinch salt, mix it quickly till the pan comes clean. Throw it onto a table. Knead it and leave it for an hour to rest. Mould it to line a tin or pie dish. Put a layer of raw bacon cut in chunks on the bottom, fill it up with cold boiled chicken cut in pieces. Add a little pepper, not too much salt. Roll out a piece of pastry for the lid and seal it off, but make a hole in the middle. Brush with egg. Bake in a hot oven (400 F., Mark 6) for $1\frac{1}{2}$ hours. After baking brush it again with egg and pour $\frac{1}{2}$ oz. gelatine mixed with a pint of boiling water or strained chicken stock through the hole in the lid. The pie is always eaten cold.

S. H. and H. H. Collins,
Broadway, Worcestershire.

CHEESE AND ONION PIE

I have been a cook all my life and am still working. I was formerly cook to Sir Bernard Docker and made many country dishes for him, I am now working for Lady Scarsdale at Kedleston Hall. I was born in the north country and we were always cooking and baking bread and pies. This pie, which is very tasty, is an old north country one. It is called Cheese and Onion Pie.

Mix 8 ozs. self raising flour with $\frac{1}{2}$ teaspoon salt, 4 ozs. butter and 4 ozs. pure lard. Mix to a soft dough with 2 or 3 tablespoons of water, flour it and roll it out. Line a pie plate with the pastry, then grate 2 large peeled onions and 8 ozs. strong cheese onto it. Season a small quantity of fresh thick cream with salt and pepper. Whip it lightly and spread it over the mixture. Cover with pastry and flute the edges securely. Brush with milk and bake in a fairly hot oven (375 F., Mark 5) for 30–35 minutes.

Mrs. Constance Bevan,
Kedleston Hall, Derby.

MUTTON PIE

When I was young money was very short. Ten shillings a week and cottage and garden was good wages for farm workers, but they were happy days and our needs were very simple. I learnt to make patchwork bedspreads and to crochet lace and shawls. I still do a lot of crochet these days. I am 76 and my family are all married with families of their own and I have 37 grandchildren and 5 great-grandchildren.

This is a very good recipe for a family using the cheaper cuts of meat as steak is expensive to buy now.

Bone 2 lbs. of neck of mutton and cut into small pieces. Cut up 3 sheep's kidneys. Put them with the meat in a pie dish, sprinkle on some parsley and 1 minced onion, salt and pepper. Pour over 2 cups of gravy and cover with pastry. Bake 1¼ hours in a hot oven to begin with then gradually lower the heat.

Mrs. M. Hughes,
Pelsall, Walsall, Staffordshire.

MEDLEY PIE

I am in my 78th year, but on Saturdays when I was eight years old I used to walk two miles to scrub my grannies white wood bedroom floors and stairs and her blue brick living room and kitchen floors, not forgetting pantry shelves, floor and four steps down to it. By the time I had finished grannies favourite Medley Pie was ready and she served it with nice mashed potatoes and greens.

For Medley Pies she greased as many saucers as required for a pie each. She covered them with a thin layer of short pastry, a layer of sliced potatoes, a little salt, then diced bacon, a layer of sliced onion, a layer of sliced apples sprinkled with brown sugar and finally a few currants and sultanas. Cover with pastry and bake until the ingredients are cooked through and the pastry brown. Very tasty.

After dinner I had quite a few more duties until I had my tea — the bottom crust off a 2 lb. cottage loaf with a little butter she had made specially for me, and with home-made raspberry jam. Then there was the journey home. Although tired and with aching limbs I always felt happy to have helped my very poorly old granny and to have sampled her favourite recipe.

Mrs. E. Adcock,
Arley, near Coventry, Warwickshire.

WORCESTERSHIRE MARROW PIE

This recipe for "A Marrow Pie" has been passed on through three generations on my father's side and comes from a little village in Worcestershire.

Cut up some marrow into pieces approximately 1 inch by ½ inch. Put a layer in a pie dish. Cut up an onion and put in a layer on top of the marrow. Cut some bacon into small strips and add to the other ingredients. Repeat the layers until the pie dish is full. Add a pinch of salt, a dash of pepper, one dessertspoonful of water. Cover the dish and bake in a moderate oven (350 F., Mark 4) until the marrow is soft. Then cover with a short crust pastry and bake until the pastry is cooked. This is delicious as a supper snack.

Mrs. Daisy Allen,
Abergele, North Wales.

NEW POTATO PIE

To eat with braised kidneys, or baked leeks or large thick slices of cheddar cheese.

Boil new potatoes for about 3 minutes. Slice and sprinkle them lightly with seasoned flour and parsley (or a very little sage or thyme). Put them into a pie dish and pour over some cream or top of milk. Cover with puff pastry, decorate it with pastry leaves, brush with milk. Bake in a hot oven (400 F., Mark 6) but reduce the heat after 5 minutes. If this is eaten with leeks also cooked in the oven this is so tasty. Or if wanted for a main meal eat it with braised kidneys or large thick slices of cheddar cheese.

Mrs. Joan Foster,
Kettering, Northamptonshire.

FISH

ELVERS

"I was born in 1890, at a village in Gloucestershire, within a few miles of the Severn, and since I can remember, from about a few years of age, the main topic down my way at Easter time has always been elvers. My dad always called them 'Manna from Heaven' ", writes *Mr. A. Phipps* from the Royal Hospital, Chelsea.

"In those days anyone who had a net could catch them but the experienced fishermen used to net them at night and hawk them from door to door, crying out 'Elvers, all alive-o', usually about 2d. lb. for the first two catches then dropping to 1½d. and even to a 1d. lb. according to the quantity of the catch. Alas, they are now about 5s. lb.

"I always liked them how my mother used to cook them; some people liked bacon with them, and some with a poached egg on top, but for me it was just the elvers, thoroughly cleaned, and fried in pure lard — which one could get then. Heat the lard to boiling point, then add the elvers, cook until white, add pepper and salt to taste, cover with a large plate, then add some boiling water to take a little of the richness off. Simmer gently for about 10 minutes, share out into hot soup plates, then with a thick slice of bread and a fork you can really get down to it, dipping your bread in the delicious juices. What a feast, fit for the gods.

"I get some sent to me every year, cooked, then frozen. I have to reheat them, and although they are very nice, and I am very grateful, they are not as good as when fresh caught.

"I have always been fascinated in the reading of how they travel to and from the Sargasso Sea, also of their journeys overland in this England of ours. They are just as prevalent as in my boyhood days, but are not so easy to get, as other nations, especially Germany, send planes to get them all alive-o to stock their own rivers with them."

Mr. Phipps,
Royal Hospital, Chelsea.

Elvers are baby eels which are considered a great delicacy in Spain. The Spaniards value them almost above caviars and truffles. They are often served fried in olive oil with garlic and chilli peppers, and eaten so hot that you need a wooden fork for them as a metal one would burn your mouth. They are well-known in the West of England and appear in most of the tributaries of the Severn with the high tides in spring time. I thought this English seasonal delicacy might be on sale in London in spring — like gull's eggs — in some of the famous fish restaurants. But I must be wrong. Said Prunier's manager: "We've never served them! I've been at Prunier's 36 years and I've never heard of them and I don't think they are ever in the market."

At Bentleys Oyster Bar they seemed to think I was a bit cracked, and I had no luck at Wheeler's either. No one, they said, ever came in and asked for any, and the manager added, for good measure. that he had never eaten an elver and had never seen one either.

It must be one of those neglected British delicacies like the lampreys, fresh water prawns, and English truffles that we can't be bothered with in this country.

BAKED HERRINGS

Take off the heads of 6 herrings and clean the fish. Place in a pie dish with $\frac{1}{2}$ teaspoon of salt, 1 teaspoon of pepper, pinch of cayenne pepper, 4 allspice, a few cloves and peppercorns, a teaspoon of grated horseradish. Add 1 gill of cold water and some vinegar. Bake in a slow oven (300 F., Mark 2) for 35 minutes. Serve cold arranged neatly on a dish, the sauce strained over them. A teaspoon of chopped chives is an improvement.

Mrs. Florence Feeney,
Yarpole, near Leominster, Herefordshire.

BREAM PIE

Scrape clean and well wash 2 freshwater bream. Make a stuffing with breadcrumbs, 1 small chopped onion and some sweet herbs and parsley, pepper and salt and a little mace and 2 beaten eggs. Stuff the fish. Sew them up and lay them in a dish lined with puff pastry. Add about 1 pint of cold water and a tablespoon of vinegar. Bake in a very hot oven (450 F., Mark 8) for about 30 minutes.

Mrs. D. N. Harris,
Amblecote, near Stourbridge, Worcs.

KEDGEREE

Old fashioned English kedgeree, one time standby of the British breakfast table, is now more often served as a supper dish, all hot and steaming and delicately flavoured with curry. You can prepare it hours beforehand then heat it ten minutes before supper.

Have a large pan of rapidly boiling salted water, throw in 8 ozs. of long grained Patna rice. Let it boil for exactly 17 minutes. Drain it in a sieve and keep it hot. Meanwhile boil 3 eggs hard, peel and cut them in quarters. Poach a couple of pounds of smoked haddock or smoked fillet gently in a frying pan in milk for 7 to 10 minutes, adding a good pinch of pepper, or mustard powder if you like your food highly flavoured. Flake the fish, throwing away any skin and bones. Stir it into the hot rice with 2 tablespoons of butter, a heaped teaspoon of curry powder and, if liked, a good pinch of cayenne pepper. Mix well, add the hard boiled eggs. Beat up 1 or 2 raw eggs in a teacup of the milk in which the fish was cooked, stir this into the kedgeree and heap it on a hot dish. Warm for about 5 minutes in the oven. It can be garnished with chopped egg yolks.

Never put a lid on any rice dish; the steam coming out of it condenses on the cold lid and drips back into the rice and makes it soggy.

GAME

GROUSE WITH MUSHROOMS

1 young grouse	1 oz. butter
1 lb. mushrooms	

Put about 6 large mushrooms, skinned and cut in quarters, inside the bird. Fry the bird in butter until brown all over, preferably in a casserole. Cut up the remainder of the mushrooms in small pieces, season with salt and pepper, add these to the casserole and fry gently. Add 2 tablespoons of cream and simmer very gently for 30 minutes. A young bird cooked in this way should not take more than 45 minutes.

Miss W. Harper,
Cropwell Butler, Nottinghamshire.

ROAST BAWN OF HARE

This was given to my grandmother by Lady Francis Gresby of Drakelow Hall, which is now, alas, an Electricity Power Plant establishment.

Skin the hare and cut off the head, neck, fore and hind legs (these can be used for soup). Stuff the back or "saddle" of the hare with a forcemeat made of thyme, parsley, basil and marjoram mixed with 2 ozs. breadcrumbs, 1½ ozs. suet, pepper and salt and bind it with 2 eggs. Cover the hare with fat bacon and secure with coarse thread.

37

Wrap it in well greased paper. Roast it for about an hour in a hot oven (400 F., Mark 6). Remove the wrapping and crisp up quickly and serve garnished with green gooseberry sauce and also a tomato and watercress salad.

Mrs. E. M. Waterfield,
Swadlincote, Burton-on-Trent.

[For Green Gooseberry Sauce see page 88].

BOILED RABBIT WITH DUMPLINGS

This is a recipe my mother used over 70 years ago and for flavour I don't think it can be beaten. We were a large family and my mother used a big oval saucepan. Into it she put 2 rabbits cut up and about 1½–2 lbs. of belly pork covered with water and brought to the boil. Season, then add sliced carrots, larger pieces of parsnip, turnip, onion until the pan is nearly full. Then my mother would make a suet dumpling for each of us which were put into the pan about 20 minutes before the rabbits were done and with boiled potatoes it was a dinner not one of us would miss.

Mrs. E. M. Gebhard,
Tile Cross, Birmingham.

VARIOUS

STILTON CHEESE

There is some confusion about the origin of Stilton cheese. It seems first to have been made in the Vale of Belvoir, or at Wymondham or at Quenby. It was already famous by 1745, probably made by several people in the area, some of whom were better known for their prime cheese than others.

Blue Stilton cheese is often said to have been made at Quenby Hall, Leicestershire, and to have first been known as Lady Beaumont's or Mrs. Ashby's cheese. With the marriage of the Quenby Hall housekeeper however, the cheese began to be sold at the Bell Inn, Stilton, and rapidly became famous. This was a well-known posting inn on the Great North Road, in Huntingdonshire, and it was much patronised by people changing horses as they travelled between London and Edinburgh. They paid the then enormous price of 2s. 6d. per lb. for Stilton cheese in the early 18th century. According to another story it was a *Mrs. Paulet* of Wymondham who made the cheese for the landlord of the Bell Inn, Stilton. He being a relative of hers named *Mr. Cooper Thornhill*.

The Melton Mowbray district of Leicestershire and the Belvoir Vale were both prosperous cheese-making areas in Victorian times and the land was reputed to be ideal for making both blue and white Stilton. The old farmhouse cheeses were mostly bought up by cheese factors, either on the farms or at Melton Mowbray and Leicester Fairs. Stilton has also been made in other parts of the Midlands too, including Derbyshire, for several generations. Blue Stilton cheese and Melton Mowbray Pies and hunting are almost synonymous.

An old Tawny Port, of course, goes very well with ripe blue Stilton but a good Claret or Burgundy would be excellent with it too, also crisp raw celery, washed and trimmed, and stood in a jug of cold water, and some wine biscuits or water biscuits.

Stilton is at its best from November to April. To get it in perfect condition it is best to go to a cheesemonger or grocer specialising in cheese. Half a Stilton or a quarter Stilton will have an incomparably better flavour than a wedge of Stilton just bought by the pound, and might not be too big for some families at Christmas. To find a whole Stilton in perfect condition one generally has to go to a restaurant specialising in cheese, or one of the famous London clubs.

People like to dig out the middle of a Stilton cheese with a special cheese scoop, but this is a wasteful habit as the large surfaces thus exposed to the air tend to dry up. Nowadays it is thought best to cut the cheese horizontally and afterwards keep the cut surface covered with a piece of greaseproof paper. Port should not be poured into a Stilton as some people think but it may be drunk with it.

LEICESTERSHIRE RED is a crumbly cheese very deep orange-red in colour, delicious with biscuits and watercress, it also makes a very good deep orange Welsh Rabbit. It was well thought of in Victorian England, but first became known in London in about 1745 at the same time as Stilton Cheese and Melton Mowbray Pies.

DERBYSHIRE cheeses are very hard, mildly flavoured very old cheeses which used to be made on the farms for working men's dinners but are now rare. The county was famous for cheese, flavoured and coloured with herbs. SAGE DERBY, once made for Christmas and harvest, has been revived. This is a curious looking piebald or striped orange and green cheese whose irregular green stripes are due to the sage which colours and flavours it. In the old days the yellow part was dyed with marigold petals. The two curds were made separately and then mixed to give striped or mottled cheese. Sometimes the green curd was cut into animal or plain figures which were pressed onto the outside of the cheese. Sometimes the sage leaves were just pressed onto the cheese in patterns which gradually became traditional.

BUTTERSCOTCH

Granny always made this butterscotch on bonfire night and it is also very good for a sore throat and is very easy to make.

"FRIED FROGS"

This recipe has been handed down for years in our family and is still enjoyed by us once a week as a change from stews, chops and fish etc. It's also quick and economical.

I don't know whether there is a correct name for this meal, I have never seen anything about it in recipe books, but we always call it "Fried Frogs". Why, I don't know.

You just fry bacon, about ½ lb. for 3 persons. Remove the bacon and into the fat slice potatoes fairly thinly with salt and pepper to season. Fill with water so that it just shows through. Cover with a lid or plate and simmer for about 30 minutes. The potatoes go down slightly in the water and form a sort of gravy. This is eaten with bread and is very tasty.

Mrs. D. Gadsby,
Burton-on-Trent, Staffordshire.

BAKED TOMATO AND CHEESE

Fill a fireproof dish with alternate layers of sliced, peeled tomatoes and onion. The English variety of the latter made a more flavoursome dish than Spanish. Add salt and pepper to taste, a knob of butter and enough water to make some juice. Cook in a moderate oven (350 F., Mark 4) until the onions are tender. Just before serving cover the top with thinly sliced cheese. Return it to the oven until the cheese has melted. When fresh tomatoes are over this recipe is quite as good using tinned tomatoes.

Miss M. Warner,
Retford, Nottinghamshire.

DOUBLE GLOUCESTER

Beer, pickled onions and the top of a new cottage loaf go perfectly with Double Gloucester cheese. This used to be made on Gloucestershire farms, particularly in the Vale of Berkeley. Single Gloucester, now seldom made, was a quicker ripening cheese made in spring when the cows were on young grass.

Those old fashioned Victorian cheese dishes with tall, flowery china covers shaped like huge slices of cheese and with a ventilation hole in the top are excellent for storing English cheese. For Gloucester Cheese and Ale slice some Double Gloucester thinly, lay it in a pie dish and spread it with English mustard. Cover it with ale, bake in the oven till the cheese melts and serve it with thick slices of hot toast made from brown bread and dipped into hot ale. The cheese should be poured over it.

In Elizabethan England the mustard for this dish came from near Tewkesbury: "his wits are thick as Tewkesbury mustard" as Falstaff says of somebody in one of Shakespeare's plays.

PORK TAIL SOUP

I thought I would write and tell you of a recipe which has been passed down to me from my great-great-grandmother and is still enjoyed by my family and parents today. My great-great-grandmother cooked for a family of 17, so of necessity her recipes had to be economical, but nourishing too. My mother tells me she was a wonderful cook, but this was one of the family's favourite dishes, and certainly nowadays we find it very useful to anyone recovering from flu and colds.

For Pork Tail Soup take:—

2 lbs. pork tails (these are sometimes referred to as "Pork Bones" and it is best to purchase the "clips" which are the thick ends of the tails, but if these are not available some of the fat should be removed from the narrower ends.)

3 ozs. lentils
1 large parsnip
water

2 large carrots
2 medium-large onions
salt and pepper

The pork tails are put into a large saucepan, and water added until it comes about one inch above the meat. Bring this to the boil, then lower the heat to simmering point. Add the lentils, peel and grate the carrots and parsnip, and finely dice the onions. Put all the vegetables into the meat and add salt and pepper to taste. Leave this to simmer for about 2 hours. Serve hot with boiled potatoes (cooked separately). The potatoes are optional as the meat and soup is delicious by itself.

This is an excellent soup for cold wintry days, and makes a pleasant change from beef stews. The aroma from the kitchen is as good as the taste and I am constantly asked "when will it be ready to eat".

Mrs. Joan Green,
Sutton Coldfield, Warwickshire.

ENGLISH BEER

Burton-on-Trent, Staffordshire, famous for its beer for centuries is said to produce the finest pale ale in the country. There are about a score of breweries producing at least 3 million barrels of beer annually. This is because of the local water which imparts a unique and distinctive flavour that you cannot get anywhere else. It comes, not from the Trent which is filthy, but from wells in the southern part of the town. The water is drawn off gravel beds rich in gypsum and has made the town famous for the flavour of its beer since the 14th century, just as the water of Speyside has made that district famous for its straight malt whiskies. Beer was exported from Burton-on-Trent to Catherine of Russia in the 17th century.

Beer is used by some hunting men to clean and brush up the pile on their black top hats, the ones which are worn with a Pink coat and white buckskin breeches in the hunting field.

Cock ale was common a century ago in Oxfordshire villages. They used to lower a freshly killed cockerel previously crushed in a mortar, feathers and all, into the big barrels of ale and leave it there for some time to mature and give strength to the beer.

Brazenose ale which is beer heated with sugar, cloves and nutmeg and has roasted apples floating in it is served at Brazenose College, Oxford, in an enormous silver tankard after dinner on Shrove Tuesday.

DERBYSHIRE OR STAFFORDSHIRE OATCAKES

These are as big as a dinner plate, thin, floppy, and though very popular in Derbyshire and Staffordshire are seldom seen elsewhere. They are more like the big Breton buckwheat pancakes than anything eaten in Scotland. At the Charles Cotton Hotel in Hartington, Derbyshire, they sometimes serve the local oatcakes for breakfast with fried egg, bacon and mushrooms. "Visitors are always surprised and delighted" *Mrs. Rhodes*, the assistant cook, told me "they buy them from the village butcher to take home." Most local people buy them ready made either to toast and eat buttered with jam or honey, or to fry with bacon and eggs. They are eaten for breakfast or high tea, keep fresh for several days and are very good.

Warm 2 pints of water to blood heat, add ½ oz. salt and 1 oz. crumbled bakers' yeast. Mix 1 lb. scotch oatmeal with 8 ozs. wholemeal flour and ½ oz. baking powder. Add this gradually to the yeast mixture stirring and beating till it's like Yorkshire pudding batter. Let it stand in a warm place for 20 minutes to "work", stirring it up if it drops down.

If the mixture seems thin add a little oatmeal, if thick a little water, Grease an iron griddle or bakestone (or an ordinary big frying pan or cookie sheet), heat it, then pour a teacup of batter in the middle so it spreads evenly. Cook it 5 minutes, turn, cook the other side, then back to the first side for 2 minutes. Cool the oatcakes on a wire sieve. They are very popular in the Potteries where some folks cover them with cheese and grill them.

WHITE PUDDING — A BREAKFAST DISH

This recipe was handed to me many years ago by my sister who in turn received it from her mother-in-law.

8 ozs. groats
1 tablespoon pearl barley
2 tablespoons rice
1 quart of milk or water

Cree* the above together until tender and all the moisture is taken up. Add 1 chopped onion, 1 tablespoon sage and a little Pennyroyal, 1 oz. of bacon fat, margarine or suet and pepper and salt to taste.

44

Mix with 1 beaten egg. Bake or boil in a basin for 1 hour. When cold slice and fry with bacon for breakfast.

Mrs. Anne Claydon,
Wingerworth, Chesterfield, Derbyshire.

To cree is to soften grain by boiling.
Pennyroyal is a small plant of the mint family, *Mentha Pulegium*, which is often used as an edging plant or growth between paving stones. It tastes of peppermint. Mint might be substituted.

MEAT

BOILED LEG OF MUTTON
Put a leg of mutton in a saucepan and nearly cover with water. Cook gently for about 2 hours. After it has been cooking for about an hour put in 6 medium sized onions, 6 carrots, 2 parsnips and 2 small swedes. Cook for a further hour with a little pepper and salt. Serve with caper sauce, which is just a white sauce with capers in it. stock can be used for soup.

Mrs. P. Hancock,
North Kilworth, Rugby, Warwickshire.

If available, a few raw veal, beef or lamb bones cooked with the meat will not only improve its flavour, but also make an excellent stock from the pot liquor. In large Victorian households a small and tender smoked ox tongue was sometimes served, boiled and hot, with the mutton. It was garnished with mashed turnips — an idea which a modern pub might emulate.

IRISH STEW
Cut 1 lb. neck of mutton or chops into pieces and slice 2 onions. Put the meat and onions in a pan with ½ pint stock and bring to the boil. Add salt and pepper and simmer for 30 minutes. Add 1 lb. potatoes and cook for 1½ hours. Serve on a hot dish with small pieces of toast.

Mrs. E. Callodine,
Heanor, Derbyshire.

LIZZIE TURNILL'S CUTLETS DE NOEL
Trim away all the fat from some cutlets. Fry them lightly. Place in a stewpan, dredge thickly with browned flour. Fry 2 or 3 large sliced onions till golden. Season highly with black pepper and scatter them over the cutlets. Add enough stock to cover the meat. Lay 1 lb. boiled peeled chestnuts on the onions. Cook slowly, covered, for 2 hours. The onions and chestnuts will be cooked by steam and their flavour will penetrate the cutlets. To serve, pile the chestnuts and

onions on a hot dish, arrange the cutlets round them. Thicken and colour the gravy and pour round. Scatter chopped capers over the chestnuts and onions and serve hot.

I have substituted "pound" for "pint" of chestnuts in this recipe which I have used many times. It is delicious.

Mrs. Isabel Turnill,
Boars Hill, Oxford.

LIZZIE TURNILL'S FILLET OF MUTTON

Cut off the thick part of a leg of mutton and bone it. Stuff it with nicely seasoned veal stuffing. Wrap the joint in a suet crust and damp and seal the edges. Then wrap it all in a cloth, plunge it into boiling water and simmer gently until cooked, 20 minutes to the pound and 15 minutes extra for every 4 lbs. To serve, turn it out of the cloth, sprinkle with brown bread crumbs mixed with finely chopped herbs. When the paste is cut it will be found to contain a nice rich gravy. Serve with caper or parsley sauce.

These old recipes come from the personal notebook of my mother-in-law, Elizabeth Turnill, the daughter and wife of a Lincolnshire farmer. It is beautifully written in copperplate style and is dated January 1888. She signed her name as Lizzie. The Cutlets de Noel and the Fillet of Mutton are old favourites with our family.

Mrs. Isabel Turnill,
Boars Hill, Oxford.

CHRISTMAS STUFFED BEEF

This recipe was used by my granny many, many years ago. She kept a country pub and gave all her customers stuffed beef on Christmas Eve. My mother carried on with this recipe for one large family and since her death I have always done the beef for Christmas breakfast (a great tradition in my family) longer than I wish to remember.

You need 5-6 lbs. brisket of beef which has been salted by the butcher for about 1 week. For the stuffing you need $\frac{3}{4}$ lb. – 1 lb. brussels sprouts, 6 good size leeks, 3 medium size onions, 1 dessert-spoon sage, 1 tablespoon thyme, 1 tablespoon parsley, a sprinkling of any other herbs and salt and pepper.

Clean well and chop the vegetables and herbs roughly, do not mince. Place as much of this raw stuffing as possible into the meat and spread some over the meat, putting the remainder in a muslin bag. Roll up and tie the meat and put it into a cloth. Fasten securely and cover completely so that water gets to it. Put the meat and bag of stuffing into a large saucepan or pot, cover with cold water; boil steadily for approximately 6 hours. Leave in the container until cold. Take out the meat and place the stuffing around it.

Miss Muriel Toon,
Syston, Leicestershire.

VICTORIAN "PIE" USING SALT BEEF

You need a shallow ovenproof dish of 1½ pint liquid capacity. Put 8 ozs. sliced cold salt beef into it, add 8 ozs. whole peeled tomatoes and pour over ¼ pint of stock. Slice 12 ozs. peeled potatoes thinly, then arrange them over the pie, leaving some of the pie filling uncovered in the centre. Sprinkle the top with nutmeg, then bake the pie on the shelf above the centre of the oven (375 F., Mark 5) for 45 minutes or until the potatoes are cooked.

Mrs. E. Knight,
Mears, Ashby, Northampton.

SEA PIE

Wash 1 lb. stewing steak and cut it into small pieces and roll them in 1 tablespoon of seasoned flour. Slice 1 carrot, 1 turnip and 1 onion and put them into a saucepan with the meat. Season with salt and pepper, add water to cover and simmer gently for 1½ hours.

Roll out ¼ lb. suet pastry into a round slightly smaller than the pan. Put in on top of the meat. Cover and cook gently for another 45 minutes. To serve, cut the crust into four, put the meat and vegetables on a dish and lay the crust on top.

Mrs. L. H. Cook,
Repton, Derbyshire.

In some households in the Colchester area a few shelled local oysters, together with their strained liquor, are often slipped under the suet pastry crust during the last 20 minutes.

OX LIVER PUDDING

My mother used to give us this pudding for dinner on very cold days. It's really delicious, much more tasty than steak and kidney pudding and so cheap and easy to make. It serves four people and is very nice with brussels sprouts and mashed potatoes.

Make a suet crust with 8 ozs. self raising flour and 4 ozs. of suet. I do not line the basin as it soaks all the gravy up. Put 1½–2 lbs. diced ox liver and 1 or 2 large sliced onions in a basin in layers. Add pepper and salt, make some gravy from stock, add half. Put a suet crust on top and foil or greaseproof paper and steam for at least 3 hours. Serve with the extra gravy.

It's a most delicious flavour and very tender.

Mrs. L. Hollaway,
Tipton, Staffordshire.

BEEF CASSEROLE

This is an old recipe of my aunt's who was the family cook for many years. She used to cook it in the old range oven and it tasted delicious.

47

potatoes cut in half and plenty of onions cut in half if fairly large. Sprinkle with sage, pepper and salt. Pour over hot stock or water with a little thickening to about half-way up the tin. Cover with foil (my idea). Place in a hot oven (400 F., Mark 6) until boiling, then lower the heat to keep simmering for about 2 hours. Remove the foil for the last 30 minutes to brown the potatoes.

Mrs. M. Toseland,
Portsmouth.

According to the Local Studies Department of Birmingham Central Library this old Midlands dish is known as Hock and Dough or Hough and Dough. Both spellings are correct but "Hough" is the more Midlands way of spelling it.

English spare ribs of pork are from the fore-end of the animal between the shoulders — usually cheap, it roasts well but has a large cut surface (without crackling) where the front leg has been cut away. A very popular cut in the Midlands it should not be confused with the U.S. cut of the same name which is just the pared down ends of cutlet bones.

BACON AND APRICOT "PIE"

Lightly brown a 1 inch thick gammon rasher on both sides in a frying pan. Lay it in a large pie dish. Place 8 ozs. dried apricots — which have been soaking in water for 12 hours previously — on top. Sprinkle a little pepper over, add 1 oz. sultanas, pour a little gravy over, cover with 6 sliced potatoes. Put a piece of greaseproof paper over all then bake in a moderate oven (350 F., Mark 4) for 1 hour. Serve hot.

Mrs. K. Greenman,
Leckhampton, Cheltenham, Gloucestershire.

MARKET DAY SAVOURY

(This can be left cooking while you go to market.)

Take 6 small pork chops, 2 pig's kidneys, 1 lb. onions, 1½ lbs. potatoes, 1 small apple, 1 teaspoon sage, 1 tablespoon tomato sauce. Peel and slice the potatoes and onions, put them in a stew jar in layers with the chops and sliced kidneys. Sprinkle sliced onion, apple and seasoning among them. Cover with a layer of potatoes. Pour over a teacup of water, put on a tight fitting lid and cook slowly for 2 or 3 hours in a very moderate oven (325 F., Mark 3). The longer you cook this dish the more savoury it will be.

Mrs. K. Greenman,
Leckhampton, Cheltenham, Gloucestershire.

STUFFED POTATOES

This dish has been used for 4 or 5 generations at least by a country family. One member thinks it was eaten over 200 years ago.

50

Scrub, but do not peel, some large potatoes and with an apple corer make a round hole right through the potato. (I have made my own scoop out of a round of metal to make the hole larger than a corer but an ordinary apple corer will do.) Now stuff the hole with strips of steak or lean pieces of lamb or minced beef or chopped kidney. Cut the piece scooped out and plug the ends, skin on the outside. Rub the outsides with salt and butter. Sprinkle with salt and parsley and bake in a moderate oven. The juices from the meat saturate the potatoes and the result is tasty and satisfying.

Mrs. Joan Foster,
Kettering, Northamptonshire.

A GELATINE OF PORK

Lay a belly of young pork, preferably salted skin side downwards on the table. Season well with pepper and cover with thin slices of pickled gherkins. Roll up as tightly as possible, tie with strong string and fasten securely in a cloth. Place the roll in a stewpan containing sufficient hot stock or hot water just to cover it. Add 1 carrot, 2 onions, $\frac{1}{4}$ turnip, 1 bay leaf, 10 peppercorns, a sprinkling of thyme and parsley and cook gently from $2\frac{1}{2}$ to 3 hours. Press between 2 dishes until cold, then remove the cloth, brush over with glaze and serve garnished with parsley.

Serve cold with hot baked potatoes in their skins and with apple preserve.

Mrs. L. Frost,
Derby.

MUCH WENLOCK "PIE"

I'm an old age pensioner now, but still enjoy my cooking, and trying out new recipes, but more often I turn back to my old and tasty dishes. This recipe belonged to my "Gran". It's really tasty and in those days the whole lot for a family of eight cost 3s. I've made it many, many times — of course cutting down the quantities.

Mince $1\frac{1}{2}$ lbs. pig's fry, 1 lb. ox liver and 3 large onions together coarsely. Add 1 tablespoon dripping or suet, $\frac{1}{2}$ teacup finely chopped sage, 1 small teaspoon curry powder, 2 level tablespoons of plain flour and 1 wineglass of ale and 1 of water. Season with salt and pepper. Stir thoroughly. Place the mixture in a pie dish or casserole.

Cut 3 large potatoes $\frac{1}{4}$ inch in thickness, place them on top of the pie overlapping each slice. Sprinkle 1 cup of fine white breadcrumbs over the potatoes and add knobs of dripping or suet. Bake in a medium hot oven (375 F., Mark 5) for $1\frac{1}{4}$ hours.

I find this delicious served with sprouts or finely chopped buttered cabbage.

Mrs. Hilda M. Connington,
Much Wenlock, Shropshire.

51

sultanas, 3 ozs. currants, 1 oz. chopped candied peel and a good teaspoonful of mixed spices. Mix thoroughly and bake in a tin which has been greased and sprinkled with brown sugar in a moderate oven (350 F., Mark 4) for about 45 minutes or until nicely browned.

My father, who was a long journeyman with two horses, used to take a good piece with him for his lunch amongst other things. He used to set off at 6 o'clock in the morning and return home about 11 p.m. and he always used to say his bread pudding was the best part of his victuals.

Mrs. A. K. Merrett,
Cheltenham, Gloucestershire.

BUTTERMILK PANCAKES

Mix 8 ozs. self raising flour, $\frac{1}{2}$ teaspoon cream of tartar, $\frac{1}{2}$ teaspoon bicarbonate of soda and a pinch of salt together. Beat in enough buttermilk to make the batter of a pancake consistency. Rub a frying pan with pork fat. Pour a small quantity of the mixture in and let it cook until bubbles rise. Turn and cook the other side. Spread with butter and eat hot.

Mrs. A. E. Bailey,
Rushall, Walsall, Staffordshire.

Buttermilk is now to be had in most supermarkets and from most milkmen.

BARLEY KERNEL PUDDING

When I was a war-time evacuee my foster mother introduced me to barley kernel pudding, it is a creamy pudding which has an unusual, crisp, nutty flavoured top when baked. Barley kernels can be obtained at any good food store.

Put 2 ozs. barley kernels in a pie dish with 2 ozs. sugar and 1 oz. butter. Pour on 1 pint of milk, stir well. Bake it in a very moderate oven (325 F., Mark 3) for two hours.

Mrs. Veronica Kearney,
Erdington, Birmingham.

BAKEWELL PUDDING

This is the genuine recipe for the famous Bakewell Pudding, as given to me some years ago by the cook at the Rutland Arms, Bakewell in Derbyshire, the hotel in which Jane Austen lived while she wrote *Pride and Prejudice*. As will be seen, a Bakewell Pudding is different in texture and much richer than the cake-like concoction called Bakewell Tart in the South.

You will need a deep tin with sloping sides, grease it, line it with puff pastry, leave it overnight, Next day cover the pastry with raspberry jam, then a rich filling made by beating 8 eggs and 8 ozs. sugar together until pale and runny and dropping off the spoon in ribbons. Melt 8 ozs. butter and run it in, beating it all together before adding 4 ozs. ground almonds. Bake the pudding in a pre-heated hot oven (400 F., Mark 6) until set.

CHRISTMAS PUDDING

This recipe was used by my great-great-grandmother a hundred and forty years ago. She lived at Dunchurch, near Rugby, and used to cook for the parents of the boys at the famous Public School when they used to visit their sons at half term. I use this recipe every Christmas and find it to be excellent. The secret of course is that each pudding must be steamed for 12 hours.

1 lb. raisins	1 lb. sultanas
1 lb. currants	1¼ lb. sugar
¾ lb. suet	1¼ lbs. breadcrumbs
2 ozs. candied peel	2 ozs. ground almonds
3 dessertspoons self raising flour	
1 teaspoon each mixed spice and nutmeg	
3 eggs	a little brandy or sherry,
	e.g. 2–3 wineglasses

Mince all the fruit. Add to the dry ingredients. Mix very well, stirring with a wooden spoon till thoroughly mixed. Beat the eggs before adding them with the brandy or sherry to the mixture. Stir again thoroughly, cover the basin with a cloth and set it aside for 12 hours in a cool place. Stir again. Pack it firmly into buttered pudding basins. Cover and steam for 12 hours. Do not allow any water to get into them when cooking as it will ruin them. Steam for another 3 hours before serving.

Mrs. B. J. Higgins,
Streetly, Sutton Coldfield, Warwickshire.

MRS. THELMA RUMBLE'S NUT BREAD PUDDING

We used to have this on Christmas Day cut in slices and spread with butter.

Mix together 2 cups self raising flour, ½ cup of chopped walnuts, a pinch of salt, ½ cup of brown sugar. Beat up an egg with ½ cup of milk and 2 tablespoons of golden syrup, add this to the dry in-gredients. Bake it in a greased tin in a very moderate oven (325 F., Mark 3) for ¾ hour or until done. Cover it with greaseproof paper to prevent over browning.

Mrs. Thelma Rumble,
Coventry, Warwickshire.

your hand. Bake them on a greased tin in a slow oven (300 F., Mark 2). The ingredients are simple and the whole art is in baking them crisp as shortbread without getting them brown.

SHROPSHIRE GINGERBREAD

Put $\frac{1}{4}$ lb. treacle in a pan with 3 ozs. butter, 2 ozs. sugar, 4 tablespoons of milk. Stand the pan on the stove until the ingredients have melted. Put 10 ozs. flour in a basin, add $\frac{1}{4}$ teaspoon baking powder, $1\frac{1}{2}$ teaspoons bicarbonate of soda, 1 teaspoon ground ginger. Mix thoroughly with the ingredients from the pan. Pour into a shallow tin lined with greaseproof paper. Bake for 30 minutes in a moderate oven (350 F., Mark 4).

Mrs. P. Hinds,
Oving, Aylesbury, Buckinghamshire.

MINT PASTRY

about 6 ozs. made pastry 2 ozs. currants
2 ozs. sugar 1 tablespoon chopped fresh mint

Roll out the pastry thinly into an oblong. Mix the currants, sugar and mint and spread on half the pastry. Damp the edges and cover with the other half. Score the top into shapes desired, fingers or squares. Brush with water. Sprinkle with sugar. Bake in a hot oven (400 F., Mark 6) until golden brown. Eat cold. This is a very refreshing dish.

Mrs. E. A. Bailey,
Rushall, Walsall, Staffordshire.

ALMOND CAKE

This is a cake my grandmother made. I think it the best almond cake I have tasted.

6 ozs. butter and margarine mixed 6 ozs. sugar
3 ozs. self raising flour 3 ozs. ground almonds
3 eggs

Soften the butter, add the flour to the butter and also the almonds, then add the sugar and lastly the well-beaten eggs. Beat the mixture well. Bake in the oven (350 F., Mark 4) for $1 - 1\frac{1}{4}$ hours.

Mrs. E. W. Booth,
Prestwood, Worcestershire.

ROUGH ROBIN CAKE

This was very popular, eaten preferably hot from the tin in slices but also delicious served cold, and it is so easy to make. This recipe was taught to me as a child and is simple enough for any child to bake.

Mix 12 ozs. plain flour, 4 ozs. ground rice and a pinch of salt. Rub in 4 ozs. butter, add $\frac{1}{2}$ teaspoon baking powder, 3 ozs. sugar, 3 ozs. currants, 3 ozs. raisins and 2 ozs. candied peel. Stir in the

milk. Keep the mixture quite stiff. Put in a greased shallow tin. Bake in a moderate oven (350 F., Mark 4) for 1 – 1½ hours.

Mrs. Baker,
Newent, Gloucestershire.

BANBURY CAKES

For the filling:— cream 8 ozs. butter with 1 tablespoon of honey. Add 8 ozs. candied peel, 1 lb. currants, 2½ ozs. allspice and ¼ oz. of cinnamon. Beat well. This can be kept in a closed jar till required.

Make some flaky pastry. Roll it out thin and cut it in squares about 4–6 inches. Put a spoonful of the mixture on each. Fold the sides to the middle, tucking in the ends. Roll again lightly to flatten. Cut a small slit on top, brush with white of egg and crushed sugar. Bake in a hot oven (425 F., Mark 7). Eat warm.

Mrs. Marie Perry,
Bourton-on-the-Water, Gloucestershire.

CUDDASKEN CAKE

This recipe has been in the family for many years and I have used it for Christmas Cake.

Beat 12 ozs. butter and 12 ozs. demerara sugar to a cream. Add 4 ozs. syrup and beat again. Beat 6 eggs one by one into the butter mixture. Add ¼ pint warmed milk and beat all together. Then add 3 lbs. currants, 4 ozs. chopped peel and 4 ozs. chopped almonds, then add 1½ lbs. self raising flour. Stir well to mix all together. Bake in a slow oven (300 F., Mark 2) for 4 hours. It should weigh 6½ lbs. and will keep for months.

Mrs. C. Richardson,
Worcester.

MUM'S MOIST CAKE

I have often been asked for the following recipe which we call "Mum's Moist Mixture". It's simple, quick, delicious and always moist even after a week, with a lovely dark colour. The secret is always use soft dark brown sugar. The ingredients are always for the same amount in weight and thus easily remembered. The recipe is for an average size cake but can be made any size according to family or need either by doubling or even halving and making into small buns. More fruit can be added if a richer cake is wanted.

Cream 4 ozs. butter and 4 ozs. soft dark brown sugar, add 2 eggs one at a time with some flour to prevent curdling then add the rest of your 4 ozs. flour sifted with a pinch of salt and a teaspoon of spice. Lastly add 4 ozs. mixed fruit. Bake for 30 to 45 minutes (320 F., Mark 3).

Mrs. R. S. Wilkie,
Hatherley, Cheltenham, Gloucestershire.

LEICESTERSHIRE APPLE SHORTCAKE

Cream 4 ozs. butter and 3 ozs. caster sugar then add 1 egg (beaten ready) and beat well together. Gradually add 6 ozs. self raising flour and mix well. It will become stiff, but do not add any milk or water. Grease a small shallow tin and put half the mixture on the bottom, then a layer of apple, then the remaining half of the short paste on top, spreading it lightly over the apples. Bake in a moderate oven (350 F., Mark 4) for about 1 hour. When cold, turn it out and cut it into squares, or keep it warm and use it as a sweet served with cream. This is delicious shortcake. Sprinkle with caster sugar.

Mrs. M. Sands,
Lazenby, Middlesbrough, Teesside.

North of England

Cheshire. Cumberland. Durham. Isle of Man. Lancashire. Northumberland. Westmorland. Yorkshire.

Agricultural Products

Yorkshire forced Rhubarb, S. Cheshire Horseradish, Dairy Cattle, Bilberries.

Dairy

Cheshire Cheese, red and white, Blue Cheshire, Lancashire Cheese, Blue or white Wensleydale Cheese, Yorkshire Curd Cheese.

Gastronomic Specialities

Roast Beef and Yorkshire Pudding with Horseradish Sauce, Tripe and Onions, Jellied Cowheel, Grouse, York Hams, Cumberland Sauce. Cumberland Mutton Hams, Lancashire Hot Pot, Liverpool Scouse, Bury Puddings, Cumberland Sausages, Brawn, Manx Kippers, Morecambe Bay Potted Shrimps, Tweed Salmon, Boiled Pickled Pork and Pease Pudding, Cumberland Rum and Mutton Pies, Hindle Wakes, Thick Gammon Rashers, Liverpool Black Tripe, Barnsley Chops, Craster Kippers, Durham Pressed Pig's Cheek, Northumberland Mittoons, Lamb's Trotters, Pan Haggerty.

Confectionery

Blackpool Rock, Gobstoppers, Penrith Fudge, Kendal Mint Cake, Treacle Toffee, Doncaster Butterscotch, Everton Toffee, Pontefract Cakes, Farrah's Original Harrogate Toffee, Ullswater Rum Butter, Peppermint Humbugs.

Pastry

Yorkshire Seed Cake, Bilberry Tarts, Apple Pie with Cheese, Curd Tarts, Eccles Cakes, Bury Simnel Cakes, Parkin, Ormskirk Gingerbread, Singin' Hinnies, Stottie Cakes, Leek Pasties, Grasmere Shortbread, Bunloaf, Aunt Maggie's Slab Cake, Yorkshire Pikelets, Chorley Cakes, Nelson Cakes.

SOUP

OXTAIL SOUP

First chop the tail into small pieces 1 inch long. Cut 2 carrots and 1 onion in thin slices. Rub a clean saucepan twice across the bottom with fresh cut garlic. Add 2 ozs. butter. Get it hot. Put in the tail, carrots and onion. Fry to a nice golden brown. Then add 5 pints of stock (or water). Boil up gently and simmer for 2 hours. Then add 3 cloves, 6 peppercorns, a sprig of parsley, 1 lump of sugar, 1 small teaspoon salt, $\frac{1}{8}$ teaspoon pepper, a small bunch of celery tops, $\frac{1}{2}$ blade of mace, small piece of thyme. Simmer another $1\frac{1}{2}$ hours.

Strain through a hair sieve. Reheat the soup. Remove the fat with a clean piece of white blotting paper. Add 1 wineglassful of port, if desired. Serve at once.

D. Cliffe,
Blackburn, Lancashire.

MANX BROTH

1 piece brisket and some bones, 4 leeks, 2 carrots, sliced turnip, 6d. parsley, $\frac{1}{4}$ cabbage, $\frac{1}{2}$ cup barley, $\frac{1}{2}$ cup dried peas.

Cut all the vegetables into small pieces. Dumplings can be added. Fill pan three-quarters full with water and simmer for 3 hours.

Mrs. V. Cavendish,
Douglas, Isle of Man.

FISH

FISH CAKES

I am fortunate because my husband brings me fresh fish from the Hull dock each week and this has been a favourite recipe ever since my father and his father sailed on the Hull trawlers.

Skin and flake about 1 lb. cooked haddock or cod and mix well with about 1 lb. creamed potatoes. Add a beaten egg, a good squeeze of lemon juice, salt and pepper and a pinch of mixed herbs and beat well. Shape into "cakes" on a floured board, brush with egg and coat with breadcrumbs. Fry in hot fat a few minutes on each side.

Mrs. Shirley Close,
Kirkella, East Yorkshire.

COD'S ROE

Buy a hard cod's roe from the fishmonger. Tie it up in a cloth to prevent breaking and boil in slightly salted water for 30 minutes or longer according to size.

Remove the skin, cut in slices, dip in flour, or better, in egg and breadcrumbs. Fry in shallow fat. Fry also some small rolls of bacon and serve one on each round of fried roe. If liked, a piece of fried tomato may be put on the roe first and then the roll of fried bacon. Send in with thin crisp toast and butter, or home-made rye bread and butter.

Mrs. M. Gilding,
Bispham, Blackpool, Lancashire.

BAKED STUFFED MACKEREL & PICKLED RED CABBAGE

Here is a recipe for stuffed mackerel that I have been cooking for over 30 years and never yet found in any cookery book.

Split and bone 1 mackerel per person, spread with sage and onion stuffing (sage, onions, breadcrumbs). Roll up and secure with a skewer or string. Place in an ovenproof dish, dot with *pork dripping*, nothing else will do. Bake in a moderate oven for about 30 minutes. Serve with new potatoes and pickled red cabbage.

Mrs. Ida Gordon,
Bradford, Yorkshire.

DEVILLED CRABS

1 or 2 large crabs	4 hard cooked egg yolks (sieved)
1 tablespoon butter	1 cup cream
2 tablespoons flour	1 teaspoon Worcester Sauce
1 teaspoon minced parsley	salt, pepper and buttered bread-crumbs

Cover the raw crabs with boiling salted water and simmer for 20 minutes. Drain off the water, break off the claws, separate shells and remove springy parts under the shell and remove the meat. Clean the upper shell of the crab. Melt the butter in a saucepan, blend in the flour. Heat until the mixture bubbles. Remove from heat and add cream gradually, stirring constantly. Cook rapidly, stirring constantly until the sauce thickens. Cook 1 to 2 minutes longer. Mix in the parsley, sieved egg yolks, seasoning and crab meat. Fill the shells with this mixture and top with breadcrumbs. Bake in a moderate oven (350 F., Mark 4) for 10 minutes until the crumbs are lightly browned.

Mrs. E. Counsell,
Livesey, Blackburn, Lancashire.

NORTHUMBERLAND PICKLED SALMON

The salmon from the River Tweed is of course famous, locally they have an unusual way of serving it in a hot pickle. The fish is cut into inch-thick steaks and poached gently in enough salted water to cover. Take them out, drain on a cloth, when cold place them in a deep dish with equal quantities of white wine, wine vinegar and the liquor in which they were boiled (called the dover). Season with pepper, nutmeg and cloves, leave it for 24 hours then serve the salmon hot, heated in the pickle liquor.

FISH "PIE"

Flake and bone 8 ozs. cooked fish then mix it with 8 ozs. mashed potatoes and 1 chopped, hard boiled egg, season, then turn it into a greased pie dish. Pour $\frac{1}{2}$ pint cold white sauce over, cover with 1 oz. grated cheese then bake in a moderate oven (350 F., Mark 4) for 30 minutes. Serve piping hot.

Mrs. Constance Buckley,
Leeds, Yorkshire.

A traditional dish for Good Friday in some parts of Yorkhsire.

MUSTARD SAUCE FOR PORK OR HERRINGS

Mix 1 tablespoon flour to a paste with a little milk, add a pinch of salt, then add the rest of the $\frac{1}{2}$ pint of milk gradually. Put a small drop of water into a pan and when it boils add the flour mixture and stir over a low heat until it thickens. Put 3 teaspoons sugar and a good lump of butter in a jug, pour over the sauce, stir well then add 1 large teaspoon mustard mixed with vinegar. Serve this with pork or herrings.

Mrs. M. Whitwam,
Bradley Bar, Huddersfield, Yorkshire.

This used to be served with a Boar's Head at Christmas in some Yorkshire pubs.

FISH CREAM

A very good steamed fish soufflé, served with parsley sauce.

Boil 12 ozs. filleted whiting in salt water for 10 minutes. Drain and chop the fish finely adding 2 ozs. soft white breadcrumbs, 2 raw egg yolks, the juice of half a lemon, 1 teaspoon butter, salt and pepper and 1 cup of hot milk. Mix well. Then beat the 2 egg whites so stiff the basin may be turned upside down without them falling out. Fold these gently into the mixture. Put it into a buttered bowl, place some foil on top. Stand the bowl in a pan of boiling water to come half-way up and so steam it for 1 hour. Then turn it carefully onto a platter and finish by pouring parsley sauce over it or by serving this separately in a sauceboat.

Miss A. Howat,
Prestwick, Lancashire.

BAKED HERRINGS

First clean and fillet the herrings, lay them flat out skin down, sprinkle with salt and pepper. On each one place a slice of onion chopped small, then sprinkle each one with chopped fresh mint, or dried mint if fresh is not available. Roll the herrings and place in a dish to bake in a hot oven (400 F., Mark 6) for 5 minutes then reduce the heat to slow (325 F., Mark 3) for 20 to 30 minutes.

They are delicious, either hot or cold, and the gravy is smashing mopped up with brown bread and butter. My mother used to do them with sage when they were 15–20 a penny.

Mr. A. Carlson,
Sunderland.

CHOPPED HERRING OR POOR MAN'S CAVIAR

Put 2 salt herrings which have been soaked in cold water, 2 matjes herrings, 2 apples (Cox's or cookers if possible) and 1 large onion through the coarse cutter of the mincer. Add 1 chopped, hard boiled egg, a slice of plain sponge cake, a little ground pepper and enough white vinegar to make it all moist but not liquid. Very good on water biscuits for an appetizer.

Mrs. Leah Dennis,
Barnsley, Yorkshire.

GRANDMA'S OYSTER CUTLETS

Soak 2 tablespoons soft white breadcrumbs in a little stock or cream. Then pound 4 ozs. cooked chicken, 1 dozen oysters and the breadcrumbs together. Add the well beaten yolks of 2 raw eggs and season well. Shape it into cutlets, coat with egg and then breadcrumbs and fry till nicely brown.

Mrs. Mary Charlton,
Fishergate, York.

SHRIMPS

Morecambe Bay and Parkgate Potted Shrimps, which are preserved in cartons and topped with seasoned butter, make an excellent topping for hot grilled plaice or for cod cutlets. The spicy butter with the shrimps melts into a kind of sauce, which also looks very appetizing.

MANX AND CRASTER KIPPERS

The Englishman's idea of a perfect kipper varies widely in different parts of the country. Fishmongers say it is difficult to sell undyed kippers to southerners who insist on those mass-produced gingery orange kippers tinted with vegetable dyes. In Lancashire everyone is mad about Manx kippers. These superb fish are specially smoked over oak chippings and only the biggest and fattest kippers are used. They are not dyed and are pale lemon in colour, for it is forbidden by Manx law (the Isle of Man has, of course, its own parliament) to use artificial dye stuffs in their preparation. Manx kippers are now so famous that they are flown out to the United States. North country people who go to the Isle of Man for Wakes Week have boxes of kippers posted home to their friends — they make a lovely present.

You can get them by writing to *Curtis, The Fishmonger, Victoria Street, Douglas, Isle of Man,* or to *Black, Duke Street, Douglas.*

Craster is a rocky Northumberland coastal village with stone quarries but it is famous for its crabs and its juicy kippers. Expatriate Geordies long for them for they are still smoked in the old-fashioned way with sawdust and no chemicals. The season begins in June when the herrings are caught fresh off the coast and goes on until September. Only the best are used for "you cannot make good kippers out of poor herrings" as they say in Craster. You can get them by writing to *L. Robson & Sons, Fish Curers, Craster, Northumberland.*

POULTRY AND GAME

MOTHER'S RABBIT SANDWICHES

We lived in the Rugby House at Hall Road, between Southport and Liverpool in the 1930's and had an old black tom cat called William (the Conqueror!) who used to catch rabbits but never ate them. He would kill them, bring them home and lay them at my mother's feet. Skinned, jointed, then popped into a heavy black casserole with a knuckle of ham costing about 6d, whole small onions and carrots, plenty of pepper and always cloves, they were slowly cooked in the oven (a coal range) and later made into a pie for Saturday night's supper. Remains were made into sandwiches for club members on Sunday afternoon, who adored my mother's "game" sandwiches. Many elderly ex-Rugby Union players will have fond memories of them. She did have a regular order for rabbits with the local poultrymonger, as William's supply was apt to be erratic.

My mother and William have been dead many years, and I'm now a grandmother myself but I still love rabbit.

Mrs. Vera Jones,
Blackpool, Lancashire.

STEWED RABBIT

The best old-fashioned recipe I can remember is stewed rabbit the way my grandmother used to cook it. She used to try and get a half-grown young fresh rabbit, skin it and gut it, wash it, cut it in joints, put it into an old-fashioned brown stew pot with a large-sized Spanish onion sliced with a couple of thick slices, home cured fat bacon cut in dice, add salt and pepper to taste, cover with cold water, put on the lid and cook slowly in a moderate oven till tender, do not allow it to boil dry at all as the rabbit, when served, should be nice and pink colour. When cooked, mix some flour and milk together, add to the rabbit and cook a little until the milky gravy thickens and serve from stew pot with potatoes and other vegetables as required and a nicer flavoured meal you never did eat.

I can still remember the good meals we had and I now am well over 60 years.

Mrs. P. W. Hawkins,
Grappenhall, Warrington, Lancashire.

POULET-A-LA-REINE

Wash a chicken with cold water and put inside it a shallot with a clove stuck in it. Put the bird in a deep fireproof casserole. Pour in enough milk to come half-way up (the quantity varies according to the size of the bird). Add a little parsley, celery, mace, salt and pepper and a bay leaf on its breast. Replace the lid and set the casserole in a very slow oven and simmer for about 2½ hours. If the bird is old you must allow longer, but it must be cooked gently. When the bird is done take it out and place on a hot dish. It will be easier to serve if jointed at this time. Take the herbs out of the milk. Melt a little butter in a saucepan and stir in enough flour to make a sauce using the milk from the casserole, stirring gently till the sauce is smooth. Put the chicken in the casserole with the sauce and it is ready to serve.

This dish can be made well in advance of the meal and any sauce that is left makes a delicious white soup.

Mrs. J. Johnson,
Knutsford, Cheshire.

YORKSHIRE RABBITS IN MILK

I was reared in Yorkshire in a village near Pontefract and can remember from my earliest days always having pig's fry every Wednesday for dinner. Another favourite in the days when fresh trapped wild rabbits cost 1s. 6d. per couple, was Rabbit in Milk. Skin and clean, and rub the flesh with cut lemon. Simmer the jointed rabbit in milk with salt and pepper, fresh rubbed sage and a little thyme and finely chopped onions. When cooked, thicken the milk by adding fresh fine white breadcrumbs and serve with potatoes mashed in butter, carrots and peas.

Mrs. T. Jones,
Llanyravon, Cwmbran, Monmouthshire.

FORCEMEAT BALLS FOR CHICKEN OR TURKEY

This is one of my late mother-in-law's recipes. She was quite a remarkable woman for she took on the job as stewardess at the Masonic Hall, Milnsbridge, a job which meant she had, at times, to cook dinner for at least 120 guests. Remarkable? Yes, you see she lost her right arm while working in the mill when she was thirteen years old; even so she got married and raised my husband and worked hard all her life.

She used to serve the forcemeat balls with chicken. She never roasted chicken, she said it made it "as dry as old sticks". She would cook it in an old brown stew pot with plenty of butter over it. Delicious.

Mix together 1 small crumbled loaf, ½ lb. suet, 1 handful chopped parsley, some thyme and sage, 1 chopped onion, 2 beaten eggs and salt and pepper to taste. Spread it in a large square Yorkshire Pudding tin greased with beef dripping and cook in a medium oven (350 F., Mark 4) until crisp and brown. Cut in squares and serve with chicken or turkey.

Mrs. M. Whitwam,
Bradley Bar, Huddersfield, Yorkshire.

ROAST GROUSE

Draw and truss the birds. If young, wipe, season with salt and pepper, put a nut of butter in each and wrap each bird in thin slices of fat bacon or fat pork. Place each on a piece of toast or bread or fried bread. Roast in a hot oven (450 F., Mark 6) for 30—35 minutes. Remove the birds and toast, skim the fat from the pan juices, add 1 oz. butter and ½ pint of stock per brace of birds. Heat fiercely stirring and scraping the pan to reduce the stock. Serve the birds on bread with red currant jelly gravy, bread sauce and fried crumbs.

Mrs. Lucie Watts,
Ripon, Yorkshire.

PIGEON PUDDING

Prepare some suet crust, roll out half and line a pudding basin. Quarter 2 pigeons. Cut up ½ lb. shin beef into small pieces, roll in seasoned flour, place in basin with a minced kidney if desired. Pour over ½ cup of stock, cover basin with crust. Tie in cloth and steam 2 hours fully.

Mrs. Benson,
Aughton, Ormskirk, Lancashire.

ROAST GOOSE

A goose needs careful buying from a man you can trust, otherwise it may be disappointingly skinny. It need not be "too rich" if you stand it on a rack in the roasting tin and baste it with dry cider or hot water. Mix some salt and pepper and rub this into the inside of the bird. Stuff it with an equal weight of peeled chopped apples and soaked stoned prunes mixed with a little sugar. It takes about 1 breakfast cup of stuffing per 1 lb. of ready to cook goose. Put the bird on the rack in a tin in a preheated fairly hot oven (375 F., Mark 5) for 20 minutes to brown, reduce the heat to very moderate (325 F., Mark 3). Continue roasting until the goose joints move readily or twist out. An 8 lb. goose (ready to cook weight) takes 4 hours, a 10 lb. goose 4½ hours, a 12 lb. goose 5 hours, and a 14 lb. (ready to cook weight) goose takes 6 hours. Baste the bird occasionally with dry cider or hot water. Pour off the surplus fat in the tin and keep it for it makes marvellous pastry.

Gravy: Make a gravy from the drippings in the pan, stirring in a little redcurrant jelly and some hot water and heat, stirring till the gravy is smooth. It will not be very thick. Pour into a warm sauce-boat.

Roast goose is traditionally served with apple sauce or apple stuffing, plain boiled potatoes, bread sauce and gravy.

WHITBY CHRISTMAS GOOSE GIBLET PIE

This is an old Yorkshire recipe which has been in the family for generations. It was a family tradition to cook a giblet pie over Christmas Eve and the "blood pudding" recipe was always added to it. My grandparents were born in Whitby, Yorkshire. They used goose's blood for it but ordinary black pudding is just as good. It is very tasty in a steak and kidney pie.

Cook the giblets and then put them in a pie dish. Mix 1 lb. of blood pudding with 1 chopped onion and a little grated suet, a little chopped thyme and sage, some salt and pepper. Steep what breadcrumbs you can in water then squeeze them dry. Add these to the black pudding with a beaten egg. After pressing the mixture dry with a fork, form it into forcemeat balls. Put these into the corners of the pie dish with the giblets. It will be nice and firm when cooked. Cover the pie dish with short crust pastry and bake it in a moderate oven (350 F., Mark 4) for about an hour.

Mrs. J. L. Croome,
Kenton, Newcastle upon Tyne.

MEAT

"COLONIAL GOOSE" from Lamb or Mutton

This is grandma's recipe, dated 1898. The joint is served with apple sauce, roast potatoes, green peas and mashed turnip.

Buy a small leg of lamb or mutton, remove the bone but leave the knuckle on. (One can ask the butcher to do this). Stuff the joint with sage and onion stuffing made from boiled, chopped onions, a little sage, salt and pepper mixed with white bread which has been soaked in hot water and squeezed out. Sew or skewer up the stuffed end of the joint and shape it like a goose — with the aid of a skewer — shaping the knuckle for the neck and back. Dust over lightly with ground ginger. Roast in a hot oven (400 F., Mark 6) 20 minutes per pound and 20 minutes over.

Hilda Towers,
Bolton-le-Sands, Carnforth, Lancashire.

ROAST LAMB WITH APRICOT SAUCE

They like good cooking in the West Riding, and the young chef at the Wilson Arms, Threshfield, gets up at 4 a.m. to buy fresh fruits and vegetables in Leeds Market. People come miles for their roast beef and Yorkshire pudding. It is thick end of sirloin roast, medium rare, carved up to half an inch thick, and served with as many fresh vegetables as possible.

They have saddle of local lamb on the Sunday night buffet "with meat jelly and enough else," he said, "with a whole York ham on the bone as well as cold salmon". Born in 1950, he has older men working under him, got the Student of the Year Award at the Thomas Danby College, Leeds, and goes back there to lecture on cooking. "We aim at speciality catering with a Yorkshire flavour" he said. On Sundays they have apple pie with Wensleydale cheese, or bilberry tart with very thick cream from *Mr. Dean's* farm down the road. The local lamb is marvellous too. "I think it's best just served with rosemary as seasoning, it makes itself" he said. For this, just make cuts in the meat with a pointed knife and thrust the sprigs of rosemary into it before roasting. "We also do apricot sauce which we find complements it. Simmer the apricots in sugar and water till soft then mix with a good thickened roast gravy, with a few entire apricot halves as garnish. Tinned ones are all right if they are decent, but we use fresh ones when we can".

YORKSHIRE LAMB CUTLETS are another of chef's specialities. Slit some lamb chops or cutlets down the fat side to make a sort of pocket. Fill this with a stuffing made by mixing chopped parsley and fresh thyme with salt, pepper, the grated rind of a lemon and some fresh breadcrumbs. Add a little egg to bind the mixture together. Stuff the chops, press the edges together. Dip them in beaten egg, then in fresh white breadcrumbs, shallow fry them very gently. They must cook very slowly otherwise the outside will be too brown before the centre is cooked.

Brian Dennison,
Threshfield, Yorkshire.

ROAST LIVER

Have 1 lb. cut off in a solid piece. Ask the butcher to gash it in the centre almost through to the other side so as to make a sort of pocket. Stuff this with a dressing made by chopping a thin rasher of bacon and 1 onion and mixing them with breadcrumbs, 1 egg well beaten and enough hot water to moisten the crumbs. Tie a string around the liver to hold it together, cover with thin rashers of bacon and bake until tender. Make a brown gravy with the fat in the baking dish. Serve with jacket potatoes and redcurrant jelly.

Mrs. E. A. Mettrick,
Wooldall, Holmfirth, Huddersfield.

LANCASHIRE HOT POT

This is my Lancashire grandmother's recipe for hot pot made in the days when coal was cheap, and mutton also. It makes a good meal for winter days and, with a bottle of "plonk", goes down very well. When my great-grandmother died, some years ago, at the ripe old age of 96, we found recipes for making wines, black puddings, cold cream and soup.

You want 1½ lbs. altogether of neck of mutton (or lamb) chops and scrag end. Ask the butcher to chop the meat. Flour it, put it into a heavy earthenware casserole or into a proper round hot pot dish. Peel and slice 2 or 3 large onions and put these on the meat, peel and cut 2 potatoes into rounds about ¼ inch thick. Put these onto the onions. Cut 2 or 3 more large potatoes into halves and make a crust of them all over the top. Flour them slightly, put seasoning into the cracks between them and add water to cover the sliced potatoes and just to touch the halved potatoes. Cook for 4 hours on the middle shelf of a moderate oven (325 F., Mark 3).

Mrs. V. L. Neilson,
Heworth, York.

PANACKALTY (Sausage Pot)

"Panackalty" is a very old north country recipe. My grandmother, also my mother used it and I now carry on the tradition as my husband and friends love it. I was born and lived in Newcastle upon Tyne, Northumberland and came down south to live 35 years ago.

To make the sausage pot have 4 large raw potatoes, sliced half an inch thick, lay them in a fireproof dish alternating with 1 lb. sausages and 2 large sliced onions. Sprinkle with sage, pepper and salt, add sufficient cold water to cover. Put on lid and bake in the oven for 30 minutes (375 F., Mark 5).

This makes a delicious savoury and economical dish for lunch or evening meal and gives a generous helping for 4 persons. If a second

71

vegetable is required serve boiled buttered cabbage — no gravy is necessary.

Mrs. Dorothy McCabe,
Brighton, Sussex.

CUMBERLAND TATIE POT

When I was a boy in the Lake District Tatie Pot was a famous dish, you used to get enormous stew jars of it in the public houses and Tatie Pot Suppers were popular local events. They also made it for Hunt Meetings, local Dales Shows, Shepherd's Meets and the like. We local lads used to eat it in quantity, in the public bar after a day on the fells and an evening drinking.

Cut 1½ lbs. stewing steak or stewing lamb in pieces and put them in a hot pot dish or deep fireproof dish in layers with 2 large sliced onions, 2 or 3 carrots, 12 ozs. black pudding, salt and pepper to your liking and about 3 potatoes sliced in thin rounds. The last layer must be potatoes. Add some hot water to come almost to the top. Start the cooking in a moderate oven (350 F., Mark 4) with a lid on but take it off about 45 minutes before the end to brown the potatoes. It takes about 2 hours altogether.

Mr. Tom Greene,
Carlisle, Cumberland.

MUTTON SAUCER PIES

Make 8 ozs. of short crust pastry and line greased saucers or small tins with it. Fill them with 8 ozs. minced mutton mixed with 1 small chopped onion, 2 large chopped mushrooms, 1 teaspoon parsley or thyme and salt and pepper. Add a little stock or milk and cover with a round of pastry. Bake in a hot oven (400 F., Mark 6) for about 45 minutes.

Mrs. E. Buckley,
Halifax, Yorkshire.

NORTH COUNTRY MUTTON AND RUM SWEET PIE

Cut ½ lb. mutton or lamb into small pieces including any fat, put it in a pie dish in layers alternately with 8 ozs. of currants, 8 ozs. sultanas, 8 ozs. of raisins, 6 ozs. of soft brown sugar and 2 ozs. of mixed peel. Season it to your taste with cinnamon, mace, nutmeg, a little white pepper and a little salt, then pour over 2 wineglasses of rum and the juice of a large lemon. Cover the pie with puff pastry and bake in a very hot oven (450 F., Mark 7) for 15 minutes then reduce it to moderate (350 F., Mark 4) for the rest of the cooking time. This is a very rich pie which is often used at Christmas instead of plum pudding.

Mrs. Isobel Middleton,
Gawthripe, Dent, near Sedburgh,
West Riding of Yorkshire.

These sweet rum and meat pies are still made in some Cumberland farmhouses between Christmas and New Year's Day, as they have been for generations. The custom and recipes themselves probably date from the Middle Ages, when spices and dried fruits were often cooked with meat. The "mincemeat" we use to fill mince pies at Christmas is in the same tradition. Though now a mixture of sugar, spices, suet, dried fruit and sometimes brandy, it used to contain meat as well; minced beef and minced tongue were included until about seventy years ago. Pork is sometimes used instead of lamb or mutton in the north country sweet pies.

We still have a manuscript in the British Museum, which was compiled by the master cooks at the court of King Richard II in about 1390. The long parchment roll mentions mace, ginger, saffron, mustard and even spikenard. There are recipes for fish cooked with chopped dates, raisins and almonds, for meat dishes flavoured with powdered ginger and sugar. They used a lot of spices as the Romans had done, though they were very expensive. Many of the recipes in this and other medieval works remind one of Oriental and Arab dishes still prepared today, a taste probably brought back by the Crusaders, for the manuscript also includes a recipe for Saracen Sauce.

STEWED RUMP OF BEEF

When I was a little girl and my granny invited the family over for dinner, I was allowed to go very early to help her prepare the meal. When the rest of my family arrived later and I opened the door for them I used to watch their faces as the delicious smell from the kitchen met them. Now I get the same looks on my own family's face when I am making granny's Stewed Rump of Beef.

Wash a rump of beef well and season with pepper, cayenne, salt, cloves and mace in fine powder. Bind it up tight and place it in a pot. Fry 3 large onions, sliced, and put them to it with 3 carrots, a turnip, a shallot, 4 cloves, a blade of mace and some celery. Cover the meat with a good beef broth or weak gravy. Simmer it gently for several hours till quite tender. Clear off the fat and add to the gravy $\frac{1}{2}$ pint of port wine and a small glass of vinegar also a large spoon of ketchup. Simmer for 30 minutes and serve in a deep dish. Garnish with carrots, turnips or pickles cut small and laid in little heaps separately. If when done the gravy is too much to fill the dish take only a part to season for serving. A spoonful of made mustard is a great improvement to the gravy.

Mrs. Meaghan,
Chorley, Lancashire.

BLACK DISH WITH MUFFINS

Cut 3 or 4 lambs' hearts and about 1 lb. of stewing steak into small pieces. Put them in a brown earthenware dish with a chopped onion, a cupful of breadcrumbs and 2 teaspoons of sage and salt and pepper to taste. Cover with water. Place a plate on top.

Traditionally this was put in the old fire oven at night and left until noon the following day, but it will cook in a slow gas or electric oven (325 F., Mark 3) in about 4 hours. My grandmother always served this with home-made Lancashire muffins but being rather lazy and busy I serve shop ones.

Mrs. Vera Burton,
Culcheth, Warrington, Lancashire.

LIVERPOOL SCOUSE

Melt 1 oz. dripping in a deep pan, put in some sliced or quartered potatoes, some sliced or quartered onions, some carrots sliced or quartered, a turnip, sliced or quartered and cook gently allowing them to absorb the fat, add salt and pepper to taste. Cut some stewing beef etc. into cubes or slices, cover the whole with water and simmer long and slowly.

Mrs. W. M. Herd,
Baldmore, Sutton Coldfield, Warwickshire.

RED FLANNEL HASH

This is a recipe I have used so many times myself and it is very good in cold weather.

You can use up any leftover cold meat, lamb's tongues, beef or mutton. Cut up the meat into small, thin pieces. Brown them with a little chopped onion in some butter over a sharp heat. When nicely browned add some mashed potatoes and chopped vegetables, turnips and leeks and pour over half a tin of soup. To this you can add a dash of Worcester Sauce, if you like the flavour. Salt and pepper to taste. Set the pan over a low heat and stir the contents occasionally. The liquids will gradually become absorbed by the vegetables and the thing to do is to keep it cooking until there is a nice brown skin at the bottom. Turn the contents over until both sides are brown and dryish. Dish up with peas or cabbage, keep the hash piping hot. Eat any kind of pickles you have with it.

Mrs. Ethel Smith,
Crowton, near Northwich, Cheshire.

BEEF ROLL

Mix all together 8 ozs. minced steak, 4 ozs. minced bacon, 8 ozs. Cumberland sausage, 4 ozs. grated breadcrumbs, seasoning and, if liked, 2 teaspoons of dried herbs. Bind with 1 large beaten egg or 2 small ones. Roll out into an oblong and tie in a floured cloth. Steam for 2 hours or, if cooked in a pressure cooker, 30 minutes.

When cold remove the cloth and slightly brown under the grill for a few minutes. This is very nice served with a salad.

Mrs. E. White,
Norris Green, Liverpool.

MOCK JUGGED HARE WITH BEEF AND FORCEMEAT BALLS

This was a great favourite of my grandmother in Yorkshire in the 1890's. She lived on a farm and had to feed the farm men in addition to her own family. In those days shin beef was very cheap. It, of course, required cooking for several hours, but as a coal oven in an old-fashioned range was used it did not involve much expense.

Cut 2 lbs. shin beef into pieces about the size of a joint of hare. Flour well and braise until brown in some good beef dripping in the frying pan. Place in a brown earthenware dish with the 2 onions with 4 cloves stuck in each, some strips of lemon rind, mixed herbs and seasoning. Cook in a slow oven (325 F., Mark 3 – 350 F., Mark 4) for 3 – 4 hours. Strain off the gravy and thicken it with the remaining flour.

Arrange the meat on a serving dish and pour over the gravy (discard the onions). Serve with red currant jelly and forcemeat balls.

For the Forcemeat Balls mix together 5 tablespoons of bread-crumbs, 2 ozs. chopped suet, 1 teaspoon parsley, $\frac{1}{2}$ teaspoon mixed herbs, $\frac{1}{2}$ teaspoon grated lemon rind and seasoning. Bind with a well beaten egg. Put some beef dripping in a roasting tin. Roast the force-meat balls for 30 minutes, turning them over as they brown.

Mrs. C. Williamson,
Thornham, Rochdale, Lancashire.

AN EASY OLD-FASHIONED SOUSE

Cut up 1 lb. shin beef and 1 dressed cowheel, put it in a large stew pan, cover with water. Bring to the boil on the stove then put into the oven to simmer gently. Simmer until all the cowheel has left the bone and the meat is tender. Pour off the liquid into a basin, mash all the meat etc. with a fork, then pour in the liquid. Season with salt and pepper, mix well then pour into basins and leave to set overnight. It is delicious eaten with all pickles, mustard, piccalilli or red cabbage.

This is one of my grandmother's recipes and I still make it.

Mrs. E. King,
Hexthorpe, Doncaster, Yorkshire.

ROAST STUFFED TRIPE

This recipe was used in our family 70 years ago.

Make a sage and onion stuffing and lay it on 1 large piece of dressed tripe. Roll up and secure with skewers and string. Cover the top with dripping. Roast in the oven for about 45 minutes. Serve with mashed potatoes. It's very tasty.

Mrs. L. Carbert,
Stockton-on-Tees, Teesside.

TRIPE AND ONIONS

Stew 1 lb. tripe in salted water with 2 large onions till tender. Strain then add a little milk and ½ lb. pork sausages placed on top of the tripe. Cook on a very slow gas until the sausages are cooked. Serve with mashed potatoes.

Mrs. L. Bishop,
Stone, near Dartford, Kent.

BAKED TRIPE

Buy 8 ozs. dressed tripe then cook it till very tender. Cut it into small pieces. Butter a pie dish and sprinkle in some breadcrumbs and chopped parsley. Put in a layer of tripe, sprinkle with salt and pepper. Add another layer of tripe and sprinkle with the rest of the breadcrumbs, 6 tablespoons in all. Beat up 2 eggs and ½ pint milk and pour over the tripe etc. Place 1 oz. of butter on top in small pieces and bake for 20 minutes in a moderate oven (350 F., Mark 4) or until the custard is set.

Mrs. J. Archer,
East Didsbury, Manchester.

LIVERPOOL TRIPE PIE WITH HAM

This is an old family recipe. It is difficult to put exact quantities down as so many can be varied depending on the larder and the family. The quantities given generally suit a family of four.

Lay into the bottom of a dish thinly sliced cold boiled, or raw ham, then put in a layer of cooked tripe with jelly adhering. Season with pepper but scant salt. Add a bit of butter. Fill the dish in layers in this manner. Put in a few tablespoons of good brown gravy. Cover the dish with good puff pastry. Brush with milk. Bake at first in a hot oven (400 F., Mark 6) to set the pastry then reduce the heat to moderate (350 F., Mark 4) to finish the cooking in 1-2 hours. Cover the pastry with a piece of greaseproof paper or foil if it seems to be getting too brown.

Mrs. R. W. Mercer,
Woolton, Liverpool.

"BUTCHER'S GOOSE" OR BONED, STUFFED PICKLED PORK IN A HUFF PASTE:

An old Christmas Dinner

This is a real old-fashioned recipe over a hundred years old, a favourite with country folk miles away from everywhere.

Take a leg of pork about 5 lbs. Your butcher will take the bone out and put it in brine for 24 hours. Soak in cold water for 2 hours, score, put on a board skin downwards. Season with pepper, salt and a sprinkle of brown sugar. Make a stuffing of sage, onions, ½ cup white breadcrumbs, ½ cup of stewed apple, pepper and salt. Make this into a roll and place down the centre of the leg. Fold over. Tie into shape with string. Now make a stiff dough of flour and water, roll out, place the leg of pork on this and wrap it up with dough. Place in a baking tin and roast in a hot oven (400 F., Mark 6) to brown the crust, then reduce the heat to moderate (350 F., Mark 4) and bake till tender on testing with a skewer. Take off the crust, sprinkle the meat with brown crumbs and brown sugar. Serve with baked potatoes, mashed swede and apple sauce.

Mrs. Wilford,
Redcar, Teesside.

CUMBERLAND BLACK PUDDING

This is a very old recipe passed down through the years. The amount I give you here will make a good bit.

Make a pan full of oatmeal porridge, boil a pan of pearl barley till nicely cooked. Cool these off then add them to 3 quarts of pig's blood or more which has been put through a strainer. You must first of all see that the blood is good and does not congeal. Stir well, add a quart of good new milk to this. Now for the fat which are really what in Cumberland we call the cracklings (from the rendered lard), the left-overs. These must not be over done, just lightly cooked to a nice light brown. Mash these up with the hand while warm to avoid hard pieces then add these to the blood, barley etc. Don't pinch for a good few of the cracklings as they improve the pudding and give it a nice flavour. Now add seasoning, salt, pepper and a large tablespoon of dried mint or more, if liked. Now put the Black Pudding into skins to cook, slowly. Have ready a pan with boiling water in the pan. Put a plate or saucer in to take it off boiling point. Simmer them gently till ready — do not boil.

Mrs. E. Horn,
Ousby, Penrith, Cumberland.

BLACK PUDDING IN A TIN

This was made by my grandmother 50 years ago. Soak a 1 lb. loaf of bread in cold water, squeeze into a bowl, add 4 or 5 onions, 2 ozs. oatmeal, 8 ozs. cooked rice, 4 ozs cooked pearl barley, 1 lb.

77

pig's fat cut in small pieces and salt, pepper and sage and marjoram, if liked. Mix well then add 1 pint blood.

Grandma turned the mixture into a large baking tin and baked till firm and set in a moderate oven (350 F., Mark 4). Slices were cut out of the tin when needed and fried with bacon.

Mrs. M. Turner,
Girlington, Bradford, Yorkshire.

In Northumberland a hot boiled suet roll filled with leeks is sometimes served with black puddings, as well as with cold joints.

LANCASHIRE BLOOD AND GROAT PIE

I am 76 and I remember my mother making eight of us a good dinner of this on a winter's day. She sent two of us to the pork butcher with a quart tea can for the blood and groats. I never hear of it now and the nearest I get to making it is with black puddings.

Cut 1 lb. stewing beef in pieces and add to 1 quart of blood and groats. Mix and add salt, pepper and a little sage. Cook till tender. Put a crust on top and bake. Serve with mashed potatoes.

Mrs. A. Jackson,
Marston, Blackpool.

LANCASHIRE BEEF AND COWHEEL PIE

Take a full "dressed" or cooked cowheel and 1 lb. good shin beef. Cut all up in small bits. Put all with the bones into a pan. Cover with water and add salt and pepper. Cook till tender. Remove the bones and thicken the gravy with flour. Put into a pie dish, cover with short pastry and bake till brown in a moderate oven (350 F., Mark 4) in about 40 minutes. This is grand with chips either hot or cold.

Miss Florrie Helmn,
Slyne, Lancashire.

A similar beef and cowheel tart with pastry above and below used to be very popular for working men's bait baskets and to take to football matches round Manchester.

CANADIAN PORK PIE (4 persons)

Mix 8 ozs. flour and ½ teaspoon salt in a basin. Rub 4 ozs. butter lightly in with the tips of the fingers. Sprinkle in a few drops of lemon juice. Moisten with a little cold water or cold milk and 1 beaten egg leaving enough to glaze the pie. The dough should be rather stiff. Roll out the pastry thinly and line with it a well greased dish or loose bottomed cake tin. Then arrange alternately in layers 4 ozs. diced lean ham, 12 ozs. diced lean pork and 1 hard boiled egg and lastly add a tablespoon of water which you have seasoned with pepper and paprika. Cover with the remaining pastry. Make a hole in the top then brush the top with the remaining egg. Bake in a fairly hot oven (375 F., Mark 5) for 10 minutes, reduce the heat to moderate (350 F., Mark 4) for 1 hour and 10 minutes.

When cooked pour into the pie a gill of nicely flavoured stock in which you have dissolved $\frac{1}{4}$ oz. of powdered gelatine and leave till cold and set. Serve with a green salad.

(The famous Mrs. Glasse gives the one with pippins and wine in her pork pie called Cheshire Pork Pie 1747).

Mrs. M. Gilding,
Bispham, near Blackpool, Lancashire.

VARIOUS

CHESHIRE CHEESE

Cheshire is the oldest English cheese, and unlike Cheddar is not imitated abroad. Crumbly rather than flaky, it is very slightly salty and is said to owe this to the salty Cheshire soil, which gives a special flavour to the meadow grass and thus to the cow's milk from which the cheese is made. There are very large salt deposits in the North-wich, Middlewich and Winsford area as well as round Nantwich, which have been flooded with water and from which brine is pumped so as to extract the salt for industrial and domestic purposes.

Farmhouse Cheshire cheese is superior to that from the creameries as it is made with the milk from only a few fields in a small area, which give it an individual flavour — one might compare it with chateau bottled as opposed to blended claret. About fifty years ago there was an annual output of about 20,000 tons of farmhouse Cheshire from about 1,200 farms, but after the Second World War only about fifty farms were making cheese, the rest was from creameries.

Blue Cheshire cheese, the epicure's dream, is really a Cheshire cheese which usually by accident rather than on purpose has provided the suitable medium for the growth of the blue mould. The rich flavour of such slowly matured cheeses which "blue" naturally is much mellower than that of cheeses where the bluing is forced artificially. You find it on a few farms in Cheshire and Shropshire.

WENSLEYDALE CHEESE

Wensleydale cheese was made originally, like that at Roquefort, with ewe's milk and it blued during ripening. It is said to have been made by the monks of Jervaulx, but, then after the dissolution of the monasteries in Tudor times, it became a farmhouse cheese, and remained so until the end of the last century when the first creamery was opened in the dales. There are only a few farmhouse cheese-makers today. White Wensleydale is soft, flaky and sometimes rather acid, the old blue Wensleydale is the one to look for, rich, creamy, and veined with blue, it spreads like butter and is delicious sand-wiched between slices of cold Christmas pudding, or to follow a brace of roast grouse from the moors.

LANCASHIRE CHEESE

Lancashire cheese used to be made in the farm kitchens and ripened on shelves near the range. Some say it is even better than Cheshire cheese for Welsh rabbit, and that made at Leigh in Lanc-ashire popularly known as the Leigh Toaster, was best of all. Sage Lancashire, like Sage Derby, is a small cheese flavoured with sage, which used to be decorated with a pattern of sage leaves, and made for harvest festivals and at Christmas.

If you are in the north do look in at Northwich Market, Cheshire, just off the M6 on a Friday. There is real farmhouse Lancashire cheese on sale, strongly flavoured and unrivalled for toasting. There is also genuine red and white farmhouse Cheshire.

They let you taste all the big cheeses to see which one is in best condition. One can sometimes buy some of the rare blue farmhouse Cheshire cheese too.

There are delicious coarse-cut black puddings tied up in sections like a bunch of grapes, as well as Cumberland sausages, coarse cut and with plenty of meat and flavour. They are not done in links, like most sausages, but go on and on like a coil of rope. Leeds market, in Yorkshire, being so near the moors also has pheasants, hares and partridges at about half the price that people pay in London.

Black puddings are a speciality of the north west, where they are of the finest quality and taste delicious. The Bury pudding is a short fat black pudding turned back on itself which is popular in Lancashire and Cheshire. They are very good fried for breakfast or boiled to eat hot. Scarlet polonies, pots of delicious brawn and very good straight sided pale pork pies are a feature of the local pork butchers' shops.

POTATO FRITTERS

Peel 1 large potato and 1 onion. Cut a thin slice of potato and on top place a thin slice of onion. Put another thin slice of potato on top. Make some batter. Dip the potato and onion "scone" in the batter and fry in hot fat. Season with salt and pepper. When brown, turn over and fry on the other side. Pepper and salt. They are lovely. You can eat them hot or cold. You can have gravy with them, have them for any meal. Put fish or meat in them.

Mrs. J. Birtle,
Preston, Lancashire.

CHAMPS

Peel and boil 2 lbs. potatoes till tender. Drain into a colander and put them back over a low heat to dry, covering with a clean towel. Chop up 6 large scallions including the white onion part, put in a bowl and pour boiling water over to scald. Drain. Put about $\frac{1}{4}$ pint milk into a small pan, add the scallions and bring to the boil. Meanwhile mash the potatoes and season well. Beat the milk mixture into the potatoes till soft and light. It must be served very hot. Pile it on a plate and make a hole in the centre and put in a big lump of butter.

We liked to take a spoonful of the potato and dip it in the butter and we drank very cold buttermilk with it.

Mrs. Ethna Flaherty,
West Denton, Newcastle upon Tyne.

Scallions are perennial plants of the onion family that grow in clumps. They are used chopped for cooking and are called Holtsers in Wales. It is also a name for gone-to-seed onions.

MASHED POTATO WITH ONION — another way

When you are having mashed potatoes try doing them like this. When they are ready beat in a bit of butter and a drop of milk, grate an onion onto a plate. Put it in the potatoes and beat all up with a fork. Add pepper and salt. They are beautiful.

Mrs. J. Birtle,
Preston, Lancashire.

YORKSHIRE EGG AND BACON PIE

Take a deep type dinner plate, line with a good pastry, then fill up with fairly lean bacon cut in small pieces. Add 2 beaten up raw eggs, salt and pepper to taste. Cover with pastry cutting two small air holes in top. Bake to a nice brown in a moderate oven (350 F., Mark 4). To be eaten cold.

Mrs. H. Blunt,
Marton, Blackpool.

CHEESE, BACON AND ONION PIE

My mother used to make this when we were children. Chop 4 ozs. bacon without the rind in small pieces. Chop 1 small onion and 4 ozs. Lancashire cheese finely. Put it all in a pan with a knob of butter and a little milk. Bring to the boil, stirring, and simmer for a few minutes. Line a buttered pie dish with short crust pastry. Pour in the cheese mixture, sprinkle with grated cheese. Bake in a fairly hot oven (375 F., Mark 5) for 15 – 20 minutes.

Mrs. L. Barnes,
Bolton, Lancashire.

POTATO AND TURNIP MASH WITH BACON

My grandmother and my mother used to make us this really nice hot meal. They used to peel and cut the turnip in small pieces and boil it on its own first until it was nice and soft, not too much. Then she used to have some potatoes peeled and cut in half. These she put on with the turnips with a pinch of salt and let them boil together until the potato was cooked. While this was doing she used to fry some bacon and then she would mash the potatoes and turnips together, put them in a casserole, pop the bacon on top and leave it all in a very slow oven (200 F., Mark 2) for the bacon juices to mix in. Then she would serve it on plates with the bacon on the top with plenty of bread and butter. It's an ideal meal. You can make as much as you want depending on the size of the family. The smell from it cooking gives you a longing for it.

Mrs. M. Pye,
Pemberton, Wigan, Lancashire.

THE DISH

It is served with bacon and egg. Or with grilled ham or sausage.

Fill a fireproof dish with layers of sliced raw potatoes and onions, pepper and salt and on each layer place a small knob of butter. Add water to come half-way up and bake in a hot oven (400 F., Mark 6) for one hour or until the potatoes are cooked through.

P. Collins,
Wallasey, Cheshire.

BREAKFAST BACON AND GAMMON RASHERS

Breakfast habits vary, and Lancashire children still get bread-and-bacon-dip with their eggs and bacon, as well sometimes as treacle "butties" for breakfast. Black treacle has for long been so popular in the north-west as to be almost a regional delicacy.

For breakfast in Cheshire people like large rashers of roll cut streaky and back bacon in one piece, "green" rather than smoked. These are cooked for 10 to 12 minutes in a hot oven (400 F., Mark 6). First melt a little dripping or bacon dip in the baking tin. When it is runny, but not scorching hot, lay in the long, long rashers, fat over lean. The eggs can be done in the oven too, if liked, in a fireproof dish in butter.

On some Cheshire farms hot buttery potato cakes, made with buttermilk, are eaten with the breakfast bacon. There is also a cheese and bacon dish which seems to have come up north from the Potteries. Fry the breakfast bacon, then fry slices of cheese in the hot bacon fat until these are brown and tacky, then eat both bacon and cheese with hot toast.

Thick gammon rashers (usually about ½ inch thick, though a full inch rasher is not uncommon) are popular all over the north-west and are served for breakfast, high tea, or supper in Cheshire public houses. Though they may be grilled it is usual to bake them in a moderate oven (350 F., Mark 4) for about 20 minutes, turning once, if the gammon is about ½ inch thick. The rind should be snipped at intervals to prevent it curling in cooking. Baked sausages, mushrooms or tomatoes are often cooked and served with them. Eggs may be broken on top of the rasher after it has been turned and will then set like conventional fried eggs.

YORK HAM AND MUTTON HAMS

A Ham as opposed to a Gammon is a hind leg of pork which has been cut off and cured separately from the side of bacon, unlike a gammon which is left on and cured with it. The Ham is usually cured more slowly and carefully and is therefore more expensive and delicate in flavour. The famous York Hams are large, weighing up to 24 lbs. and are rather long in shape because of the way they are cut off the bacon flitch. (A flitch is a side of bacon which has had the hind leg removed before curing.) York Hams are dry salted and lightly smoked and the original ones are supposed to have got their taste from being smoked in the sawdust left after building York Minster. Nowadays the name is often used loosely to describe any boiled ham. Mutton Hams are traditional to Cumberland but now very rare, the legs of mutton used to be pickled with salt, brown sugar and juniper berries before smoking. They are a delicacy similar to the smoked mutton so popular in Norway. In Oslo wafer-thin slices of smoked mutton are served in restaurants and much appreciated, the meat has a strange, almost candlewax, taste to which one quickly becomes accustomed and then likes it very much. Perhaps the Norwegian and the Cumberland specialities have a similar Norse origin.

NORTHUMBERLAND LEEK PASTY

They grow giant leeks in cottage gardens from Bishop Auckland to Amble, and sometimes make them into boiled leek puddings to serve hot and steaming with a cold joint, or with some of the excellent local black puddings. They also make a very good Northumberland Leek Pasty which is quite unlike the Cornish ones. This old north country dish is not really so different from the much better known French *tarte aux poireaux*.

Line a greased Swiss roll tin with short crust pastry. Sprinkle 8 ozs. chopped bacon or ham on it, and 1 lb. well washed, then chopped and scalded leeks. Beat up 2 eggs and 4 tablespoons milk, a little salt and pepper. Pour this over the vegetables and bacon. Top with pastry, sealing the edges with milk and crimping them with a fork, brush over with milk. Bake in a hot oven (400 F., Mark 6) for 20 minutes.

GRANDMOTHER'S PICKLED RED CABBAGE

In Lancashire pickled cabbage is always served with hot pot and usually with a cottage pie and such dishes as celery baked with cheese sauce, and so on.

Take 1 hearty red cabbage. Remove the stalk and the outer leaves. Slice it in rounds ¼ inch thick, place these on large plates or meat dishes and cover them with a handful of salt and leave overnight in a cool, clean place. Drain off the salt. Now put a half teaspoon of sugar in the bottom of each screw-topped jar. Press the salt cabbage into each jar to the neck. Put a little pickling spice in a clean piece of old linen and tie up with cotton. One little bag for the top of each jar. Fill up with *cold* malt vinegar and screw the tops on tightly. Ready for serving in one week's time.

Mrs. D. Kean,
Padgate, Lancashire.

CUMBERLAND SAUCE

Peel and chop fine 3 shallots, boil for 2 minutes. Peel and cut the rind of 1 orange and 1 lemon in strips, boil 5 minutes.

Mix the peel and the drained shallots with the juice of the orange and half the lemon, add a pinch of ground ginger and a pinch of cayenne pepper, then 6 tablespoons of melted red currant jelly and 5 tablespoons port. Mix well.

Serve with cold meat or venison.

Mrs. Gardiner,
Keswick, Cumberland.

APPLE BATTER

This is sometimes served for high tea in Yorkshire with thick gammon rashers which may be baked at the same time.

Sift together 4 ozs. self raising flour, 2 ozs. sugar and a good pinch of salt. Mix it to a smooth batter with ½ pint of milk and add 1 lb. peeled, cored and thinly sliced apples. Melt 3 ozs. butter, grease a Yorkshire pudding tin with some of it, stir the rest into the batter which pour into the tin. Bake it in the centre of a hot oven (400 F., Mark 6) for 20 minutes. Then reduce the heat to moderate (350 F., Mark 4). Bake for a further 20 minutes.

Mrs. Appleby,
Grassington, near Ilkley, Yorkshire.

TREACLE TOFFEE (LANCASHIRE)

Cover the bottom of a pan with water, then add 8 ozs. black treacle, 8 ozs. sugar, 8 ozs. best butter and 2 teaspoons of vinegar. Stir it over a low heat till the sugar has melted then till boiling. Boil for 15 minutes stirring all the time. Test for setting in a little cold water. Take it off the stove. Pour the liquid toffee into a shallow greased tin. Leave it till cold and set, then break it up with a hammer or kitchen weight.

Mrs. Doris Young,
Debdale Park, Manchester.

Tom Trot is the name of a dark treacle toffee made in Swaledale, Yorkshire, to eat round the bonfire on Guy Fawkes night. The recipe is not dissimilar to this one, but when the toffee is cooked enough to set in a little cold water, as above, it is poured onto a buttered dish and then worked with the hands and pulled and twisted into long lengths until the toffee is bright and clear. These twists are broken in pieces when cold. Peg's Leg is a striped Irish toffee which used to be popular in Liverpool and was widely sold on market stalls in Lancashire and Cheshire about thirty years ago. It was sometimes flavoured with peppermint.

Pontefract or Pomfret Cakes are liquorice sweets.

ULLSWATER RUM BUTTER

Melt 1 lb. butter, add 1½ lbs. soft brown sugar, 2 teaspoons of grated nutmeg. Pour in a wineglass of rum, stir until it begins to thicken, then pour it into a pretty china bowl and leave it to set.

Mrs. Brown,
Carlisle.

OLD CHESHIRE RUM SAUCE FOR CHRISTMAS PUDDING

Beat up 1 tablespoon of sugar with 2 egg yolks, adding the strained juice of a lemon, a wineglass of rum and ¼ pint of water, heat, stirring till it thickens — something like zabaione. If it boils it curdles.

Mrs. Emily Howarth,
Chester.

ELDERFLOWER "CHAMPAGNE"

Mrs. Appleby, who lives in a cottage in Grassington, with a dramatic view of the river, is an authority on old Yorkshire recipes, nettle beer, yarrow wine, cheese cakes, frumenty and Scarborough muffins. She was good enough to offer me a glass of her elderflower "champagne" on the hot June afternoon I visited her. It had been made the previous Saturday. I was a bit wary at first as I was driving. "But it's not intoxicating," she cried, "it's what they take to the hayfields." We had it in wine glasses and, as a matter of fact, it was quite delicious. A nice, cool, fizzy drink the colour of lemon squash, perfect for hot summer days and quite easy to make.

Put 4 heads of elderflowers, 1½ lbs. of sugar, 2 tablespoons of white wine vinegar or ordinary distilled white vinegar into a large bowl with a gallon of cold water. Squeeze, quarter and add 2 lemons. Let it stand for 24 hours, stirring occasionally before straining and bottling it in screw-top bottles. It's ready to drink in a few days' time.

Mrs. Appleby,
Grassington, Yorkshire.

CHUTNEY

This is my oldest recipe for Chutney, It is lovely with all the cold meats (pork pie, pig chap, brawn, cold pork and particularly with bacon). I have made quite a few hundreds of jars over the years for charities, O.A.P. Clubs and it is very popular.

Slice 2 lbs. green tomatoes up fine and put on a meat dish and sprinkle well with salt. Leave overnight. Next day drain off the water from the tomatoes and put them in a pan. Next, peel and chop 1 lb. onions, peel and chop 2 lbs. cooking apples removing the cores, of course. Add 1 quart of vinegar, ½ lb. brown sugar, some sultanas, a 4 oz. packet of dates, chopped, and 1½ teaspoons of ground ginger. Add 1½ ozs. pickling spice which has been tied up tightly in a muslin bag. Boil altogether and simmer until it is thick. Take the bag of pickling spice out and then put the chutney in warmed jars. This quantity makes about 10 lbs. and will keep a year but is usually eaten up before January.

Mrs. D. Griffiths,
Blaxton, near Doncaster, Yorkshire.

EGYPTIAN CHUTNEY

2 lbs. rhubarb	2 lbs. dates
1 lb. onions	1½ lbs. sugar
1 quart vinegar	2 tablespoons salt
1 teaspoon cayenne pepper	1 teaspoon ground ginger
1 oz. mustard seeds (washed)	few cloves of garlic

Cut the rhubarb and onions into small pieces. Put the dates through the mincer, also the garlic. Mix all well together and simmer until tender. Bottle when cold. The onions can go through the mincer.

Mrs. M. Sands,
Lazenby, Middlesbrough, Teesside.

BENGAL CHUTNEY

The Bengal Chutney handed down from my grandmother was her favourite chutney. The Egyptian Chutney I make every year in August. It is very easy to do and very useful for a large family.

1½ lbs. brown sugar	¼ lb. salt
¼ lb. onions	¼ lb. ground ginger
½ lb. mustard seed	1½ lbs. stoned raisins

1 oz. garlic   2 ozs. eschalots
½ oz. cayenne pepper
6½ lbs. cooking apples (Bramley seedlings are the best to use) weighed
after peeling and coring.
3 pints vinegar — boil and let get cold.

Bake the apples in a slow oven. The garlic, eschalots and onions
must be pounded, mustard seed must be soaked and dried. Mince
the raisins. When the apples are cold and in a pulp mix all the other
ingredients thoroughly and blend well together then bottle and
keep for a few weeks before using.

This recipe is very old and very useful where there are apple
trees in the garden as fallen apples can be used.

Mrs. M. Sands,
Lazenby, Middlesbrough, Teesside.

CHUTNEY (no cooking)

1 lb. stoneless dates   1 lb. sultanas
1 lb. apples   1 lb. onions
1 lb. brown sugar   1 pint vinegar
1 tablespoon salt   3 dashes of pepper
small bag of pickling spice   small piece of whole ginger

Mince the first four ingredients (dates, sultanas, apples and onions).
Stir together with the sugar, vinegar, salt, pepper, spices and ginger.
Leave for 24 hours. Remove the bag of spices and ginger. Bottle.
This is delicious with cold meat.

Mrs. G. Messenger,
Thornhill, Dewsbury, Yorkshire.

YORKSHIRE MINCEMEAT (with brandy)

My grandmother was born in Bendigo, Victoria, Australia in
1856, that is 115 years ago and this recipe was brought to Australia
from Ilkley, Yorkshire. I think that the original meat ingredient may
have been pork but my grandmother and my mother and myself
use mutton and very delicious mincemeat it is. We keep it in the
'fridge for at least six weeks and it keeps quite all right in an Australian summer. But before the days of refrigerators my mother made it
and I never ever heard of any going bad. We used to take out what
we needed for a pie then smooth the remainder down and put a drop
of brandy on it.

3 lbs. boiled mutton   1 lb. raisins
3 lbs. minced apple   1 lb. currants
½ lb. lemon peel   ½ teaspoon salt
1 bottle of essence of lemon   sugar to taste

Mince all together, if not moist enough add a little of the water
in which the meat was boiled. I always boil a small leg of mutton.

I then have enough over for a meal and then stock for broth. Just put it in a jar and tie a paper over it and use as required.

We always pinched spoonfuls as children and just ate it, but of course it goes in pastry.

Mrs. A. Sopp,
Melbourne, Victoria, Australia.

WESTMORLAND MINT CAKE

Boil 1 lb. granulated sugar with $\frac{1}{4}$ pint of milk, stirring all the time until it reaches the soft ball stage. Beat the mixture for 2 minutes until it goes cloudy, then boil until a hard ball is reached, 260 F. on the sugar thermometer. Off the heat, add some peppermint essence and stir until it thickens slightly. Then pour it into wetted tins and cut it before it is quite cold. Wrap in toffee paper.

NORTH COUNTRY GOOSEBERRY SAUCE

The old north country Gooseberry Sauce is delicious with bacon, ham or cold meats.

Put 2 lbs. demerara sugar and 1 pint vinegar in an enamel pan with 3 lbs. topped and tailed gooseberries, add $\frac{1}{4}$ oz. ground cloves. Bring it all gently to the boil, stirring, until the sugar melts then boil until it thickens in about 40 minutes. Bottle and seal.

Mrs. Johnson,
Hexham, Northumberland.

YORKSHIRE PUDDING

Yorkshire Pudding is still eaten with thick gravy as a separate dish before the main meat course in its home county. Onions which have been chopped up and soaked in vinegar the week before are often served with it. After the meal a fresh lot of onions is usually prepared for the following week. In other parts of the country the Yorkshire pudding is usually served with the roast beef. In Yorkshire some people swear by Yorkshire pudding that is flat and rather soggy, others insist on having it puffy, some like it half and half. It is best cooked in the oven in a deep meat tin in smoking hot dripping and is served cut in portions. For the last few minutes, when it has risen, some cooks like to place it on a brass trivet in front of a hot fire to set. For a good pudding you must have a good hot oven, very hot fat and not too much of it. Some cooks make their puddings with half milk and half water so they will be crisp. In the old spit roasting days the pudding was put in a dish under the joint and as the meat turned on the spit the juices dripped onto the pudding. In a modern oven without a spit a somewhat similar effect can be got by raising the meat on a trivet or wire rack over the dish of pudding, towards the end of the roasting time.

Break 1 egg into 4 ozs. plain flour mixed with 1 teaspoon salt, beat it in the mix $\frac{1}{4}$ pint milk and $\frac{1}{4}$ pint water. Add just enough of it to the flour to make it of a beating consistency, beat well, let it stand for 30 minutes before adding the rest of the liquid. Get the tin with the fat so hot that blue smoke rises from it before the mixture is poured into it. Cook the Yorkshire Pudding at once in a very hot oven (450 F., Mark 8).

SEASON PUDDING

When Yorkshire pudding is served with pork or with roast lamb herbs are often added to the batter (chopped onion and chopped sage and sometimes thyme and parsley) to make Yorkshire Season Pudding. This is popular all over Lancashire and Yorkshire and often served *first*, piping hot, before the roast.

"This recipe was given to me over 35 years ago by my husband's grandma, an old lady, about 89 years old. We lived in Preston, Lancashire, then, but wherever I've lived no one seems to have heard about it" writes Mrs. Dorothy Austin from Hertfordshire, "yet it is so simple to make. Our Christmas dinner is not complete without it, even though I make it dozens of times during the year — every time we have pork, chicken and so on. It's called Season Pudding." Take 1 breakfastcup of plain flour and mix it with $\frac{1}{2}$ teaspoon of salt, gradually beat in 2 eggs and then 1 pint of milk (day before's) to make a Yorkshire pudding batter. Then add 1 medium-sized onion, chopped fine, 2 ozs. suet, 1 thick slice of bread made into breadcrumbs. Mix well and add 1 level dessertspoon of chopped sage and 1 level dessertspoon of thyme, or to your taste. When the pudding is mixed, pour it into a hot, greased meat tin 12 inches x 12 inches. Put it at the bottom of the oven to cook slowly for about $1\frac{1}{4}$ hours. Then bring it to the top of the oven and cook until brown and crisp.

Serve with gravy only at the beginning of dinner.

Mrs. Dorothy Austin,
Birchanger, nr. Bishop's Stortford, Herts.

SEASONED PUDDING AND BEDLAM EATING

I was brought up in a small village in the West Riding of Yorkshire where nearly every householder, including my father, kept a couple of pigs. These were killed a short time before Christmas, and the bacon and hams were cured and hung on the beams in the kitchen to be eaten later. The spare ribs and pig's cheeks were left in salt on the cellar stone for use over Christmas, but the pig's fry was always eaten within a couple of days of the pigs being killed. This was cooked in a huge earthenware stew pot and was always served with Seasoned Pudding. This was made like a Yorkshire pudding but with oatmeal, suet, chopped onion and sage added to the batter. It was made in huge quantities and as children we were sent, with portions of the pig's fry and pudding straight from the oven to our various friends, who returned the compliment when their own pigs were killed later. For some reason unknown to me this feast was locally called a Bedlam Eating and although now sixty years later I still cook pig's fry and seasoned pudding, it never tastes quite as good as it did when we were children.

Mrs. A. Whitehead,
Lightcliffe, near Halifax, Yorkshire.

SAVOURY PUDDING

This is cut into squares and served hot — before the meat — and with a good thick gravy in Lancashire and Yorkshire. Very good with roast goose or duckling.

Soak 8 ozs. stale breadcrumbs in hot water for 30 minutes. Drain and beat out any lumps with a fork. Boil 2 large English onions in salted water then chop them coarsely. Mix together 8 ozs. fine oatmeal, the bread, 8 ozs. chopped butcher's suet, the chopped onions, ¼ teaspoon mixed herbs, ½ teaspoon powdered sage, some salt and pepper. Beat up 2 eggs and add these last. Melt some dripping in a pudding tin to form a thin layer at the bottom. Place in the pudding and spread evenly. Bake in a moderate oven (350 F., Mark 4) for about an hour. Cut it into squares and serve it hot with a good thick gravy.

Mrs. Kathleen Clegg,
The Coppice, Oldham, Lancashire.

NORTHUMBERLAND PEASE PUDDING

Soak 1 pint yellow split peas overnight in rainwater. Tie them loosely in a clean cloth and then boil them in rainwater for 2 hours. Rub them through a sieve and add 2 ozs. butter, pepper and salt to your taste and 1 large egg. Put the pease pudding into an ovenproof dish and bake in a moderate oven (350 F., Mark 4) for 45 minutes. To be served with roast beef or roast pork.

Miss A. Howat,
Prestwick, Lancashire.

Pease Pudding, though popular all over the British Isles, is almost "the national dish of the north-east" as everybody in Newcastle tells you, and one sees 40 lb. and 50 lb. bowls of freshly made, delicious pease pudding in all the butchers' shops in Newcastle and Gateshead. The flavour is superb and the little tins of it people buy down south would be unthinkable to the Geordies. Everybody buys a bit of pease pudding, or pork stuffing in Northumberland. They have it with all kinds of pork cuts, with sausages, or with white puddings, and with slices of cold roast pork. Some like it with sandwiches, others have it with the rolled "green" bacon which they buy for boiling.

PUDDING

ALMASPITE

My granny was a housekeeper in one of the old halls — this is her apple tart with almond crust.

Stew 1 lb. dessert apples with only enough water to prevent burning and sweeten to taste. Sift 6 ozs. flour into a basin. Rub in 4 – 5 ozs. butter. Mix an egg yolk with about 2 tablespoons of soured cream. Stir into the flour mixture. Knead till smooth then chill for 30 minutes. Brush a 7 inch sandwich tin lightly with melted butter. Divide the pastry into two equal portions. Roll half into a round to fit the tin. Line the tin, then trim the edge and ornament to taste. Prick the base well with a fork. Bake well in a moderately hot oven (400 F., Mark 5 – 6) for about 10 minutes.

Meanwhile mix 2 ozs. ground almonds with 2 ozs. caster sugar. At the end of 10 minutes spread the inside of the pastry case with strawberry jam. Cover with half the almonds and sugar. Beat the egg white to a stiff froth. Fold in the apples. Spread evenly in the case. Sprinkle with the remaining almonds and sugar mixture. Then cover with the remaining pastry. Brush the top with egg white. Bake in a moderately hot oven (400 F., Mark 5 – 6) for 20 minutes or so, leave until cold. Decorate round the rim with whipped cream, then top the cream with plenty of glacé cherries to taste.

Mrs. M. Gilding,
Bispham, Blackpool, Lancashire.

YORKSHIRE CREAM CHEESE PUDDING OR SOUFFLÉ

This cream cheese pudding is the filling for the curd cheese cakes (tarts) my grandmother used to make when I was a child in Yorkshire. It serves four.

Separate 2 eggs and whisk the whites into peaks. Mix together 8 ozs. curd cheese, 4 ozs. sugar, 1½ ozs. raisins or sultanas (or half a cup of drained, crushed pineapple) and the 2 egg yolks. Fold in the egg whites. Pour into a shallow, buttered fireproof dish and bake as for a soufflé. The top should be golden brown. Serve immediately.

I've lost count of the times I've served this pudding to guests with success and passed on the recipe, quite unknown, especially in Canada and the U.S. and recently in England since I came to live here.

Mrs. Jan Williams,
Tunbridge Wells, Kent.

When made in a 1¾ pint straight sided, flat bottomed fireproof china soufflé dish, this pudding puffs up into a delicious soufflé. It can also be flavoured with rum.

COLD WATER PUDDING

This is one of my mother's favourite puddings taken out of her personal recipe book, compiled while she was parlour maid in 1902, which I still treasure though she has been dead nearly 35 years.

Beat 2 ozs. butter to a cream. Add 4 ozs. caster sugar, 4 egg yolks well beaten. Mix all well together. Then add 8 tablespoons of cold water, the juice of a lemon, the grated rind and lastly the 4 stiffly beaten egg whites. Put the mixture into a fireproof dish and stand it in another dish containing water. Put a plate on the top and bake slowly for 20 minutes. It is really delicious.

Mrs. B. Warburton,
Pocklington, Yorkshire.

ASH WEDNESDAY FRITTERS

Crumble $\frac{3}{4}$ oz. yeast into $\frac{1}{2}$ pint warm milk and let it rise. Melt 1 oz. lard and pour into the yeast mixture. Add 12 ozs. plain flour, 3 ozs. currants, $1\frac{1}{2}$ ozs. raisins, 1 saltspoon cinnamon, 1 saltspoon salt, 1 tablespoon sugar, the rind of half a lemon and 1 chopped apple. Beat into a smooth batter. Fry in spoonfuls till golden brown on both sides. Serve hot, sprinkled with sugar and lemon juice.

Mrs. C. Benson,
Southport, Lancashire.

GRANNY'S ORANGE DELIGHT WITH WHISKY

Allow one large orange per person. Wash the oranges, cut a slice from the top to make a lid. With sharp scissors or a thin bladed sharp knife cut out the centre part of the orange segments — just as if you were coring an apple, taking care not to puncture the skin at the base of the orange. Pack this centre as hard as you can with sugar then pour on about one tablespoonful of scotch whisky or as much whisky as the sugar will absorb. Replace the lid and leave in a cool place for several hours. Serve with sponge biscuits and a small spoon to scoop out the delicious fruit.

Mrs. J. Hughes,
Bury, Lancashire.

AMHURST PUDDING

Well butter a pudding dish and line with thin slices of bread and butter.

Peel and slice some sour baking apples, fill the dish with them. Sprinkle with brown sugar and a little powdered clove and cinnamon. Cover the apples with slices of bread and butter. Turn a plate or dish over the pudding so as to cover it closely. Bake in a moderate oven (350 F., Mark 4) for $1\frac{1}{2}$ hours. Serve with cream sauce.

Miss M. Deveney,
Wheatley Hills, Doncaster, Yorkshire.

SWEET YORKSHIRE PUDDING

My old grandmother's favourite pudding:—

Mix up a Yorkshire Pudding, just add a nice helping of mixed dried fruits, a little lemon peel (or marmalade). Cook in a very hot oven. When cooked, sprinkle a little caster sugar on top. So simple and nice.

Mrs. E. Pussey,
Tankerton, Kent.

RASPBERRY VINEGAR FOR BATTER PUDDINGS

Put 4 quarts of raspberries into a stone jar, then pour over them 1 quart of vinegar. Let it stand for 4 days, uncovered, stirring twice a day, then once a day for 4 days, keeping it covered. Strain through a flannel bag. Boil the liquid gently for 10 minutes, having first dissolved in it 3 lbs. loaf sugar. Bottle. Serve with batter pudding.

Mrs. M. R. Pamment,
York.

MOTHER'S CHOCOLATE PANCAKES

Mix 2 ozs. dry fine flour with 2 tablespoons milk, the whites of 2 eggs and the yolks of 4 eggs beaten separately. Add a tablespoon of sugar and a pinch of salt. Beat the batter well for 30 minutes with 2 tablespoons of cream. With this batter fry some very thin small pancakes, browning them on one side only. Lay them on a plate with the unfried side uppermost. Grate over each a layer of chocolate (milk or plain), enough to cover the pancakes entirely. Roll up the pancakes. Dust with sugar and lay on a buttered tin. Set the tin on a trivet and bake for 20 minutes in a moderate oven (350 F., Mark 4).

Mrs. A. Sellen,
Sale, Cheshire.

MARROW PUDDING

Chop half the marrow of a beef bone, take out the largest pieces, then chop up the rest very small. Put it into a basin and mix it into 4 ozs. of stale, plain cake. Pour 1 pint boiling milk on the cake and leave to soak. Whisk 3 eggs to a stiff froth. By this time the cake will be soaked; beat it quite smooth, give the eggs another whisk and pour them into the cake. Add a few currants, some candied orange and lemon peel cut small, about a quarter of a nutmeg, grated, half the peel of a fresh lemon, grated and sufficient sugar to sweeten. Put it all into your dish, lay the pieces of marrow over the top with a few more currants and citron peel cut in very thin slices and bake in a warm oven.

Mrs. Lila Jenkins,
Harworth, Doncaster, Yorkshire.

YORKSHIRE BURBRIDGE PUDDING WITH THICK CREAM

I have been thinking of childhood days in Yorkshire, and fascinating visits to a housemaid's old mother in her cottage — a special treat. We could hardly understand a word she said, for cats were "tettins" and birds were "grunnins" (pronounced the Yorkshire way). It was also a privilege to be allowed through the kitchen door at home then. Happy days! Yorkshire Burbridge Pudding was a favourite one I have never come across since. This is not exactly what my "granny used to cook", but it was written down for me by a dearly-loved old cook who went to my tartar of a grandmother as a tweeny at the age of 14, straight from a farmhouse in Lincolnshire. It was not until she retired in her seventies, after being handed down to me, that she began to use her real name again — my grandmother did not consider Georgina a suitable name for a servant and dubbed her Mary instead.

Mix 4 ozs. demerara sugar, $\frac{1}{2}$ teaspoon bicarbonate of soda, 4 ozs. chopped suet, 1 tablespoon strawberry jam, 4 ozs. fresh breadcrumbs and 1 egg all well together and steam for 3 – 4 hours. It was served with thick cream, and not even the younger members of the family could manage a second helping.

Mrs. Kate Sawle Daly,
London, S.W.1

YORKSHIRE BEASTINGS TART

When the calves came in the spring mother would buy a quart of beastings, which is the first milk drawn from the cow after calving. Add sugar and pour it into a pastry lined dish. Add a knob of butter and a little grated nutmeg. Bake as you would a custard. No eggs are needed, it sets like a custard, firm enough to cut.

Mrs. T. Jones,
Cwmbran, Monmouthshire, South Wales.

"Beistyns", "Bestys" or "Firsttings" or "Beastings" is as thick as double cream and golden yellow. It is not now sold commercially. Farmers sometimes give away a jug of it to their friends. Beastings are used on some farms to make Yorkshire Pudding.

APPLE PIE FILLING   I

When making an Apple Pie, instead of cutting the apples up or cooking them before you put them to the pastry, slice them with a potato cutter and sprinkle sugar on. It makes the apples like a jelly. Put the pastry on top.

I have tried them this way since I was a little girl at school and we learned it in cookery class.

Mrs. J. Birtle,
Preston. Lancashire.

APPLE PIE FILLING II

Chop 3 apples, add 1 beaten egg, ⅛th pint cream, spice, sugar, raisins and currants, sufficient to make a firm filling.

Mrs. R. W. Mercer,
Woolton, Liverpool.

RATAFIA PUDDING WITH WINE SAUCE

Put enough water into a stewpan to come rather more than half as high as a 3 pint mould, of whatever shape you please, and put it on a low heat. Remove the warmed mould and butter the inside well. Stick stoned raisins and glacé cherries on the butter to make it look ornamental. Arrange ratafias to cover the whole of the inside of the mould. Cut 6 small sponge cakes in half, and put them in, mixing a few ratafias and cherries among them; then put in more ratafias till the mould is about three parts full. Now whisk 7 large eggs lightly. Pour upon them 1½ pints of sweetened boiling milk. Whisk well and pour into the mould. Tie a cloth over the mould or put a cover on and put this into the boiling water in the stewpan. It will take rather more than an hour to boil, turn it out onto a dish, pour wine over it and send some to the table in a sauce boat. It must be sent to the table as hot as possible and is served with wine sauce.

Wine Sauce

Into a clean pan put 2 ozs. of butter. Put it on the fire and when melted stir ½ tablespoon of flour into it until it is quite smooth; mix by degrees a wineglassful of water, ½ wineglass of brandy and 2 wineglasses of white wine, with enough moist sugar to sweeten it; mix these together, put them on the fire, keep stirring it till thick (it ought not to boil), pour it into a sauce boat and send to the table.

Mrs. Lila Jenkins,
Harworth, Doncaster, Yorkshire.

BAKING

DOUGH CAKES

Oh the heavenly smell of baking day! My mother had an enormous yellow bowl which held a stone (14 lbs.) of flour, and in addition to the big crusty loaves of bread, she used to make several kinds of Dough Cakes for us. When the dough was kneaded and risen she would cut out a large lump of it, take a handful of lard (home rendered in a large brown crock) a handful of currants and raisins, mix them into the dough and knead it into flat, round cakes. She baked these in the oven bottom, turning them over to brown on both sides to make "Fatty Cakes". Then sometimes she would cut off a large lump of dough and roll it out as thin as possible. It was baked in the oven bottom and turned and it made scrumptious oven bottom cakes which we ate hot from the oven, cut through and spread with butter and golden syrup. Or she would take another lump and knead a large lump of butter, large raisins and peel and sugar into it. This made 2 fruit cakes in loaf tins. Then my sister and I would have a small piece to roll into a short length, tie in a knot, put two currants in one of the ends, and out of the oven would come two little ducks. All this variety from the large bowlful as well as the big crusty loaves of bread.

Mrs. M. Leach,
Harden, Bingley, Yorkshire.

STOTTY CAKE

My grandmother used to bake a special cake for me when I was a boy in Darlington. Flat, two-inches thick, and made, I think, from ordinary dough though it had air spaces and the crust was an unusual colour. I wanted the recipe so my wife could bake it and wrote to the *Northern Echo* asking if they knew what it was. Letters poured into the *Daily Express* office with recipes for the cake, known variously as stotty, flat, new, yeasty and oven bottom cake. Most were similar with flour, sugar, yeast and water. Some added lard.

My wife, Billee, baked two cakes, one with lard and one without. "Marvellous" I said, "although it's better with lard." It's amazing really, I normally write about serious matters on defence and I never get a letter. I write about stotty cakes and I'm flooded out. Some people were really kind and asked me to visit them. I got a letter from Nurse Cherry, of Richmond House, Richmond, who wrote "I'm only 90".

Mr. Chapman Pincher,
Daily Express.

NEW CAKE

"New Cake", often called "lard cake", is made from ordinary bread dough. Roll it out and cover it all over with pieces of lard, fold it up and again roll out, repeating this three times. Put in a hot oven. It is best eaten at once, but I do not advise people who suffer from indigestion to eat very much.

Mrs. Ethel Spencer,
Barnard Castle.

When done it may be covered with a clean towel to bring out that lovely muffin texture.

NEW CAKE

New Cake is the same as Stotty or Oven-Bottom cake. In my family it has always been known as New Cake, but the usual name on Tyneside is Stotty. It is made by taking a piece of plain bread dough, rolling thinly and pricking with a fork. Traditionally it was baked on the bottom of the oven with the loaves on the shelves above, but in a modern gas or electric oven it has to be placed on a greased baking sheet and baked higher in the oven.

This was the bread that was eaten new, split and buttered or dipped in fat and served with bacon, the loaves being kept until the day after baking.

Mrs. M. Snape,
The Peth, Durham.

PLAIN CUMBERLAND TEA LOAF

— a nice change from shop bread.

Sift 12 ozs. plain flour, 4 ozs. cornflour and 1 oz. sugar together. Add 1 teaspoon of salt and leave it in a warm place. Cream 1 oz. yeast with another 1 oz. sugar and add 1 tablespoon of warm milk. Leave it to prove, or rise. Melt 2 – 3 ozs. butter and set aside to cool slightly before adding to the remaining warm milk — about $\frac{3}{8}$ of a pint altogether. Make a well in the centre of the warm flour mixture and pour in the yeast, 1 beaten egg and the butter with the rest of the milk. Beat all well with a wooden spoon. Flour the hands and knead the dough well. It should be very light and only just possible to handle it without the hands sticking to it. Set it aside in a warm place until the dough has risen to twice its original size then divide it into four. Knead again lightly into round but rather flattened loaves, and place them to rise on a warmed baking tray, covered with a good dry cloth. When well risen bake in the centre of a good hot oven (400 F., Mark 6) until golden brown, probably for 15 minutes.

Mrs. M. Gilding,
Bispham, Blackpool, Lancashire.

CHRISTMAS LOAF

First wash 1½ lbs. currants and leave them to drain for at least 4 hours. Cream 1 lb. of butter with 8 ozs. of granulated sugar, 8 ozs. of brown sugar and 1 lb. of black treacle. Cream them well. Beat 8 large eggs very thoroughly and add them to the mixture, also 1 cup of wine. Mix well then add 1 lb. 4 ozs. of self raising flour, 1 teaspoon of mixed spice. Mix, then add the currants and, if liked, 2 ozs. of ground almonds last. Mix all well and leave before putting into 3 large loaf tins lined with paper. Bake for 2½ hours in a fairly slow oven (325 F., Mark 3) on the middle shelf.

It can be left without looking at. This mixture is very nice with 1 lb. currants and cooked for 2 hours. You may notice I have not put much flavouring in. If liked, $\frac{1}{2}$ teaspoon ground nutmeg could be added but we like it without. It makes a very light Christmas loaf without too much fruit.

Mrs. Holt,
Blackpool, Lancashire.

BUNLOAF

This is an old recipe the family calls "Grandma's Bunloaf". My grandmother was married in 1848 and I copied it when I married in 1923 from her "receipts". It keeps well and is quite unlike the dark bunloaf sold today.

Mix $1\frac{1}{2}$ lbs. plain flour with 8 ozs. ground rice and 4 level teaspoons baking powder and $\frac{1}{2}$ teaspoon salt. Rub in 1 lb. lard and add $1\frac{3}{4}$ lbs. caster sugar, 8 ozs. each large-stoned raisins, seedless raisins, currants, sultanas, 2 ozs. chopped peel, 3 teaspoonfuls mixed spices. I use a mixture of cinnamon, mace, allspice, with just a pinch of cloves, but I *grated* nutmeg for grandma nearly 70 years ago. Mix with 4 eggs and milk to make a slightly stiff batter. Bake at (350 F., Mark 4). 1 lb. tins take about 45 – 55 minutes.

Mrs. E. Kay,
Wallasey, Cheshire.

BILBERRY TART

It is back-breaking work picking bilberries, which are no bigger than currants and grow in ones and twos in bushes round your ankles, on Ilkley Moor, for instance. Years ago in the West Riding they used to gather them with rakes, but now they mostly come from Poland. They are so popular all over the north of England, right up to the Scottish border and down to the Midlands and in Wales — anywhere that the bilberries used to grow wild — that the Poles have specially chartered boats which put in regularly to Hull during July and August with over 10,000 baskets a week when it is a good crop. There are less even of these now though than there used to be for Poland is processing the fresh bilberries in increasing quantities, freezing and bottling them instead of sending them here fresh.

This is a real regional delicacy. They are mad about them in Manchester, but I'm told you can't sell fresh bilberries in the south of England or in Lincolnshire or over the Scottish border. I think they are gorgeous. I remember munching them all raw and purple and rolled thick in sugar as a child in Cheshire. They make luscious summer pudding and Yorkshire miners say there is nothing like a bilberry tart for taking down the pits as they don't go mouldy in the coal mine like other fruit.

Grease an ordinary enamelled metal dinner plate or picnic plate, or old tart tin. Line it with short crust pastry crimping the edges with a fork. Fill it to within an inch of the edge with bilberries previously picked over, rinsed in a little cold water and drained. Add 2 table-spoons of sugar, arrange strips of pastry about ½ inch wide in a pattern across the top. Bake it in a fairly hot oven (375 F., Mark 5) for about 15 minutes. In Derbyshire a little chopped fresh mint is often added to the bilberries.

It can also be topped with pastry if liked. This should be sprinkled with a little sugar before baking.

AUNTIE MAGGIE'S SLAB CAKE

(Though the recipes vary a little, Auntie Maggie's Slab Cake is popular all over the north of England, but no one now seems to remember who Auntie Maggie was.   S.H.)

Prepare an 8-inch to 9-inch cake tin by lining it with foil or silicone paper or with buttered greaseproof paper. Cream 12 ozs. butter and 12 ozs. sugar together and add 5 eggs, one at a time, well beaten. Then 1 lb. sultanas and 4 ozs. ground almonds. Lastly mix in 1 lb. self raising flour with half a nutmeg grated and a drop of lemon juice. Put it in a papered tin with blanched almonds on top. Bake in a slow oven (275 F., Mark 1) for about 3 hours.

Mrs. Calvert,
Bury, Lancashire.

YORKSHIRE CUT AND COME AGAIN CAKE

This is very popular in the West Riding where they eat it with cheese. "A bit of spice and a bit of cheese" in the words of the old Yorkshire rhyme, "a glass of cold water and a penny, if you please". Mrs. Bolton, head of the homecraft department, Thomas Danby Technical College, Leeds, says this was an old temperance song and that there was something in the first verse about not drinking beer. A lot of people in Leeds, she adds, have the cake for high tea, and you often get a slice of Wensleydale cheese and a piece of Cut and Come Again Cake on your plate at the same time.

Rub 6 ozs. soft butter into 10 ozs. of self raising flour, then add 6 ozs. soft brown sugar, 4 ozs. currants, 6 ozs. sultanas, 3 ozs. stoned raisins, 1 oz. chopped peel, ¼ teaspoon powdered cinnamon. Then just mix it to a soft consistency with 4 beaten eggs and a little milk. Some cooks also add a tablespoon of rum or brandy to the cake mixture, but this is optional. It is one of those free and easy recipes where you can vary the ingredients a bit to your liking. Put it in an 8-inch cake tin and bake it for 1½ hours in a preheated oven (350 F., Mark 4 – 5).

Mrs. Bolton,
Leeds, Yorkshire.

PLAIN CHRISTMAS CAKE

This recipe for Christmas Cake was my aunt's who was born in 1871 and died in 1946. I well remember the ritual when she had got the end product in the oven and her strict instructions if we children had occasion to leave the room. Don't bang the door! and then the moment of truth when she went in like a bull-fighter, knitting needle in hand to make a test and running her finger and thumb down it after withdrawal. She was the eldest daughter of a master dyer and lost my grandmother when she was quite young and had to act as mother to a family, comprising her father, two boys and six daughters. She was the wife of a Leeds solicitor who died in 1911. I think she added a drop of rum.

Cream 1 lb. butter and 1 lb. sugar together until white and fluffy. Sift 2 lbs. plain flour, 6 teaspoons baking powder and a pinch of salt together. Add them to the butter and sugar alternately with 8 well beaten eggs. Add 1 lb. currants, 8 ozs. raisins with 2 ozs. candied lemon peel last. Finally add 2 tablespoons of rum with a little milk if the mixture seems too stiff.

Bake in a moderate oven (350 F., Mark 4). 1 lb. sized tins take about 45 – 55 minutes. Take out the cake and cool it on a wire rack.

Mr. Frank Ellison,
Leeds, Yorkshire.

YORKSHIRE FRUMERTY — for Christmas

In the Yorkshire Dales Christmas Eve was always celebrated with bowls of frumerty followed by cheese and spice cake and mince pies, and my earliest recollections of Christmas at grandma's was the candles on the table which were not lit before midnight when a male member of the family went outside with a piece of coal in his pocket and holly in his buttonhole and on the stroke of midnight he would enter, kiss my grandmother and wish everyone a happy Christmas and Christmas was duly "let in". The carol singers would sing and then come into the house and frumerty and all the good things were served. Happy days!

Place 8 ozs. wheat (pearl if possible) with 3 pints of water and a pinch of salt in a slow oven. The wheat needs to simmer for several hours until it is a soft creed and no water is left. (You can pour off any surplus). Add 2 pints of milk, currants, raisins and sultanas and a little nutmeg to taste and sweeten to your taste. Cook for another 2 hours and thicken with cornflour or arrowroot. Serve with cream and rum.

Mrs. Gladys Mottershaw,
Saffron Walden, Essex.

WILFRA TARTS

Wilfra Tarts were little jam tarts and curd cheese cakes eaten in Ripon, Yorkshire in Wilfra — or Wilfred — week, the first week in August. People used to get up at four in the morning to bake them on the feast day (that of St. Wilfred, patron saint of Ripon Cathedral).

Every household had large meat dishes full of cheese cakes and jam tarts placed just inside the doors of the cottages and passers-by were asked to help themselves.

CHEESE CAKES (using rennet)

Take 1 quart of milk, warm it to blood heat, add 1 teaspoon of rennet (to be bought at any chemist's shop). Leave it to stand when the milk will turn into curds and whey. Then strain it through a cloth till the whey runs out. The milk must never boil nor get really hot else it will not set. In grandma's day the whey used to be a drink to give a beautiful complexion.

Sweeten the curds with 3 tablespoons sugar, add 1½ ozs. raisins, 1½ ozs. currants, some chopped, mixed candied peel and 2 beaten raw eggs.

Line a not too deep flan type dish with a good suet crust pastry. Fill this with the curds mixture. Leave the top open except if fancied for a couple of narrow pastry strips laid over the curds mixture. Bake in a moderate oven (350 F., Mark 4) till the pastry and curds are cooked through.

Note: Nowadays the curd is usually bought from the grocer or baker. The above gives about 8 ozs. curds. A tablespoon of golden syrup may be substituted for 1 tablespoon of sugar.

Mrs. H. Blunt,
Marton, Blackpool, Lancashire.

HOW TO MAKE CURD FOR TARTS (using vinegar)

I am giving you a recipe of my mother's. I was 84 last February and I remember quite well her making curd tarts. She used to warm a quart of milk in a pan to blood heat and put about a tablespoon of vinegar in it, to break it to make the curd. When cold, she strained the curd through a sieve. She then slipped 1 egg into it, 2 ozs. of sugar, 2 ozs. of sultanas, 2 ozs. of currants and mixed it all together. She would make little tarts, or big ones.

Sometimes you can buy curd now in Yorkshire at pork butchers' shops.

Mrs. J. Phillips,
Bingley, Yorkshire.

SMALL RICE CAKES

Grease 18 small tins. Cream 4 ozs. butter and 4 ozs. sugar well together till white. Add 2 well beaten eggs. Sift 3 ozs. self raising flour and 1½ ozs. ground rice together and stir in lightly. Put in the prepared tins. Bake in a hot oven (400 F., Mark 6, 375 F., Mark 5) for 10 minutes, reduce the heat slightly and cook more slowly for another 5–10 minutes. To test if they are done press the centre of a cake with your finger, and it should spring up again.

Mrs. Doris Young,
Debdale Park, Manchester.

GRANNY'S PARKIN

Melt 8 ozs. butter, 6 ozs. soft brown sugar and 8 ozs. black treacle or golden syrup slowly. Mix 1 lb. plain flour and 1 teaspoon bi-carbonate of soda and 1 large teaspoon of ground ginger and stir in 12 ozs. medium oatmeal. Mix well. Add 3 large beaten eggs. Stir well. Bake in a Yorkshire pudding tin for about 45 minutes in a fairly low moderate oven (350 F., Mark 4).

Mrs. Major,
St. Anne's on Sea, Lancashire.

YORKSHIRE PARKIN

Around the 31st October the kids in the West Riding of Yorkshire, like kids all over the country, become affected by a curious klepto-mania called "chumping". That's their term for finding, stealing, liberating, anything which will burn.

A real choice "chump" used to be an old pit prop, bent by years underground supporting a sagging black roof above the grimy faces of generations of coal miners. That would burn a treat on the 5th in honour of Guy Fawkes — and he was a Yorkshireman too!

With the smell of the bonfire even now I can smell parkin. It was and still is served round the bonfire with beer or mulled wine for the grown-ups and dandelion and burdock for the children.

This is really a granny's recipe because it was handed down to my mother-in-law by her mother and for all I know to her by her mother. Which takes us well back in the last century because mother-in-law is 80 now.

What you need: 4 ozs. self-raising flour, 8 ozs. treacle, warmed — Golden Syrup does quite well — 8 ozs. medium oatmeal, 2 teaspoons ground ginger, 2 ozs. butter, 1 egg, 4 ozs. brown sugar, 2–3 table-spoons of milk. What you do: Grease a Yorkshire pudding tin; chuck the flour and the oatmeal in a basin and sort of stir it about. Rub the butter in, chuck in the sugar and the ground ginger and mix the whole caboodle around. Bung in the syrup or the treacle and the egg — without its shell — and stir around with the little bit of milk until you get a soft paste — not too runny.

Slurp the whole mess into the prepared baking tin and shove it into a moderately slow oven (325 F., Mark 3) to bake for 1 hour. Fantastic.

Mr. Robin Esser,
Daily Express.

PARKIN AND SOUL CAKES

Parkin is that dark, spicy gingerbread made all over Yorkshire, Lancashire and Cheshire for Guy Fawkes' Night, and eaten all through November in the north. It is baked in a Yorkshire pudding tin and should be made at least a week beforehand and left to mature. In Yorkshire it is sometimes eaten with cheese.

The Lancashire Parkin used to be called Harcake or Soul Mass Cake and is traditionally associated with All Soul's Day, November 2nd. "Har" is the Norse name for the pagan god Odin.

In Cheshire and parts of Shropshire the children go souling at the end of October, singing from house to house and getting money, nowadays usually "a copper for the guy". At one time, however, they used to be given sweet buns called "soul cakes". These are meant to be eaten on All Soul's Day. "A soul cake, A soul cake" you chant as you eat it, "Have mercy on all Christian souls".

I have no north country recipe for Soul Cake but the following recipe comes from Shropshire.

Three lbs. flour, 4 ozs. butter (or 8 ozs. if the cakes are to be extra rich), allspice to taste, and sufficient new milk to make it into a light paste. Put the mixture (without the sugar or spice) to rise before the fire for half an hour, then add the sugar and allspice enough to flavour it well; make into rather flat buns and bake.

This is the recipe of Mrs. Mary Ward, who is known to be the last person who kept up the old custom of giving "Soul Cakes" at Pulverbatch. She died in 1853 at the age of 101. Mrs. Ward is reputed to be one of the "pretty girls" for which Church Pulverbatch is famed in the local ditty. On her 100th birthday she was dressed in her bridal dress of yellow satin and received Holy Communion with her friends and neighbours. She never had a day's illness in her life and died very deaf but in other ways sensible to the last.

Shropshire Women's Institute Cook Book.

GRASMERE GINGERBREAD

This recipe has been handed down for many generations in a Westmorland family.

Mix 8 ozs. self raising flour, $\frac{1}{4}$ oz. ground ginger, 1 oz. chopped preserved ginger, 3 ozs. white sugar, $\frac{1}{2}$ teaspoon lemon rind and $\frac{1}{2}$ teaspoon baking powder with 5 ozs. warmed butter and the yolks of 2 eggs. Add 1 tablespoon syrup. Press into a tin. Brush the top with the white of the two eggs and sprinkle on 2 ozs. finely chopped almonds. Bake for 30 minutes in a medium oven (350 F., Mark 4).

Mrs. J. Rowling,
Purley, Surrey.

FAIRGROUND GINGERBREAD

This recipe for Gingerbread, as sold at country fairs, was given to me by an 80 year-old aunt who died about 20 years ago.

Crumble up 4 ozs. butter or lard into 2 lbs. plain flour, mixed with 8 ozs. brown sugar, 2 ozs. ground ginger and ½ oz. ground caraway seeds. Then mix to this 2 lbs. of black treacle and 3 well whisked eggs and, last of all, ½ oz. of bicarbonate of soda dissolved in a small cup of warm water. Stir the whole thing briskly together.

Well grease a shallow tin or two tins and half fill as this gingerbread will rise up high and be very good and light. Put it in a moderate oven (350 F., Mark 4) and bake for 1½ hours. When cold, cut up into thick squares and you will have a delicious gingerbread.

Mrs. Dorothy Watson,
School Lane, Fulford, York.

BIRTHDAY CAKE

— as made in the early 1860's. This is cooked in a frying pan to eat hot and buttered —

Rub 6 ozs. lard into 1 lb. plain flour. Add 4 ozs. scalded and dried currants, ½ teaspoon salt, 1 teaspoon baking powder. Mix it to a stiffish dough, using a half cup of milk and water. Knead a little. Roll it into a round cake about ½ inch thick. Set this aside till the girdle iron or thick-bottomed frying pan is hot, grease this lightly and put on the cake. Cook on a medium heat one side for 15 minutes. Cut down the middles and turn each half over. Cook 15 minutes. While still warm split each half and butter well. Sprinkle with brown sugar and a pinch of nutmeg. Put two lids on and cut into portions. Keep warm till needed.

Mrs. Wilford,
Redcar, Teesside.

The West Country

Cornwall, Devonshire, Dorset, Somerset and parts of Hampshire and Wiltshire.

Livestock and Agricultural Production

Devon Lamb, Dairy Cattle, Cider Orchards, Watercress Farms.

Dairy

Farmhouse Cheddar, Dorset Blue Vinney, Clotted Cream, Ilchester Cheese, Cornish and Devon Butter, Creamery "cottage" cheese. Fresh Cream.

Gastronomic Specialities

Gull's Eggs, Scallops or Queens, Dorset Crabs, Brixham Lobsters, Helford Oysters, Devon Lamb, Bath Chaps, Roast Badger, Venison, Rook Pie and Figgy 'Obbin, Chicken Pie, Cornish Pasties, Pilchards, Mackerel, Weymouth Red Mullet, Truffles, Lampreys.

Pastry

Cornish Saffron Cake, Honiton Fairlings, Bath Olivers, Dorset Knobs, Lardy Cakes, Somerset Apple Cake.

Confectionery

Bristol Stem Ginger. Spiced Dartmouth Crab Apples.

Farmhouse Draught Cider, Plymouth Gin (or Old Tom, sweeter than London Gin), "Jungle Juice", Bristol Sherry, Bristol Rum. Mead, Metheglin, Sloe Gin, Sparkling Perry, Bottled Cider.

FISH

GRILLED DORSET CRAB

The landlord of the Chapelhay Tavern, a small pub in one of the back streets of Weymouth, has a pair of scales on the bar for crabs and lobsters and does a roaring trade in local shellfish. People weigh out their own and he sells 4 cwt. – 5 cwt. of crabs a week at very reasonable prices. Some go to the Channel Islands and one window cleaner from Reading takes 20 lbs. of crabs every week. The one I got was as big as a dinner plate and tasted delicious grilled with curry butter and garnished with watercress.

Get the fishmonger to open the crab, remove those bits known colloquially as "dead men's fingers" which it would be indelicate to eat. Take out all the rest of the meat yourself, cracking bits of shell when necessary. Some is white and flaky, some yellowish and crumbly, but all delicious. Pull off the legs, crack the claws with a 1 lb. weight, and before putting the meat back in the crab shell crack and break off the extra rim of shell around the main carapace.

You will see what I mean when you have the crab in your hand. There is a serrated line which breaks easily. Just tear along the dotted line and it's done. Stuff the crab with its own meat, sprinkle with salt and pepper, brush all over with melted butter, toast it under the hot griller for about 10 minutes. Serve it piping hot with 4 ozs. of melted butter mixed with the juice of half a lemon and a large teaspoon of curry powder. This does marvellous things for the crab and I know you will enjoy it.

TORBAY SOLE IN DEVONSHIRE CREAM (Delicious)

The Torbay Sole — or Witch or Megrim — is at its best from July to February, after which it is spawning and goes all flabby and lovesick. Cheaper than Dover Sole it has not quite so fine a flavour but is delicious baked in dry cider, or stewed in clotted cream. According to the famous Eliza Acton whose *Modern Cookery for Private Families* was published in 1845 and was a best seller for the next seventy or eighty years, this was once the normal way of cooking them at Penzance. She writes of grey mullet done in clotted cream with parsley and lemon juice, and of soles, eels and turbot cooked in the same manner.

I myself poach the fillets of sole in a fireproof dish in the oven. Four medium fillets need about half a glass of slightly salted water and take 8 to 10 minutes in a preheated moderate oven (350 F., Mark 4). Put a paper on top to keep them moist. When cooked drain them well and put them back in the oven for a moment to dry. Just before serving pour over them $\frac{1}{4}$ pint clotted cream mixed with a dash of lemon juice, a little salt, cayenne pepper, grated nutmeg, a tablespoon of butter and the yolk of an egg. Heat the sauce very gently, stirring all the time, for about 4 minutes. Do not let it get too hot or you will just have very rich scrambled egg. Pour it over the fish.

MARINATED FISH

This is an old recipe that originally came from Cornwall's fishing folk. Now you rarely see or hear of it being made.

Scale and clean the fish, do not split them open. Cut in two or three pieces according to the size of the fish and lay in a baking dish (an earthenware casserole is preferred as it bakes slowly) for about 4 hours, adding pickling spice and bay leaves to the fish, cover with vinegar, pepper and salt. Fill up the dish with layers of fish, bay leaves and pickling spice until it is full. To cook, put on a cover and put into a slow oven (300 F., Mark 2). It can be eaten after 2 hours cooking but the longer it cooks the better it tastes.

Any fish can be used if desired. Mackerel or herring are particularly good. Conger eel can be used.

Mrs. D. Pryor,
Troon, Camborne, Cornwall.

106

COLD POACHED DEVON AND CORNWALL MACKEREL

Fresh caught mackerel may be gutted and boiled in sea water for 10 minutes gently. Let them get cold in the cooking liquid. Ordinary salty water will do if no sea water is available. Drain and serve with Oxford Brawn Sauce or Gooseberry Sauce.

GRILLED MACKEREL or BASS WITH FENNEL

Mackerel taste and smell delicious when stuffed with a few bits of fennel and grilled over fennel twigs. The grill pan may be lined with foil to prevent it from smelling afterwards of fish. Fennel stalks should be laid under the fish and will scorch and burn a little whilst grilling. Fennel is often to be found growing wild by the seaside in this country. The Cornish Bass, a similar fish to the *loup de mer* of the Mediterranean, is delicious when cooked in the same way.

J. Daniels,
Bridport, Dorset.

STAR GAZY PIE

Take as many fresh herrings or mackerel as will fill a moderate dish. Scale and open them. Remove the bones. Lay them flat on the table, season with salt, pepper and chopped parsley. Roll them up neatly or lay flat in a buttered pie dish, sprinkle with breadcrumbs. Cover the contents with a few slices of streaky bacon. Pour over all 6 well beaten eggs mixed with 2 spoons tarragon vinegar or, if preferred, a quarter pint of thin cream. Cover the dish with a good pastry crust. Bake in a well heated moderate oven (350 F., Mark 4) for about 1 hour. Arrange the fish so the heads stick up through the pastry crust.

Mrs. Hilda Bovey,
St. Blazey, Cornwall.

This was originally a dish for pilchards.

PILCHARDS

Pilchards, or "Fair Maids" as they were once known in Cornwall, are the same fish as the Portuguese sardines which we now import fresh frozen in such large quantities for fashionable London restaurants. Crisp fried fresh sardines are delicious and should become increasingly popular. The pilchard fishing however has been in decline for years, partly because the catches are spasmodic. Either there is none at all or a glut. The pilchard run is for about 2 months after which they disappear. You'd imagine that with deep freezing it would be no more of a problem than the seasonal glut of peas and strawberries, but, though many London fishmongers now sell quantities of the deep frozen sardines — which are practically the same fish — people say there's no market for pilchards. Prices paid to fishermen are 30% less than they were 15 years ago and hardly any are landed now. In Mevagissy the old pilchard curing stores, where for more than half a century thousands of tons of pilchards were cured each year in 9 foot deep vats for the Italian market, was cleared away some years ago to make room for a car park. The Italians no longer buy our salt pilchards but no one seems to have bothered to find out why. Nowadays almost the only outlet for Cornish pilchards is for fish paste. Many of the Cornish pilchard people went into canning a few years ago but were beaten by the South Africans who can deliver them here at about 2d. per can cheaper than Cornish pilchards and, indeed, those familiar red cans of pilchards and tomato you buy at the grocers come from South Africa as you will discover if you read the small print on the label.

Surely somebody can find a market for Cornish pilchards which are to the Duchy what the haggis is to Scotland, part of its tradition.

When I was on the little Island of Bornholm in the Baltic a few years ago I dined sumptuously on a vaste cold buffet entirely composed of smoked, cured, pickled or cooked tiny Baltic herrings, a fish very similar to the pilchard.

BAKED COD

Clean the fish well and place it in cold salted water for about half an hour. Dry thoroughly and stuff with forcemeat made as follows: 1 oz. butter, 1 oz. suet, 1 oz. bacon fat, 4 ozs. breadcrumbs, 1 teaspoonful of chopped parsley, 1 egg, salt, cayenne and nutmeg. Then sew up the fish, dip in egg left from the forcemeat and cover with breadcrumbs. Bake from 45 minutes to an hour (according to the size) in the baking tin with good beef dripping, and baste continually. Best in a moderate oven (350 F., Mark 4).

H. J. Bunney,
Saltash, Cornwall.

MEAT, POULTRY AND GAME

FARMHOUSE CIDER

The old draught farmhouse cider which has been part of the everyday life of the west country for centuries is becoming more and more difficult to get. Farmers can't sell it because, as more and more pubs are taken over by the brewers, their new owners insist on the sale of factory cider to the exclusion of the old farmhouse "scrumpy" and though this may be very good it is not the same thing at all. Farmers are immensely proud of their cider which many of them have been making on their farms for hundreds of years. Some of the old ones are as clear and pale as a glass of brandy, having been kept to mature till they have lost their sweetness and become what is known as hard cider, very dry with a faint taste of tannin from the apples.

Years ago farm labourers used to drink the draught cider for their breakfast and have free glasses of it with bread and cheese at dinner time. It is made from pure apple juice fermented naturally and is not sweetened in any way. This is not only a marvellous drink but very good for cooking and it will be a great pity if it is allowed to die out. The same thing is happening, however, in Somerset, Herefordshire, Devonshire and Dorset. Even the old cider orchards are being grubbed up as the sale of cider apples to the factories is not very profitable. Much of the apple pulp for factory cider is imported from France.

Jungle Juice, a popular drink in pubs in Dorset, is simply a glass of cider with a tot of gin poured into it. It is extremely potent.

Plymouth Gin, very popular in the Navy, is less dry than London Gin and has a bland taste. It is often served as pink gin with a dash of Angostura bitters.

Mead and Metheglin are made from honey and are a revival of a drink which was popular several hundred years ago in Cornwall.

DEVON LAMB – THE SADDLE

Devon lamb is very tender, very expensive and has a flavour beyond belief. It is flown over in quantity to the big Paris restaurants for Easter, is delicious with the early asparagus or those delicate *mange-tout* peas which are so young and tender one eats the whole thing, pods and all. They should be boiled and served with a little butter, the lamb is best plainly roasted, slightly underdone.

A saddle consists of both sides of the loin joined by the backbone, and normally weighs 4½ – 8 lbs. It is particularly delicious hot as it is carved with the grain of the meat. Imagine the pleasure of eating a thick loin of lamb chop served to you in long, pink succulent slices. They result from carving the meat lengthways with the grain, whereas the loin and best end of lamb are carved parallel with the rib bone — the other way.

I like my lamb roast only 15 minutes per lb. and really pink and underdone inside as they have it in France. But a lot of English people object to this and 20 – 23 minutes per lb. might be a safer time to cook it. Stand the meat in a roasting tin without the rack. Brush it with 1 oz. of melted butter. Put it in the centre of a very hot oven (450 F., Mark 8). Reduce the heat to moderate at once (350 F., Mark 4) and roast it to the times specified. The flavour of the meat may be increased by moistening it with a little red wine an hour before roasting it. Baste it with 2 tablespoons of water and some salt five minutes before serving.

Make a clear gravy in the roasting tin and strain it into a really hot sauceboat. Salt, pepper, a pinch of sugar, and the juice of a large orange can be added to it. Since the carving may take a little time, have the plates, platters and gravy as hot as possible. To carve, steady the joint with a fork plunged into the centre of the back. With the sharpest possible carving knife find the ridge on each side of the backbone. At this point cut down through the meat holding the flat of the knife against the bone. Make two long cuts each side of and parallel to the backbone and go on cutting wedge shaped slices. Each can be divided in half if they are too long.

"I knew one cook, from my days as a scullery maid in big kitchens," writes Miss Rose Ellery of Puddletown, Dorset, "who would take a saddle of lamb, cut the meat away from the bone and stuff it with pâté de foie gras. She then tied the meat back in place and roasted it. A good cheese sauce (made rather thick) was poured over the top and then it was browned under the grill before serving".

DEVON ROAST BEEF DINNER

This is a Devonshire meal from about 1860. My grandmother's recipe for a special roast beef dinner prepared from a piece of sirloin of beef, potatoes, onions, salt, pepper and suet pastry. Peel and cut up the onions, place them in the bottom of a baking dish. Peel and halve the potatoes and place them on top of the onions, add salt and pepper to taste. Cover with cold water. Place the sirloin of beef on top. Now mix a suet pudding with 12 ozs. self raising flour, 4 ozs. suet, a little salt. Mix to a stiff dough. Place in one end of the dish with the other ingredients. Bake in a hot oven for approximately 1½ hours.

Result: a delicious meal if served with a second vegetable. No gravy is needed as the juice from the meat goes down to the water at the bottom of the dish. It is still a great favourite in my family after all these years.

Mrs. Sybil Cowan,
Watchet, Somerset.

Allow 15 minutes per lb. in a hot oven (400 F., Mark 6), joints under 4 lbs. slightly longer.

CORNISH UNDERROAST — for 4 people

Cut 1½ lbs. beef skirt or chuck steak in pieces and roll it in seasoned flour together with 4 ozs. ox kidney and 1 sliced medium onion. Stew gently for 1½ hours. Adjust the seasoning and add 4 ozs. mushrooms; place in a pie dish.

Peel 4 or 5 large potatoes, cut them in half "flat" ways and place them on top of the meat in the dish so as to cover it. Bake in a hot oven (400 F., Mark 6) for approximately 1 hour, or until the potatoes are nicely browned. Serve with one other vegetable.

Mrs. A. W. Frostick,
St. Erth Hayle, Cornwall.

BEEF STEW WITH CHEDDAR CHEESE DUMPLINGS

Slice 2 onions and fry them in 1 oz. lard until browned. Remove the onions, add 1 lb. stewing beef, 1 oz. flour, salt and pepper and ½ teaspoon brown sugar to the pan. Stir in ¼ pint brown ale. Turn into a casserole, cover and bake at 325 F., Mark 3 for 2¾ hours.

For the dumplings: place 4 ozs. self raising flour, salt and pepper, 1½ ozs. shredded suet, 1½ ozs. finely grated Cheddar cheese into a bowl. Mix in enough water to make a slack dough. Divide into eight portions and place these on top of the stew. Cover the dish again and continue cooking for 15 to 20 minutes. Serve with boiled potatoes, diced carrots and turnips.

Mrs. M. Higginson,
Clevedon, Somerset.

SQUAB PIE

"My husband's people (who were from a very old Devon family) used regularly to make a squab pie," writes Mrs. Olive Chave of Tiverton, Devon, "and there was a rhyme which went with it.

Apples, onions, mutton and dough,

Make as fine a pudding as any I know.

Said of course in really broad Devon dialect, which if spoken by a genuine Devonian can sound like a foreign language.

"A large brown fireproof dish was used, and filled with layers of sliced apples, sliced onions, sliced mutton flavoured with pepper and salt. Add a little water and cover with a short pastry. It was cooked in a large oven rather like an old-fashioned baker's oven. This, of course, can be cooked in a modern oven, but according to my husband the flavour is not like his mother's original pie!"

Mrs. Olive Chave,
Tiverton, Devon.

Squab Pies are very like the Fidget or Fitchett Pork Pie traditional to Shropshire though in South Devon Villages the meat for the pie was often flank of beef or just butchers' trimmings. But there were more elaborate squab pies, some with a layer of cream immediately under the pastry. Young squabs are also young pigeons. Sometimes these were used for the pie with mutton, onions and apples.

Occasionally young cormorants carefully skinned were substituted for the pigeons.

111

DEVONSHIRE DISH

I should like to pass on a dish my grandmother brought to London when she married a wheelwright in 1840. My mother often gave it to us: "Devonshire Dish".

You get any meat left over from the joint, get a fairly large baking tin and put slices of the meat in it with potatoes, sage, onions and mushrooms (if available). Cover with $\frac{1}{4}$ pint stock. Repeat this till the tin or casserole is full. Put another $\frac{1}{4}$ pint of stock in and finish with potatoes and sage and seasoning. Bake for 1 hour in a fairly hot oven (375 F., Mark 5).

The flavour of this is quite out of this world.

Mrs. Daisy Fenner,
Greatstone, New Romney, Kent.

GRANNY'S WILTSHIRE TATTIES

As children granny used to make us what she called "Granny's Wiltshire Tatties" (potatoes). She also packed them in grandad's dinner "bag".

Wash and then bake the required potatoes in their skins in the oven, and, when cold, cut a hole in the top of each as large as a half-crown. Through this remove with a small spoon all the potato, leaving only the rind. While the potatoes are cooking make a mixture of ham, chicken or any other cold meat available, add parsley, breadcrumbs and lemon peel, thoroughly mixed, with pepper and salt. Fill the potato jackets with this mixture, moistening with a good brown gravy. Stand the potatoes upright and bake in a moderate oven (350 F., Mark 4) for 20 minutes then allow to cool. Delicious.

Mrs. Hilda Glasson,
West Harnham, Salisbury, Wiltshire.

MEAT AND POTATO PUDDING

This is a recipe of my mother's who left us many years ago. It was my favourite meal as a child and is also that of my son who has two children so I don't think it will die out for many years.

Skin thinly and slice some potatoes, 1 onion according to size and taste, about $\frac{1}{2}$ lb. or $\frac{3}{4}$ lb. beef skirt cut small. Put into a basin a layer of potato, a layer of onion sliced thin, then the skirt. Now add pepper, salt and a little flour to thicken the gravy. Cover with cold water. The basin should be about three-quarters full. Now fill with more potato and put on top a layer of suet crust. Tie down with a cloth, place in a large saucepan of boiling water. Boil for 3 to 4 or more hours according to size of the pudding. Add more boiling water so the saucepan won't boil dry. Serve with any vegetable.

Mrs. E. Brace,
Newton Tracey, Barnstaple, North Devon.

CHICKEN PIE

Divide a large chicken into joints, cut off the legs and wings at the first joint. Boil these for 2 hours with the backbones, neck and gizzard with a little parsley, thyme and marjoram (which remove after 15 minutes). Then strain for stock. Parboil the liver and chop finely. Cut 8 ozs. ham or bacon into small pieces about the size of a walnut and slice 2 hard boiled eggs. Arrange the raw chicken, ham and eggs in alternate layers in a pie dish with a grate of lemon rind and a sprinkle of the chopped chicken liver between each layer. Repeat till full. Pour over about ¾ pint of the chicken stock till the dish is three-quarters full. Bake in a slow oven (300 F., Mark 2) for 3½ hours. Take out. When nearly cold cover with puff pastry and bake in a hot oven (400 F., Mark 6) to cook the pastry. Serve hot or cold. This is enough for 7 – 8 persons.

Mrs. D. M. Atkinson,
Newbridge Hill, Bath, Somerset.

BOILED CAPON WITH OYSTER SAUCE

Simmer a 7-8 lbs. capon or chicken with a salted pig's foot prepared for cooking, 1 large sliced onion, 1 sliced carrot, a few celery stalks, a bayleaf, a sprig or pinch of thyme, a few parsley stalks, 6 peppercorns, no salt, in a pot just big enough to allow the contents to be barely covered with water. When cooked, the bird should be very tender but firm, and the meat should be falling off the trotter. About 15 minutes to the pound though some judgement must be used. If the stock reduces too much during cooking add a little water, but don't overdo the water and don't keep lifting the lid off the pot every five minutes.

For the oyster sauce you need 1 pint of strained stock from the chicken or capon reduced over a quick fire until you have ¾ pint, 1 oz. good flavoured butter and 1 oz. strong flour, ½ gill double cream and 2 small oysters for each person.

Make a sauce by melting the butter, add the flour and cook over the fire for a few minutes but do not colour. Now add the stock a little at a time, the stock can be warm but not boiling, and while adding the stock keep stirring briskly until it has all amalgamated with the roux and the result is a smooth, medium thick sauce, easy to pour but not too runny. Now taste and season with salt and pepper as required, add the cream, stir in the oysters. (If fresh oysters are used, add the oyster juice free of grit and shell. If frozen, allow to defrost slightly and add. If canned, add a little of the liquor if not too salty.) Keep the sauce hot but do not allow to boil.

Serve portions of the bird coated with oyster sauce. Garnish with bacon rolls and puff pastry or fried bread crescents and a small bunch of watercress. Small croquettes and buttered brussels sprouts could accompany this or rice, either plainly boiled or cooked like a pilaff with some of the stock.

John Stewart,
Buckfastleigh, Devon.

BOILED FOWL

This is one of our favourite dishes, especially in the winter. Put a boiling fowl into a large saucepan with cold water to cover. Bring it to the boil then simmer for about 2 hours. Add salt and pepper, onions to your liking and simmer for another hour. Then add some macaroni and peeled, sliced potatoes and simmer again until all is well cooked.

Mrs. L. Tucker,
St. Thomas, Exeter, Devon.

DEVILLED CHICKEN OR PHEASANT

This is one of the recipes from my scullery days in a big house. Cut the cooked chicken or pheasant into the pieces required. Heat in a little stock. Take and mix 1 teaspoon freshly mixed English mustard, 1 tablespoon of Harvey or Worcester Sauce, ½ pint whipped cream. Put the pieces of meat into a soufflé dish and pour the above mixture over it. Bake at (400 F., Mark 6) for 5 minutes.

Quails used to be served on a bed of rice with pimentoes. The breasts were turned outwards and the little legs turned over with a bunch of watercress in the middle; but one never hears now of teal, widgeon and shoveller ducks, all the wildfowl seem to have died out.

We used to serve Crème Brûlée on Sundays for lunch, browning the top with a salamander.

Miss Rose Ellery,
Puddletown, Dorchester, Dorset.

OLD SOMERSET ROOK PIE WITH FIGGY PASTIE

Take 6 rooks which have been skinned, using only the legs and breasts, as all the other parts are bitter. They should be put to soak in salt and water overnight. In the morning drain away the brine and put the legs and breasts in a good sized pie dish, adding some pieces of fat bacon cut in chunks. Cover with weak stock and season well with pepper and salt.

For the paste take 1 lb. flour, 8 ozs. fat, 4 ozs. currants, 4 ozs. stoned raisins. Rub the fat well into the flour, adding pepper and salt, then add the currants and raisins. Mix well and add sufficient water to make a stiff paste. Roll out to about ¾ inch thick then place right over the pie, letting it come well over the sides. Place a piece of greaseproof paper right over the pie and then your floured pudding cloth on top. Tie down well and see that the water has no chance of getting in. There must be sufficient water in your boiler to cover it.

Do not put the pie in till the water is boiling. The pie takes a good 3 hours to cook and is delicious served with gooseberry jam.

Mrs. A. E. Sorrill,
Torquay, Devon.

"Figs" in old – Cornish are raisins. The pastry is a very interesting one and probably medieval in origin.

BAKED STUFFED HARE IN MILK

This is the way my mother used to cook young hares and rabbits in my girlhood. They always tasted delicious and were a change from stews, pies and jugged hare.

First stuff the hare, preferably with home-made sage and onion stuffing, and sew the stuffing in. Place the joint in a baking tin, smother with seasoned plain flour. Slice 4 ozs. of butter and lay on the top together with a couple of rashers of bacon. Pour on ½ pint full cream milk. Cover and cook.

This was always cooked in a coal oven so I suggest 2 hours at 375 F., Mark 5. Take the cover off for the last 15 minutes and to make the gravy just add a cube and make gravy in the normal way.

Mrs. H. Wright,
Burton, Chippenham, Wiltshire.

RABBIT CUSTARD DORSET FASHION

Wash a young rabbit, cut it into joints and flour well. Put 8 ozs. breadcrumbs with a little chopped sage, 1 chopped or minced Spanish onion, some grated lemon peel together and season well. Add a beaten egg and sufficient milk to make the mixture the consistency of custard. Pour this over the rabbit and cover with a greased paper lid. Bake for 2 – 3 hours in a moderate oven (350 F., Mark 4).

Mrs. B. M. Anderson,
Minehead, Somerset.

RABBIT WITH MUSHROOMS AND CREAM

Melt 1 oz. butter in a saucepan, put in 8 ozs. peeled, fresh mushrooms and stir on a low heat until soft, then lift them out and heat another 1 oz. butter in the saucepan. Now put in a young rabbit cut in small, neat pieces. Brown it slightly and add 2 tablespoons chopped onion, salt and pepper. Put the lid on and cook for 10 – 15 minutes, moisten with a cupful of slightly warmed thin cream, add a bunch of herbs and cook again for 30 minutes or until the rabbit is tender. About 10 minutes before the rabbit is ready, return the mushrooms to the pan and let all simmer together for the remainder of the time. Remove the bunch of herbs. Arrange the rabbit and mushrooms on a hot dish, strain the sauce and pour it over.

Mrs. P. F. Jones,
Yeovil, Somerset.

Also suitable for chicken.

PIGEON PIE

Prepare 3 pigeons and boil whole for 1 hour in a large saucepan of lightly salted water. Drain and leave to cool.

In a heavy pan fry one large onion, floured and sliced in rings. Remove from the fat and arrange in a pie dish with the sliced meat of the pigeons in alternate layers with the onions. Add two sliced hard boiled eggs in a layer to cover the top. Make a gravy in the pan used for cooking the onions by adding a little flour to a table-spoonful of fat and seasoning to taste. Brown over a little heat and add the stock from boiling the pigeons until a nice thick gravy is obtained. Add enough to half fill the pie dish. Cover the whole with a short crust pastry and bake for 30 minutes in a hot oven (400 F., Mark 6). Use the remaining gravy hot when serving.

Mrs. M. A. Dickens,
Exeter, Devon.

CORNISH POTATO LOAF

Boil 2 – 3 lbs. of potatoes, mash and mix with butter and 2 teacups of flour. Bind with milk and use them to line the bottom and sides of a large loaf tin, making walls an inch thick and reserving some for the top. Chop up some cooked vegetables, add cooked meat, corned beef or sausage meat — approximately 4 ozs. – 8 ozs. — and mix well. Moisten with a little gravy and pack into the tin. Place the remainder of the potato crust on top. Brush over with egg and bake in a moderate oven (350 F., Mark 4) until nicely browned.

Mrs. T. Palastre,
Calstock, Cornwall.

PORK CASSEROLE OR "VARMERS VAVRIT"

My gran was a Devonshire woman and was a cook before her marriage. She just loved to cook and I spent many wonderful hours with her in her kitchen. People say I'm a "fab" cook but I owe it all to her. This recipe is for Pork Casserole but called "Varmers Vavrit" (Farmer's Favourite) by my gran.

Fry 1 large chopped onion until golden and then put in the casserole. Fry 1 lb. lean pork, cut in small pieces until nicely coloured and put that into the casserole too. Slice 8 ozs. tomatoes and finely shred a small cabbage (or half a big one). Quickly fry together until the cabbage is limp. Place in the casserole. Stir together with ½ pint stock and $\frac{1}{2}$ teaspoon sage. Season with salt and pepper. Put on a cover. Cook for 2 hours (200 F., Mark 1). Serve inside a ring of mashed potatoes.

Mrs. Doreen Williams,
Castle Mayne, Basildon, Essex.

MARKET DAY DINNER

My grandmother and great aunt used to cook this dish in the oven at the side of the fire before going off to market. We call it Market Day Dinner.

Place 6 small pork chops, 2 sliced pig's kidneys, 1 lb. peeled and sliced onions, 1 peeled, cored and sliced apple in a dish. Add 1 teaspoon of sage and a little salt and pepper. Cover with 1 lb. peeled and sliced potatoes. Add a cupful of water. Cook covered for 3 hours in a very moderate oven (325 F., Mark 3).

Mrs. M. Hall,
Chippenham, Wiltshire.

BATH POLONIES AND BATH CHAPS

Bath polonies are something like Italian Bologna sausages but much smaller. They have a delicious flavour and a thin layer of fat next to the red skin.

Bath Chaps are made from the pig's cheek which has been pickled with sugar and spices and smoked like a ham. These are usually sold cooked having been boiled till tender, skinned and covered with breadcrumbs. Nice for a picnic.

FRIED PIG'S BRAINS

Thinking back to the pig killing days, this recipe was my father's favourite supper snack.

Take a set of pig's brains, place them in a basin and cover with cold water and add about a dessertspoon of salt. Let it stand for half an hour or so. Meanwhile dice two large onions and fry until soft. Now strain off the brains and remove the skin that holds them. Toss the brains into the pan with the onions and chop all together with a knife or cooking spoon. Fry until golden. Serve on fried bread, if liked. My father preferred it with a crusty point torn from a freshly baked loaf.

Mrs. I. D. Hurley,
Milton Abbas, Blandford, Dorset.

VARIOUS

WATERCRESS

There is an ancient and celebrated watercress farm on the chalk springs all round the village of Bere Regis, where much of "Far From The Madding Crowd" was filmed. The cress is grown in specially constructed beds, then bunched and labelled and hydra-cooled under immaculate conditions before being despatched to market. It arrives even in Edinburgh within 24 hours of being boxed. The Jesty family has been growing watercress for well over 100 years and a lot of the men who cut the cresses are sons and grandsons of the men who worked for *John Jesty's* grandfather. The beds are irrigated by water from springs and artesian wells. It comes glugging up out of the chalk, sparkling and bubbly, the clearest water in the world, at a constant 52°F. so that it is warm enough for the cresses to grow even in winter. Sluices take the surplus water to the river Bere, a tributary of the Piddle, which, everybody says, is not only full of crayfish but lampreys like many streams in Dorset. Nobody catches them but scientists, though in France lampreys are stewed in wine and eaten at banquets.

There are six or seven weeks each spring when watercress is at its best. Though one can get it all the year round it never seems so good as in early May when the leaves are all big and dark and peppery and taste delicious in hot bacon sandwiches. The Jestys also have a trout stream, white in spring with water buttercups, not more than 20 feet from the sitting room window but John never catches any, "They are all friends" he said, "it would be like eating the cat."

"Watercress is delicious chopped into scrambled eggs" he went on "and it makes a particularly good soup with ham stock. The two flavours complement each other and make something you will not otherwise have." Watercress is also absolutely perfect, I think, to eat raw with hot juicy grilled kidneys, or fresh mackerel or underdone fillet steak. Put a small bunch on each plate, the slight peppery taste sets them off perfectly.

MRS. JESTY'S WATERCRESS SOUP

For this chop 2 bunches of watercress, fry one chopped onion gently in 1 oz. of butter so it melts rather than browns, adding the watercress and cooking it gently for about 3 minutes. Stir in a table-spoon of cornflour, cooking for 2 more minutes and gradually stirring in 2 pints of ham stock or if unavailable the stock from bouillon cubes. Add salt and pepper and let it simmer for 10 minutes. Before serving stir in 2 tablespoons of cream.

Mrs. Jesty,
Bere Regis, Dorset.

Watercress is excellent, too, with a nice hot plainly roasted farmhouse chicken.

Lay the washed cress over the hot meat dish just before serving, sprinkle it with salt and a little lemon juice. Put the chicken on top, pour some of the pan juices from the roasting pan over it. Eat chicken and cress with their flavours intermingled.

BAKED MARROW WITH CHEDDAR CHEESE

Choose a young vegetable marrow, peel and slice thinly into small squares. Peel and slice thinly a large onion. Grease a pie dish and pile up with layers of marrow, onion and fresh breadcrumbs. Add a pint of milk and salt and pepper to taste.

Grate a nice tasty cheese on the top and bake in a moderate oven (350 F., Mark 4) for about 1½ hours. This is a delicious dish eaten with bread and butter for a late tea or supper. My grandmother used to make it, also my mother and now myself. It is at least 130 years old.

Mrs. C. E. Norton,
Newton Abbot, Devon.

CHEESE PUDDING

Put into a saucepan ¾ pint of milk, let it come to boiling point. Mix in a basin 1 breakfast cup of breadcrumbs, 3 oz. of grated cheese, 1 oz. butter, a little salt and pepper. Pour the boiling milk over these. Beat two eggs till light and frothy and add them. Pour into a buttered pie dish. Bake in a moderate oven (350 F., Mark 4) 20 – 30 minutes.

Mrs. K. Strugnell,
Melksham, Wiltshire.

BOILED, STUFFED CABBAGE, WITH GRAVY

Take a good sized cabbage and cut out the heart. Chop up some cold veal or any cold meat finely. Mix it with herbs and breadcrumbs. Season highly with salt and pepper and bind together with a beaten egg. Fill the cavity in the cabbage with the stuffing. Tie the leaves together firmly and then boil for 1 hour.

Serve hot with breadcrumbs sprinkled over the whole and good gravy poured around it.

Mrs. C. Lawes,
Ford, near Chippenham, Wiltshire.

BAKED, STUFFED WHITE CABBAGE

Prepare 1 firm white cabbage weighing 3 – 4 lbs. as follows: Cut off the tight outside leaves and put in boiling salt water. Cut the remainder in quarters and shred finely discarding the stalk and add to the water for 10 – 15 minutes.

Prepare the filling by finely mincing 1 lb. best stewing steak or left-over from the joint, 1 onion and 2 rashers of lean bacon. Mix with an egg, 1 tablespoon of flour and 2 tablespoons of thyme using tepid water to make a soft consistency. Add salt and pepper to taste. Line a fireproof dish with some of the large leaves. Spread the meat filling then the fine chopped cabbage topping it with large leaves. Dot with butter. Cover with a lid or foil. Bake near the top of the oven for 1½ hours at (350 F., Mark 4) for 1 hour then reduce to (200 F., Mark 2). Serve with potatoes and white sauce flavoured with nutmeg.

Mrs. Henny Allen,
Truro, Cornwall.

HOME PRESERVED MUSHROOMS

Peel some freshly gathered mushrooms. Put them in a baking tin in a cool oven to dry until they are shrivelled, then put the dried mushrooms into an air-tight biscuit tin. When you want them, make a gravy from stock or a soup square and while lukewarm put the mushrooms in and bring slowly to the boil. They will swell twice the size and taste like the freshly gathered ones.

Mrs. C. Lawes,
Ford, near Chippenham, Wiltshire.

BANANA PORRIDGE

Mash 6 bananas finely. Take a tablespoonful of cornflour, mix with a little cold milk, add a pint of boiling milk to it then stir in the banana pulp adding sugar to taste. Boil the whole together for 5 minutes stirring all the time till thick. Serve very hot.

This is a delicious breakfast porridge and very nourishing.

Mrs. L. Hughes,
St. Dominic, Saltash.

WEST COUNTRY CLOTTED CREAM AND ONION PIE

Make a standard short crust pastry with 8 ozs. of plain flour, 2 ozs. butter, 2 ozs. lard and a pinch of salt. Line a sandwich tin or fireproof glass plate, approximately 7 inches in diameter, with the pastry. Fill with finely chopped onions, and with parsley if desired. Add 2 ozs. of Devonshire cream. Cover the whole with pastry and cook in a moderate oven (350 F., Mark 4) for 1 hour when the onions should be cooked. Serve while hot.

This is a very old and very tasty dish, very economical in price and provides a very warm meal in cold weather enjoyed in many west country homes by outdoor workers.

Miss Marion Majestic Moorey,
Forest Gate, London, E7.

WEST COUNTRY CHESTNUT AND BACON PIE

Short crust pastry, chestnuts and bacon, about half of each, and a sauce.

Boil 1 lb. chestnuts, then skin and peel them but leave them whole. Mix with 1 lb. cooked, diced bacon and ¾ pint white sauce. Put into a pie dish, cover with short crust pastry and bake in a moderate oven (350 F., Mark 4) for about 25 minutes.

Miss R. Mitchell
East Grinstead, Sussex.

AUSTRALIAN CHRISTMAS TOMATO PIE

My recipe is old in that my grandmother always made it for us and I have had it every Christmas lunch since I can remember. I came to live here from Australia a year ago. A commonplace dish at home and evidently unknown over here which amuses and surprises me. Here is what I do.

Scald the tomatoes briefly in boiling water to peel the skin off and core. Slice a good number of tomatoes and onions. Put them in layers in a buttered casserole, tomatoes first with generous knobs of butter on top, plus sugar, ground pepper and garlic salt, then thinly sliced onion. Continue like this to the top. Add nothing more except chunky breadcrumbs all over the top for the last half hour of cooking so they are crisp and golden. Cook for about 2 hours in a moderate oven (350 F., Mark 4). It often bubbles over the top so place a tin dish underneath.

Mrs. John Robinson,
Barnstaple, Devon.

LEEK OR LIKKY PIE WITH CREAM

Peel and wash 6 large leeks well. Parboil them for 15 minutes in salted water. Cut 1½ lbs. pork belly into inch squares about ¼ inch thick. Drain the leeks and slice them up. Fill a pie dish with alternate layers of pork and leeks. Season slightly with salt and cover completely with milk. Cook in a hot oven (400 F., Mark 6) with a foil cover on top for about 1 hour. Remove from the oven, cool slightly, stir in ¼ pint cream. Cover with puff pastry and cook in a hot oven (400 F., Mark 6) till the pastry is cooked. Serve with creamed potatoes and thin slivers of carrots.

This pie was often made when I lived with Cornish folk.

Mrs. E. Penson,
Yatton, Bristol.

SMOKED FOOD

There is a place on the Old Racecourse at Totnes, Devon, where they smoke duck, chicken, eels and mackerel over oak chips and apple wood. They smoke cheese for the Ilchester people and do smoked venison pickled in Burgundy and olive oil to the *Duchess of Bedford's* recipe. The smoked duck and chicken are expensive but delicious instead of cold meat with salad.

Smoked mackerel is cheaper and nice for starters with horseradish sauce and a plate of brown bread and butter.

CORNISH EGGS

Melt a couple of tablespoons of butter in a shallow fireproof dish in the oven. Break in the eggs being careful to keep the yolks whole. Sprinkle with a little salt when the egg whites are set. Put a spoonful of clotted cream on each, return the dish to the oven for a few moments.

If liked the eggs can be fried crisp in butter in a pan, then the cream added.

J. M. Fish,
Newlyn, Cornwall.

ONION SOUP

Being one of a family of 11 this soup was a great favourite of ours on a cold winter's night.

Take 15 onions, boil in 5 pints of water with a knuckle of veal or lamb, a blade or two of mace and some pepper. When the onions are quite soft take them out and rub them through a fine sieve and work in 4 ozs. of butter and flour. When the meat is boiled so that it leaves the bones, strain the liquor on the onions and boil gently for 30 minutes. Remember to stir well when the butter and flour are added to the onions.

Mrs. L. G. Windsor,
Willsbridge, Bristol.

A very similar soup is made in the west country called Kettle or Kiddley broth. The old-fashioned soup kettle still used in some parts of Wales, as well perhaps as in Cornwall, has a wide stumpy spout and a much wider lid than a tea kettle. It is ideal for a meat and vegetable broth for the soup can be poured easily through the wide spout leaving the meat and vegetables for another dish.

GINGER BEER

During the hay making and the harvest — the two busiest seasons of the year — workmen and farmers alike gulp down this drink, often preferring it to cider.

Put 2 lbs. sugar, 2 ozs. cream of tartar, 1 oz. well bruised root ginger and 2 sliced lemons into a large container. Pour on 2 gallons of boiling water, and when lukewarm rub in 1 oz. yeast. Strain and bottle the next day, when it is ready for use.

Mrs. E. Venner,
North Petherton, Bridgwater, Somerset.

TEAR ALONG THE DOTTED LINE

MARROW JAM

Cut 5 lbs. marrow into 1 inch cubes and to every 1 lb. of marrow allow 1 lb. preserving sugar, which should be put with it in layers in a preserving pan and left for 24 hours. Then add 4 ozs. chopped crystalised ginger and the finely cut rind and the juice of 3 lemons. Simmer for 3 – 5 hours, stirring from time to time. This is an excellent old-fashioned jam and very popular with my friends.

Mrs. E. M. A. Watson,
Sherborne, Dorset.

DUMPSIDEARY JAM

The Dumpsideary Jam is West Country and has a delicious flavour. My mother used to make it when suitable fruits were available. She was a wonderful cook and used to help her granny to cook when about six years old and only gave up not long before she died as the effects of arthritis and a stroke made it difficult.

3 lbs. pears   3 lbs. large plums
3 lb. sharp apples — all weighed after peeling etc.
1 small lemon to every 3 lb. fruit (or 3 lemons)
a few cloves   ½ oz. cinnamon.
sugar   water

Peel and core the apples, cut in quarters. Peel etc. the pears, cut smaller. Save the peelings of both. Stone the plums and put the stones with the cloves into a muslin bag. Scrub the lemons and grate the rinds*. Mix and weigh the fruit. Put the apple and pear peelings into a saucepan with the plum stones etc. and 1 pint water. Simmer for 30 minutes and strain. Put this liquid into a preserving pan with 1 lb. sugar to every 1 lb. of prepared fruit, let the sugar dissolve slowly then add the fruit, also the kernels of the plum stones and the cinnamon. Bring to the boil slowly and boil until the jam will set.

* I strain the lemon juice and add it to the fruit while cooking.

Miss Rosemarie Gibaud,
Elson, Gosport, Hampshire.

PICKLED WALNUTS

Do this in July when the skins are green and the insides are soft. Make the brine, 12 ozs. of salt to ½ gallon of water, leave your green walnuts in it for 10 days. Don't forget to stir it morning and evening and be sure to put them in 2 fresh lots of brine during this time. After 10 days rinse your walnuts in fresh water and set them out on trays in the air for a day to go black and then put 2 teaspoons of pickling spice and 4 chopped up nutmegs in a bit of white cotton.

Boil them in 2 quarts of vinegar. Pack your walnuts in warm jars and strain your hot vinegar over. This will pickle about 100 walnuts.

Miss Wright,
Bradford-on-Severn.

The neighbourhood of Bath and the Vale of Pewsey have been famous for their walnut trees for generations.

CHEDDAR CHEESE

This is the one most imitated abroad, in Canada where it has been made on a commercial basis since about 1864, in Australia and in New Zealand and the United States (where about 900,000,000 lbs. of Cheddar are made annually) and now even in France for export to Britain.

Excellent farmhouse Cheddar is still made in quantity in Somerset and Dorset however, a great deal of it round Wells and Shepton Mallet. Some of the well matured ones, more than a year old and tasting faintly of apples, are exquisite. The cheese is perfect to eat plain for lunch with a glass of rough cider, some Dorset Knobs or Bath Oliver biscuits, Devon butter and a dish of pickled onions.

A great deal of the English Cheddar that one sees now in the supermarkets is unfortunately only block Cheddar, made by a quicker, simpler method, it is very mild and usually rather soapy.

BLUE VINNEY CHEESE

Blue Vinney or Dorset Blue Veiney is a hard, dry, crumbly cheese now very rare and difficult to find though it was once seen in nearly every farmhouse cheese store in the south west. It is a skim-milk cheese with a harsh open texture which goes crumbly and breaks in pieces when really blue. The name comes from the old west country word for mould, "vinew", pronounced vinney. How the mould was produced was a closely guarded secret of the Dorset cheesemakers. Sometimes, however, it is so copious that the cheese seems to be blue all over. It has a pungent, very attractive, flavour and was already well known and liked in the 18th century when the Dorset cheesemakers suddenly became famous.

Dorset Blue, a different but softer and very good cheese something in flavour between Stilton and Gorgonzola is now being made in Dorset.

BATH OLIVER BISCUITS

The famous Bath Oliver biscuit, thin, hard and cream coloured, goes perfectly with wine and cheese. It was invented in the early 18th century when Bath was a fashionable watering place by a Dr. William Oliver (1695-1764) whose portrait is still stamped on each biscuit. He was a fashionable physician and philanthropist with estates in Cornwall, who settled in Bath in 1725, after studying medicine at Leyden and Cambridge. He knew everybody, had numerous patients among the landed gentry and was responsible for building the Royal Mineral Water Hospital in Bath, and was appointed physician to it.

He gave the secret of his famous biscuit, shortly before his death, to his coachman, Atkins, together with £100 and ten sacks of the finest wheat flour. Mr. Atkins opened a shop in Green Street and rapidly made his fortune. For many years the biscuits were manufactured by Fortt's who claimed to have the original recipe, but they are now made by one of the large biscuit firms. They are a little thicker than they used to be.

PUDDING

CLOTTED CREAM

Pour 2 quarts of milk into a wide, shallow pan and leave it for 24 hours when the cream rises to the top. Lift it very gently onto a warm stove without shaking for this would break up the cream. Leave it on a very low heat to clot — the lower the better — it must not boil at all or there will be a thick skin on it. When it has clotted a solid ring begins to form round the edge and the cream looks all ribbed and wrinkled on top. Exactly how long it will take depends on the width of the pan, the heat of the cooker and so forth. When clotted lift the pan off the fire as gently as possible, leave it in a cool place for 24 hours then skim off the clotted cream into a dish. Those bottles of gold top Channel Isles milk produce beautiful clotted cream.

CHOCOLATE À LA PRALINE

Dissolve ¼ oz. gelatine in a little hot water, then dissolve ¼ lb. chocolate with 3 yolks of eggs, 1 oz. sugar, a little vanilla flavouring. Do not let it boil. Put aside to cool. Whip ½ pint cream, also the whites of the eggs to a stiff froth. When the chocolate mixture is cold add the cream, gelatine and lastly the egg white. Put in a dish and sprinkle with chopped nuts.

Mrs. W. Force,
Bradminch, Exeter, Devon.

RÖTE GRUTZE — Red Porridge

This is my favourite pudding served in my German grandparents' house.

Boil 1 lb. red currants and 1½ lbs. raspberries with a little water until all the juice has been extracted. Rub it through a hair sieve.

125

Return the juice to a saucepan, add 4 tablespoons sugar and simmer for 8 minutes, stirring occasionally. Remove from the heat, add 3 tablespoons of semolina and $\frac{1}{4}$ teaspoon grated vanilla pod and a large pinch of salt. Stir well, return the mixture to the heat, boil it for 2 minutes, stirring all the time to prevent it from sticking. Then lower the heat and cook it slowly until it is thickish, always stirring. Remove from the heat and pour into the serving dish while still warm. Eat it when cool with or without cream.

Mrs. A. B. Phillpotts,
Ashburton, Devonshire.

SWEET PUMPKIN PIE WITH DEVONSHIRE CREAM

Peel and remove the seeds from one medium pumpkin. Cut the flesh into $\frac{1}{2} - \frac{3}{4}$ inch cubes. Simmer in a covered pan until tender. Drain well and put into a pie dish. Add 2 tablespoons brown sugar, 4 ozs. currants, $\frac{1}{2}$ teaspoon grated nutmeg and a little lemon juice. Cover with short crust pastry and bake in a fairly hot oven (375 F., Mark 5) for 30 minutes.

Serve with clotted or double Devonshire cream.

Mrs. M. A. Dickens,
Alphington, Exeter, Devon.

SWEET VEGETABLE MARROW PIE

This recipe was given by my grandmother to my mother and thence to me. It is very luscious and much too fattening!

Peel and remove the seeds from a vegetable marrow. Cook as you would normally in the quantity preferred. Drain and sweeten to taste with brown sugar, nutmeg and plenty of butter, mashing the whole lot together to a purée. Make a pie of it using short, short pastry top and bottom. Don't forget to sprinkle a little nutmeg and brown sugar on the top after brushing with milk. Bake for about 30 minutes.

This is really delicious, but, funnily enough, no one ever seems to have heard of it bar me!

Mrs. Daphne Hickson,
Buckland St. Mary, near Chard, Somerset.

LEMON SAGO AND THICK CREAM

Soak overnight 1 cup of sago in 6 cups of water with 1 cup of brown sugar, the grated rind of 2 lemons and 2 tablespoons of syrup. Boil it, stirring over a medium heat until clear. Add the juice of the 2 lemons. Stir and set overnight—not in the refrigerator. Serve with a layer of thick cream.

Mrs. Lena Thomas,
Marazion, Cornwall.

WESTFIELD PUDDING

Sometimes one is unable to enjoy Christmas Pudding because it is too heavy, but this is a lovely substitute and in no way weighty.

Soak 2 tablespoonfuls sago overnight in 1 breakfast cup milk. Add 1 cup breadcrumbs, ¾ cup sugar, 1 cup sultanas, ½ tablespoon melted butter, 1 teaspoon bicarbonate of soda and a little cut peel if liked. Mix well and steam for 3 hours.

Mrs. Ruby W. Carey,
St. Newlyn East, Newquay.

RICH PUDDING

This is a rather rich pudding and is ideal for those who do not like the traditional Christmas pudding.

Put 10 ozs. breadcrumbs into a basin with 4 ozs. sago, 7 ozs. grated suet, 6 ozs. moist brown sugar, the grated rind of half a lemon, ¼ pint of rum and 4 eggs. Stir these ingredients well together then add 2 more eggs and 4 tablespoons cream and beat well. Butter a large basin, cover the bottom with a few breadcrumbs, then a layer of ratafias, a layer of the above mixture and a layer of sponge cake spread thickly with jam. Continue with layers in this way until the basin is full, being sure to end with a layer of the mixture on top. One will need 4 small sponge cakes, 8 ozs. jam and 2 ozs. ratafias. Cover with foil and bake in a fairly hot oven (350 – 375 F., Mark 4 or 5) for 1 – 1¼ hours. Serve with cream or custard sauce.

Mrs. M. Sheppard,
Knowle, Braunton, North Devon.

"FIG" PIE

My mother (who came from Cornwall) says the large raisins used in the pie were always called figs when she was a girl.

Line a deep pie plate with short crust pastry. Cover the bottom with a good layer of stoned raisins (not the stoneless sort). Beat up two eggs and pour over the raisins. Put on a lid of pastry. Brush with milk and sprinkle with caster sugar. Bake for about half an hour at 400 F., Mark 6 until brown and the egg has set. Eat cold.

Mrs. O. Wilford,
Ruddington, Nottingham.

ORANGE PUDDING

Take the weight of 2 eggs in butter, sugar and of 1 egg in flour. Cream the butter and sugar together, add the yolks of the eggs, the grated rind of 1 orange and half the juice, then add the flour. Whip the whites of the eggs, add last. Grease a basin and line with pieces of orange. Pour in the mixture and steam for 1 hour.

For the sauce, boil ½ pint water, add some orange juice and grated rind, thicken with a little cornflour. Add sugar to taste.

Mrs. W. Force,
Bradminch, Exeter, Devon.

STICK-TO-THE-RIB PUDDING

I first sampled this pudding as an evacuee in Somerset and it has been a firm favourite of mine since, although I've never been able to find the recipe in a cookery book. I make it as follows.

8 ozs. self raising flour   4 ozs. suet
pinch salt   approximately 8 ozs. peeled chunks
                                               raw cooking apples
demerara sugar   cinnamon

Sprinkle the cinnamon over the pieces of apple then roll them in the demerara sugar making sure that each piece is coated. Then mix all the ingredients, including the pieces of apple, together and use just enough water to bind. Put in a buttered basin, cover and steam.

Incidentally it's called "Stick-to-the-rib Pudding" and believe me, it does.

Mrs. Audrey Cory,
Upminster, Essex.

SYLLABUB

The juice of 2 or 3 lemons the equivalent to ½ gill of juice. Sweeten well. Add ¼ pint thick cream. Whisk together until fluffy but not too thick. Fold in a stiffly whipped white of egg. Put it in individual dishes and decorate to taste, i.e. nuts, cherries etc.

Place in a refrigerator or cool place and serve when thoroughly chilled.

Miss P. Martin,
Beaminster, Dorset.

DEVONSHIRE JUNKET

"When I was a child in North Devon we used to have a delicious giblet pie, principally chicken giblets and added steak and onions, covered with a golden crust made with real Devon butter. And then to follow there was often a Devonshire Junket flavoured with rum and covered with Devon cream and ratafia biscuits. Gorgeous."

Mrs. V. Keizer,
Harrow, Middlesex.

You add a tablespoon of sugar and a tablespoon of rum to 2 pints of warm milk (which must not boil nor ever have been boiled), just at blood heat. Stir in 2 teaspoons of rennet (from good grocers), pour it into a china dish and leave it in a pleasantly warm place for some hours to set. Then spread clotted cream over the top, sprinkle a little grated nutmeg and sugar over it and garnish with ratafia biscuits or good apricot jam with white kernels.

BAKING

OLD ENGLISH CIDER CAKE

Beat 4 ozs. butter and 4 ozs. sugar to a cream. Add 2 well beaten eggs, then 4 ozs. plain flour sifted with 1 teaspoon bicarbonate of soda and $\frac{1}{2}$ – 1 teaspoon nutmeg. Pour over all 1 teacup of cider beaten to a froth and mix thoroughly. Stir in another 4 ozs. plain flour and mix well together. Bake in a shallow well-greased tin in a moderate oven (350 F., Mark 4) for about 45 minutes.

This cake, when properly made, is delicious with a distinct flavour quite unlike any other.

Mrs. H. Glasson,
West Harnham, Salisbury, Wiltshire.

SOMERSET APPLE CAKE

This cake is also very popular in Dorset.

Place 8 ozs. self raising flour and 4 ozs. butter in a bowl and rub well together and add 4 ozs. soft brown sugar and a pinch of salt. Chop 2 good cooking apples small after peeling and coring, add a little ground ginger and a little lemon juice. Make a hole in the flour, add the apple mixture and stir well, then add 2 beaten eggs and enough milk to make a nice mixture but not too wet. Mix it all together and pour it into a well buttered tin, a flat but not shallow one. Sprinkle a little flour into the tin after greasing and shake it out just before adding the mixture. Sprinkle the top with caster sugar and bake in a fairly moderate oven (375 F., Mark 5) till a golden brown. Serve hot with real cream (or a little syrup if liked).

Mrs. Rosina Male,
Vergan, Truro, Cornwall.

GOOSEBERRY CAKE

Top and tail 12 ozs. gooseberries and if they are large cut them in half. Mix 8 ozs. self raising flour and 6 ozs. butter together. Add 6 ozs. sugar and 2 eggs to make a stiff cake mixture, then add the gooseberries. Bake for 1 – 1$\frac{1}{2}$ hours in a moderate oven (350 F., Mark 4).

When cooked either cut it in half and spread with butter and caster sugar and eat it while still warm or, if eaten cold, leave the cake as it is and sprinkle the top with caster sugar. Do not keep it about long, it must be eaten fresh and is a very good cake.

Mrs. D. Holloway,
Sherborne, Dorset.

HONITON FAIRINGS (or Brandy Snaps)

Melt 6 ozs. butter, 6 ozs. golden syrup and 4 ozs. sugar in the top of a double saucepan with hot water below. Sift 1 teaspoon ground ginger and 4 ozs. flour together and add these to the mixture with 2 teaspoons of brandy. Take a large well greased baking sheet and drop teaspoons of the mixture on it. Put them far apart as it does spread in cooking. Bake your fairings in a preheated moderate oven (350 F., Mark 4) until they are a nice brown. Take them out, let them cool slightly and as soon as you can pick up the pieces with a knife wrap each quickly round a suitable piece of stick or the well greased handle of a wooden spoon. When rolled let them cool and harden, but they stiffen very fast as they cool so you must roll them very quickly. The ones on the tray, if necessary, can be put back in the oven for a moment to soften.

These biscuits are always sold at Honiton Fair. You can fill them if you like with whipped cream.

Mrs. E. Porter,
Axminster, Devon.

CORNISH GINGERBREAD BISCUITS

Melt 1 lb. treacle (golden syrup), 8 ozs. butter, 8 ozs. lard and 1 lb. sugar, then stir in 2 lbs. flour, 1 oz. bicarbonate of soda, 8 ozs. lemon peel, 1 oz. cinnamon and 1 oz. ground ginger. Mix well. Butter your palms and roll small pieces of the mixture into balls. Drop on to papered trays. Bake in a preheated moderate oven (350 F., Mark 4) till brown. Remove when cold and store in an air-tight tin.

Mrs. Lena Thomas,
Marazion, Cornwall.

CORNISH SAFFRON CAKE

Set 2 ozs. yeast to rise with a little sugar and 1 tablespoon flour in a warm place. Soak about 5p worth of saffron — it used to be 3d. worth 60 years ago! — in a little boiling water. Mix 3 lbs. flour and a pinch of salt with 1 lb. lard, 4 ozs. butter and 8 ozs. sugar. Add 1 lb. currants, 4 ozs. sultanas, 4 ozs. peel. Add the yeast sponge and make a soft dough. Set this to rise for 3 hours. Knead into round "loaves" and place in warmed cake tins. Set to rise for 20 minutes longer. Bake in a moderate oven (350 F., Mark 4) for 1 hour. When this was baked in an old Cornish range there were no thermostats! — only coal and sticks, and what cooks they were to achieve perfection.

Mrs. Lena Thomas,
Marazion, Cornwall.

Saffron, the dried stamens of the autumn crocus (*Crocus Sativus*) is very expensive as it takes about 4,000 flowers to produce an ounce of it, though it is only required in small quantities. "As dear as saffron, m'dear" is an old Cornish saying. It is used a lot in Italian and Spanish cooking, but Cornish people say it was introduced to them by the Phoenicians, like so much else. Saffron was once used for colouring cheese and butter and dyeing cloth. Saffron biscuits are also made in Somerset for Easter.

JOSEPHINE CAKE

Rumour had it that Josephine liked this cake made when travelling around to visit Napoleon on his campaigns. How did my ancestors get it? Wish one knew the story.

Mix together 4 ozs. butter, 4 ozs. caster sugar, 3 well beaten eggs. Add 6 ozs. flour with 1 teaspoon of baking powder (less if self raising flour is used). Add 6 drops of essence of lemon. Beat well. Pour half the mixture into a greased and lined cake tin, then sprinkle over 2 ozs. glacé cherries and 2 ozs. citron peel, cut small and floured. Add the remainder of cake mixture and bake in a moderate oven (350 F., Mark 4) for about 45 minutes.

Miss Rosemarie Gibaud,
Elson, Gosport, Hampshire.

WILTSHIRE LARDY CAKE

1 quarter of dough from the bakers. Put it in a warm place to rise for 2 hours then roll it out and spread all over with a layer of lard and brown sugar. Fold over and roll again with a spread of currants and mixed spices. Make into a round and put into a cake tin and make a coburg loaf. Bake until a golden brown. They are delicious hot for tea in the winter.

Mrs. Tabitha Cheal,
Ashford, Kent.

See also Northumberland Stotty Cake.

SCRATCHINS CAKE

This was always made in our grandmother's time after the pigs were killed. The "scratchins" are the crisp, tasty pieces of fat which are left in the rendering tins after the pig fat has been reduced to lard. They are eaten hot on rounds of toast and any that remain allowed to cool before being finely chopped ready for cake making. The making of a "scratchins" cake was always a great treat. This is the recipe.

Wash and dry 8 ozs. large raisins and add to 6 ozs. demerara sugar, 8 ozs. scratchins and 1 lb. S.R. flour. Grate the rind of 2 lemons and mix all well together. Beat up 1 egg, pour on 1 pint of milk and a dessertspoon of vinegar and use these to mix the dry ingredients to a dough. Turn into a greased tin and bake for about $1\frac{1}{2}$ hours in a moderate oven (350 F., Mark 4).

Mrs. A. E. Sorrill,
Torquay, Devon.

LIQUID YEAST

This is wonderful for bread making and for scones etc. It was used in the Goldrush days of Australia and Klondyke where normal yeast was not available. It will keep indefinitely, is cheap to make and economical to use (for cakes and pastry also).

At least 1 pint *screw top* beer bottle or similar strong bottle, some raisins and potato water.

After boiling the potatoes, drain off the water and retain until luke warm. Pour into the bottle. Leave about 2 inches space from the top. Put in about 4 or 5 raisins and screw the bottle tightly. Keep in kitchen at an ordinary temperature. Shake occasionally (not too hard). After about 45 hours the yeast is ready to use. When using mix with the ingredients instead of water and always leave about 2 inches of stock yeast in the bottle. Top up with potato water again — no raisins and the yeast will be ready in 24 hours. If not unstoppered it will be ready for use any time and will keep perfectly sweet. When the kick has gone out of it after a week or two add a few more raisins. Wonderful for bread making with a little milk powder added. *Care in unscrewing the stopper is needed as it is very lively like champagne.*

Mr. Lionel Helmore,
Exmouth, Devon.

HORSERADISH CREAMS

Make cheese biscuits with 1 oz. each of flour, margarine or butter and grated cheese, salt and a little water. Mix together grated horseradish seasoning and whipped cream. Pile the mixture on the biscuits. Top with paprika pepper.

Miss Rose Ellery,
Puddletown, Dorchester, Dorset.

YEAST CAKES OR BATH BUNS

These are delicious eaten buttered and with cheese. My grandparents were farmers and I can remember when it was pig killing time, the home fed pork that we shared. I remember fat bacon bought from the butchers which my mother fried until crisp and we ate it with laver — a seaweed — which the local fishermen picked off the rocks.

Prepare 1 oz. yeast by placing it in a cup or small bowl, sprinkle it with a little flour and sugar (just enough to cover the yeast). Add enough warm milk and water to fill the cup to about three-quarters full, they must be at blood heat, and feel neither hot nor cold when tested with a clean finger. This is ready to use when the yeast has risen to the top.

While the yeast is rising put 1 lb. plain flour into a bowl with ½ oz. of butter and 3 ozs. sugar. Rub the fat into the flour and sugar, add a pinch of spice and salt and 3 ozs. currants. Make a well in the centre and put in the yeast, add an egg, then add enough luke warm milk and water to make a soft mix. Leave to rise in a warm place covered with a clean cloth for about an hour. Turn out onto a floured board, cut into four and knead into cakes. Leave to rise for 15 minutes. Bake for 30 minutes (375 F., Mark 5).

Mrs. D. M. Atkinson,
Bath, Somerset.

For Bath Buns, sprinkle with sugar nibs 15 minutes before baking and brush over with sugar and water syrup after baking.

DORSET KNOBS

One can see Dorset Knobs being baked at Morecombelake, a very small village clinging to the hillside four miles west of Bridport. A gorgeous beery odour of hot freshly made bread flows out from the bakery, *Keith Moores* and his cousin *Ivor* use the same recipe as their grandfather Sam, who made them on a farm out in Stoke Mills about 100 years ago. They are the only people producing them now. "They used to be made in the old faggot oven", *Keith Moores* says in his soft Dorset voice, "using the receding heat to dry them out and make rusks, didn't they cousin? We make them by hand and cannot do enough, but it is difficult to get a machine that will do it without changing the recipe." *Cousin Ivor* agrees with him. They think theirs may be an old recipe, fashionable in Weymouth when George III came there for the bathing in 1789, popping his royal head under the water to the strains of the National Anthem. Locally, the farm workers have always eaten Dorset Knobs for breakfast before milking, and the older Dorset folk still dunk them in their tea.

They are, however, a superb cheese biscuit or rusk, crisp, dry and crunchy and as perfect with the now rare local Blue Vinney cheese as with a hunk of ripe farmhouse Cheddar or Double Gloucester, a thing for epicures ... Being hand-made, however, and only in Morecombelake they are scarce and hard to get. You can buy them, by post, from the *West End Dairy, 35 West Street, Bridpord* (3203), *Dorset,* or in London from *Fortnum and Mason in Piccadilly, W.*1, or from *Harrods in Knightsbridge, S.W.*1.

CORNISH PASTY

Pastry rolled out like a plate,
Piled with turmut, tates and mate
Doubled up and baked like fate
That's a Cornish Pasty.

Make some pastry from 1 lb. plain flour, 8 ozs. lard and suet mixed and ½ teaspoon of salt. Add a little water to make a nice pastry dough. Roll out the pastry ¼ inch thick and cut in rounds the size of a large tea plate. Fill each pasty with 4 ozs. raw meat cut small, chopped potato, onion or turnip, salt and a lump of butter the size of a walnut. Shape into a crescent, wet the edges and crimp them together. Brush with milk. Bake for 1 hour first in a hot oven (450 F., Mark 6) then after 15 minutes reduce the heat to moderate (350 F., Mark 4).

Mrs. Hilda Bovey,
St. Blazey, Cornwall.

CORNISH PASTIES

My brother was at Exeter and is now headmaster of a school in Cornwall. When the students are going home they break their journey to see my sister-in-law and get her to make some Cornish pasties to take home. This is how she makes them.

The pastry should use a third fat to flour. (It must not be as rich as short crust, or it will go to pieces). Cut this into rounds with a tea plate and put a layer of thinly sliced potato, swede and carrot in the middle of the pastry, then a small amount of onion, if liked, topped by a layer of minced beef. Season to taste and pull the edges of the round together with floured fingers and crimp it. This is a thing which only comes with practice. You use the two thumbs and two first fingers. Give the pasty a slight pressing then turn over. Bake for 1 hour in a hot oven (400 F., Mark 6) for the first 15 minutes, then reduce the heat to moderate (350 F., Mark 4). Eat in your hand, *not* with a knife and fork.

Miss M. Strong,
Swindon, Wiltshire.

The large ones often called Sallakee Pasties.

DEVON PARSLEY PASTY

I spent most of my early years in Devonshire, and I so liked this that I have made it, over 36 years of married life, whenever I have sufficient parsley. The dish, a main meal one, seems to be peculiar to a certain area in Devon. I have never come across it anywhere else, nor has anyone apparently heard of it.

Make a good round short pastry from 1 lb. self raising flour, 8 ozs. lard, a pinch of salt and milk and water to mix to a good dough. Roll it out to $\frac{1}{4}$ inch thick as far as it will go. On one half pile as much parsley as the dough will take when the other half is folded over to make at least one 12-inch long pasty. You *must* pile on the parsley, plenty of it. Turn up and over the edges of a pasty and lightly brush the top with milk and bake in a moderate oven (350 F., Mark 4) until the pasty is nicely browned, then place it on a large dish. While piping hot, slit the top of the pasty right across the length and pour in $\frac{1}{4}$ pint of raw double cream and serve at once. Add a dash of pepper and salt if liked.

This is a meal fit for the gods.

Mrs. Louise Shaw,
Burnham-on-Sea, Somerset.

The South Coast

Kent, Surrey, Sussex, the Channel Islands and parts of Hampshire including the Isle of Wight and Wiltshire.

Agricultural Products

Southdown Lamb and Mutton, Surrey Capons, Romney Marsh Lambs, Hops, Strawberries, Apples, Honey, Medlars, Quinces and Cob nuts, Tomatoes, Cherries.

Gastronomic Specialities

Whitstable Oysters, Dover Sole, Medway Smelts, Tonbridge Brawn, Worthing Seakale. Truffles, Kentish Pudding Pies, Ashdown Forest Partridge Pudding, Rabbit Pudding, Chicken Pudding, Suet Roll with Roast or Boiled Beef, Sussex Well Pudding. Ormers, Channel Islands Conger Eel Soup.

Pastry etc.

Tonbridge Wells Romary Biscuits, Flead Cakes, Folkestone Pudding Pies, Maidstone Cherry Brandy, "Rum and Black" Pub Drink, Cherry Wine, Barley Water.

FISH

CONGER EEL SOUP from Guernsey

Put the head and tail of a conger eel, a piece of salted pork, about 4 ozs. carrots, 4 potatoes, 1 parsnip and $4\frac{1}{2}$ pints water in a pan. Bring to the boil, then simmer for 30 minutes. Strain. Have ready 1 white cabbage, $\frac{1}{2}$ pint green peas, 5 sprigs parsley, 2 sprigs thyme, 2 onions, and the petals of 5 marigolds. Boil gently for 20 minutes until the vegetables are soft, add $\frac{1}{2}$ pint milk, 1 tablespoon butter, salt and pepper. Bring to the boil and the soup is ready.

This is from a notebook of my mother's. She was nearly 86 when she died in 1962. Although I haven't had this soup for years, I have only to close my eyes and I can see the green peas and marigold petals floating on top of a delicious creamy mixture that we had when we were a largish family.

Miss M. Fenton,
Highgate, London.

FISHERMAN'S RICE SOUP

Put $2\frac{1}{2}$ quarts of water into a soup pot and bring to the boil. Add $1\frac{1}{2}$ lbs. fish — trimmings or small fish or different kinds — which has been cut into pieces. Then add 1 onion and some pieces of carrot and celery. Add 1 blade of mace, 6 cloves. Leave them to boil for 1 hour. Strain. Have the pot washed out, put the stock back into it. Add 2 cut and skinned tomatoes and 4 ozs. rice. Boil for 20 minutes longer, season well. If a few oysters or shell fish are added at the end do not let it boil, only heat thoroughly. Garnish with chopped parsley.

This soup is delightful.

Mrs. F. Hersey,
Albourne, near Hassocks, Sussex.

SMELTS

In the days when salmon used to run up the Thames there were smelts and whitebait too in plenty. Smelts are still found in the River Medway but the ones in the shops mostly come from Holland. It is a beautiful little fish with greenish skin. When very fresh people say it smells of violets or perhaps ferns or cucumbers. It has a delicate taste and "eats very well" as the old cooks used to say.

Clean and wash the smelts. Pat them dry in a towel, then shake them up, one at a time, in a paper bag of seasoned flour till coated all over like a nicely powdered nose. Deep fry them in a pan of hot oil till golden brown. Put them on a hot dish and eat them crisp and hot with hunks of lemon and thinly cut brown bread and butter.

JOHN DORY

This fish is dressed in the same way as turbot, which it resembles in firmness but not in richness. Clean the fish thoroughly, cut off fins but not the head, (that is a delicacy on its own). Lay it in a fish-kettle (if possible), cover with warm water, add salt to taste, bring gradually to near boiling point and simmer gently for fifteen minutes. Serve it hot, garnish with cut lemon and parsley and melted butter. If liked, lobster, anchovy, or shrimp sauce.

Mrs. B. M. Russell,
Portslade-by-sea, Sussex.

DOVER SOLE

There is some marvellous fish on the south coast. The world famous oyster beds at Whitstable have been in continuous cultivation for at least 2,000 years and their oysters, though expensive, are superb.

Then, a large plain grilled Dover sole is one of the glories of British cooking, a classic dish which, like bacon and eggs, one can never have too often. Though chefs have devised hundreds of recipes for this lovely fish, when it is at its best, it is exquisite plainly grilled.

If, however, a waiter tries to sell you a grilled Dover sole in Scotland or the border counties either it is not a Dover sole or it has been frozen. They are not caught in these icy waters, but, like the nightingale, are only found south of a line drawn through somewhere like Burton-on-Trent. Neither are they caught on the other side of the Atlantic, so that when Americans talk about eating Dover sole, they are unlikely to have tasted it in its full perfection as we have.

They sell marvellous fish in all the little fishing ports along the south coast, straight out of the sea at about half the price you would get it in the shops. The last time I went down to Folkestone harbour I was just in time to meet *Mr. Lala Taylor*, skipper of the *Jacqueline Roberts*, which had just come into port. He looked more like a fisherman than one would believe possible in huge sea boots, orange windcheater and a pair of those gold ear-rings which are still so popular with the younger, as well as the older, fishermen. He had just brought in 50 stone of glittering plaice and Dover sole which he had caught at 4 o'clock that morning off Dungeness. They had only just stopped wriggling when they went into my shopping basket.

The modern domestic griller is too small to grill soles for more than 1 or 2 people. If there are several of us I cook plaice, Dover sole and lemon sole like the local fishermen. I just dip them in seasoned flour then put about a tablespoon of butter in the frying pan, when it has melted and sizzling in go the fish. I fry them about 3 minutes per side, or more according to how big they are, then I flip them onto a plate. I melt a little more butter in the frying pan, squeeze a bit of lemon into it — very important, it does a lot to the flavour — and pour all this over the fish. I don't bother with chips and things, just salad on a side plate and a little brown bread and butter.

Hastings also produces superb flat fish, but it used to be known too, for its gurnet or gurnard, a smallish fish which one can often buy from fishermen on the beach. Cut off the heads, shake the fish in a paper bag with a little seasoned flour, pour melted butter over. Grill them in a grill pan lined with foil turning the fish twice. Serve piping hot with parsley butter.

HERRINGS

Wash, scale and gut the fresh herrings. Sprinkle with salt and dip once in vinegar; skewer with tails in mouth. Put into boiling water, simmer for fifteen minutes (very gently), take out and drain. Arrange on a hot dish, garnished with parsley. These are excellent served with mustard sauce.

Lilian Sauyer,
Strood, Rochester, Kent.

SOUSED HERRINGS (to eat hot or cold)

Wash, remove the heads and split down the side 3 or more fresh herrings. Pull out the backbone — all the bones will come away easily. Roll each fish round a piece of roe, sprinkle each fish with salt, pepper and slightly dust with flour, pack into a baking dish.

138

Add a bay leaf, 10 peppercorns, 2 cloves and cover with half a breakfast cup of liquid — 3 parts vinegar to 1 part water. Cover with a lid and bake in the oven (300 F., Mark 3) for 1 hour. These can be eaten hot or cold.

Mrs. D. Robinson,
Blackwater, Camberley, Surrey.

RYE BONFIRE NIGHT

They have a bloater barbecue in the ancient town of Rye in Sussex, usually on the first Saturday in November, as part of the Guy Fawkes celebrations. There is nearly always a great torchlight procession with fireworks, tableaux and I once saw a great paper dragon belching forth smoke and, for all I know, the rich odour of bloaters. Then there's boat burning on the Town Salts, when some well known personality lights an enormous bonfire, with the Last Post sounding as Guy Fawkes perishes in the flames.

Last, but not least is the Bloater Boat, with a charcoal fire amidships and a rich odour of sizzling fish wafted across the breeze. It is an old fishing boat, of iron so it will not burn, with a charcoal fire amidships. They have been cooking bloaters on charcoal in Rye on bonfire night for hundreds of years. The chief cook and bloater boy — *Roger Brown*, a lorry driver and skin dresser by profession the time I was there — sells about a hundred bloaters and seven hundred rolls during the celebrations. They put the bloater heads on the fire with the charcoal to make it burn up. The flavour is indescribable but luscious. Some like their bloaters hard-roed, some like them soft. It's a matter of opinion.

"We catch the herrings off the coast here in Rye Bay, said *Mr. Brown* "salt them overnight and smoke them in a special shed 25 per spit over a fire of oak sawdust."

You eat the bloaters in your fingers, beginning either at the tail and working from left to right, or starting at the head and working anti-clockwise. This is a lovely thing for anybody's Bonfire Night. The bloaters are quite easy to do on the end of a stick or toasting fork in any bonfire — and they give you a tremendous thirst. If you cannot get bloaters you might try kippers, though these being softer will be a little trickier to cook.

"Of course, all this bonfire stuff is older than Guy Fawkes really" a Rye policeman told me, among a fusillade of Chinese squibs, "Hundreds of years ago we used to drag burning French boats through the town. The French invaded this part of the coast several times and the Rye-ers raided the French coast in the thirteenth century and it's been going on ever since . . ."

Nobody mentioned Boney.

MEAT POULTRY AND GAME

Mrs. CHAMP

Mrs. Champ is a bird-like woman of 76 who has spent nearly all her life as cook for "the best people". She can still rattle off the appalling list of her duties as a 13-year-old room maid to the Duke of Buccleuch in Kettering more than 60 years sgo. Creeping down from the attics at 4 a.m. to light fires and help prepare lunch for the gentlemen going shooting. Cleaning coppers in the scullery with sand and vinegar and soft soap. "At night you used to have to scour the big soup pots with taps on. They threw the bones in and they boiled all day. I was so little I had to have a stool to stand on for two or three hours at a time, with the grease dripping down my arms."

In between times she gutted hares and plucked pheasants.

The next year she was scullery maid to the 10th Earl Ferrers. Six in kitchen, lady housekeeper kept, wages £9 a year and not a stitch of uniform found. The estate was so large his lordship had a private clergyman and filled his own church with tenants. It was an assured, arrogant world, utterly free from any sense of the ridiculous.

"On Sundays you lined up behind the housekeeper in the vestibule hall in a long black dress and bonnet with a black veil tied over the face. At 10.50 sharp you fell into rank, housekeeper first, personal maid second, housemaids third, other ranks behind. A footman opened the outside door and you followed the housekeeper into church. The women went to the left, the men to the right, the men in smocks and the estate manager in silk hat and frock coat. At 11 o'clock on the dot his lordship and the ladies came into church, followed by the butler and two footmen who took his lordship's hat and gloves at the door. The butler opened the high box pews for her ladyship, the first footman opening those opposite for his lordship. The Sunday school children seated on forms rose to their feet, the girls curtsied, the boys stood to attention. The verger locked the church door, the organ started and played his lordship into his seat and the service began.

"At the end they all filed out with as much ceremony as before. You raced upstairs, threw off your black frock and went sharp back to work. That was your Sunday. And of course the work piled up when you were gone" said *Mrs. Champ*, "you may depend on it."

"I have had plates thrown at me, buckets of water thrown over me. What for? Nothing. Cooks got in tempers, they had so much to do they got excited."

She has memories of vast greasy meals eaten by other people, huge jacks, 6 ft. long, full of roasting game, spitting fat, which worked by clockwork. "I was tipping scuttles of coal in all the time" she says. She spoke about the black stove, the hot plate, general range, two huge ovens and pipes to other ovens for keeping plates hot.

"After black-leading the stove we were like spotted dicks." It was difficult to marry in service, almost impossible to have children without losing your job, but *Mrs. Champ* now lives in a cottage at the gates of a manor house where she was once cook, and where *Horace Champ*, her 83-year-old husband, was gamekeeper. She has cooked in houses in Albany, flats in Paris and in castles in Wales for oil magnates and aristocrats, getting her jobs from *Massey's Superior Agency for Nobleman's Servants*, 100 *Baker Street*.

In the last war, however, when the big house where she was cook/housekeeper was requisitioned by the Navy, she joined the W.R.N.S. and stayed on there to become Chief Mistress at Arms, something like a regimental sergeant-major. There are pictures of her in uniform before the house with her Wrens (some from the best families) lined up meekly behind her. You could see she thoroughly enjoyed it.

In her day everything came in from the home farm, game, vegetables in season, whole sheep to be cut in joints. The old pheasants were boiled and served deliciously in celery sauce. "There are too many casseroles nowadays" *Mrs. Champ* said, "they wouldn't have it in my time, too much repetition."

Mrs. CHAMP'S BOILED PHEASANT WITH CELERY SAUCE

Put a brace of pheasants in a large pan with herbs, seasoning and hot water to cover. Bring to the boil, skimming off the scum. Let them simmer gently for 1½ hours. Meanwhile wash, de-string, dice and boil your celery till just tender. Melt 1 oz. butter, stir in 1 tablespoon flour, then gradually stir in about ¾ pint of milk. Heat, stirring, till smooth and thick. Add salt, pepper, a little ground mace or nutmeg. Stir in the diced celery and a little cream before pouring the sauce over the pheasants. No other garnish.

I asked *Mrs. Champ* if people didn't decorate them with the tail feathers. "No tails!" cried *Mrs. Champ*. "In a gentleman's house, you must never over-decorate the food. Nothing showy, like in a restaurant, for the gentry. They're trying to sell the stuff. In a nobleman's house everything must be plain, for someone with a palate. When serving chicken you don't put bread sauce, it's too common. Vegetables are the thing. Diced potatoes with the pheasant and tiny brussels sprouts plainly covered with butter. For the third vegetable, diced carrot."

TO MAKE GAME SOUP FROM PHEASANT WATER

Put it in a pan with the raw pheasant giblets, 8 ozs. shin beef very finely chopped, a bay leaf, bouquet garni, sliced onions and carrots, 12 peppercorns, a little salt. Bring it to the boil and simmer for about an hour. The beef will clear the soup and there will be no fat on it. If there are four to dinner, when cooked, strain the soup into a clean

pan and boil it violently to reduce it to the exact quantity for four.
Serve it quite plain without any bits and pieces.

Mrs. Champ,
Milstead, near Sittingbourne, Kent.

CHICKEN BRAWN OR COLLARED FOWL

Get a large fowl, draw and clean it, strip all the flesh off the bones
and beat it flat with a large knife on a board. Sprinkle with a little
salt and pepper. Lay a few rashers of streaky bacon all over the fowl
("green" or home cured bacon is the best as it gives a better flavour
to the brawn). Now start to roll it like a suet pudding, then tie it
tightly in a clean cloth. Place the giblets and bones in a saucepan,
also the fowl, cover with cold water, add a bunch of parsley and a
sprig of thyme. Add a little salt and pepper, bring to the boil.
Simmer for 2 hours. Take the cloth off the meat and place in a cool
mould, press down with a heavy weight. The next day it will be ready
for the table. If the stock is saved after the brawn is taken out add
a little pot herbs and pearl barley. This will make a delicious soup.

Dorothy Gabbott,
Bexhill-on-Sea, Sussex.

Some butchers and poultry men can still be found who will bone
a fowl for you.

IRISH STUFFING FOR PORK OR GOOSE

Boil 2 lbs. potatoes (peeled weight). While still hot mix in 1 lb.
breadcrumbs, 3 large chopped onions, some sage, pepper and salt
binding together with a little lard and milk, not too moist, rather
dry. Place under the bird or joint of pork in the roasting dish, or
stuff the goose with it. **Mrs. Shannon,**
Fishbourne, near Chichester, Sussex.

KENTISH CHICKEN PUDDING

Grease a pudding basin and line it with suet crust. Cut up a
chicken into small pieces and flour them. Cut a few slices of cooked
ham into strips $\frac{3}{4}$ inch long and 2 inches wide. Chop some parsley
(leaves, not stalks) and scatter it with the ham and a few button
mushrooms, salt and pepper amongst the pieces of chicken until the
suet lined basin is full. Cover with a thin steak of veal or pork. Pour
one teacup of cold water over all and cover with a suet crust. Pinch
the edges together and cover all with a piece of buttered paper, then
with a cloth and tie securely. Boil for 3 hours, never allowing the
water to boil dry. Serve the pudding turned out of the basin.

Joan Houghton,
Hildenborough, Kent.

A similar pudding is sometimes prepared with a rabbit or a
partridge or a couple of pigeons.

142

DUCK PIE

Cut off the wings and legs of a good young duck and boil the remainder for 15 minutes. Cut it up while hot saving the gravy that runs from it. Take the giblets, adding to them a few anchovies, a large pat of butter, 1 blade of mace, 6 peppercorns, 2 onions, a small piece of toast, a small bunch of herbs and a pinch of cayenne pepper. Heat all this together until the butter has melted, then add ½ pint boiling water and let all stew gently until the giblets are tender. Strain these and then put into the pie dish. Let the gravy stand until cold, skim off the fat, adding the "juice" from the cut up bird. Pour into the pie dish adding the duck portions, well seasoned with pepper, salt and butter, cover with flaky pastry. Bake in a moderate oven (350 F., Mark 4). This is far preferable to roast duck.

Mrs. Ducker,
Maidstone, Kent.

CHICKEN AND LEEK PIE

Put a chicken in a saucepan, cover with cold water. When boiling add 1 large quartered onion, 1 stick of celery, mixed herbs and salt. Simmer for 1½ hours, remove the chicken, strain the stock into a basin, leave until set into a jelly. Trim the green off a bunch of small well-washed leeks, scald the white part with boiling water, split and cut into 1-inch long pieces. Carve the chicken into neat joints, lay it in a pie dish with 3 slices of cooked tongue, the leeks and a little chopped parsley. Moisten with some of the chicken jelly. For the pastry put 6 ozs. flour in a basin, make a well in the centre and add 3 tablespoons of dripping dissolved in 1 gill of boiling water, mix thoroughly with a spoon. Knead, then roll out to cover the pie dish. Bake in a quick oven (400 F., Mark 5) till the pastry is a light golden colour.

Miss M. Sadowski,
Hove, Sussex.

ROAST VEAL

Wash 2 – 3 lbs. neck of veal thoroughly and rub with salt, cover with a thin layer of dripping. Make a stuffing from 2 ozs. suet, 1 slice of cooked chopped bacon, 1 small chopped onion, 1 tablespoon soft breadcrumbs, 1 tablespoon chopped parsley, a little grated lemon peel, pepper and salt to taste. Spread this forcemeat with a knife over the veal, as evenly as possible. In the centre of this place 3 hard boiled eggs. Roll the meat and tie with string. Roast in a moderate oven (350 F., Mark 4) for about 2 hours. Serve very hot with a good brown gravy and redcurrant jelly.

Mrs. I. Hunter,
Dover, Kent.

CALF'S HEAD

Bone the head, cut into pieces and blanch. Leave the tongue whole. Cover with water in which you have put a handful of flour. Simmer for 3 hours with onion, carrot, pepper and salt to your own taste. Serve with the following sauce.

Mix 1 egg cup olive oil and $\frac{1}{2}$ egg cup vinegar together with a little dry mustard. Add salt and pepper. Chop 1 hard boiled egg very finely, 1 small onion finely, a little parsley and a small gherkin and add to the sauce and serve.

Mrs. E. Staples,
Southampton.

A calf's head is difficult to buy nowadays from the butcher but it makes an excellent dish which, in France, is considered a great delicacy.

BRAIN AND CHEESE PASTRY SQUARES (delicious)

Clean and bring a large set of brains to the boil. Strain and return them to the saucepan in hot salted water. Cook them gently until tender. Strain them and remove any bits of skin that may be left. Chop the brains, mix with chopped parsley and pepper. Heat some butter in a pan and sauté the mixture very quickly. Let it cool. When cold beat a little stiffly whipped cream into the mixture. Roll out some short crust pastry to a thickness of about $\frac{3}{16}$ inch. Cut it into 3 x 3 inch squares. Place a spoonful of the mixture on one square, brush the edges with milk and cover it with the top square. Press round the edge gently making any design you like. Make a circle in the middle of the square by piercing it with a fork. Cover completely with beaten egg (using a brush). Place the squares in a fairly hot oven (375 F., Mark 5). Have some grated cheese ready and when the squares are nearly cooked sprinkle the tops quickly with the cheese. Put them back in the oven until the cheese is golden and soft. Garnish them with very small sprigs of parsley poked into the centres of the squares to give the appearance of a tiny brush.

Mrs. K. J. Hopkins,
Hastings, Sussex.

SALT BEEF WITH PEASE PUDDING

Soak 8 ozs. split peas overnight in cold water. Next morning strain the peas and tie them up in a piece of muslin, put in cold water with $2 - 2\frac{1}{2}$ lbs. salt silverside or brisket. Bring to the boil and simmer for $1\frac{1}{2} - 2$ hours. Add small whole carrots and onions 30 minutes before the end. Press any liquid from the peas and mash them with butter and pepper, adding salt if required. Slice the meat and serve it with the vegetables and pease pudding, potatoes can be added if wished.

144

(Always put split peas into cold water and never add salt until the water is boiling).

Mrs. G. Salisbury,
Ryde, Isle of Wight.

SALT BRISKET OF BEEF — HOW TO PICKLE IT

Boil 3 ozs. salt, 1 oz. brown sugar, 2 teaspoons pickling spices, 1 teaspoon mixed herbs, $\frac{1}{2}$ teaspoon nutmeg and $\frac{1}{2}$ flat teaspoon cinnamon in half a pint of water. Leave to cool. Rub 3 lbs. boned and rolled flank of beef with 1 teaspoon saltpetre, roll it in the pickle mixture and turn it every day for a minimum of 6 days, then drain and simmer it with carrots, onions, turnip and parsnip for about 3 hours. Put in some dumplings 30 minutes before the meat is cooked. Thicken the stock with plain flour and serve with pease pudding.

Mrs. W. E. Paine,
Ringwood, Hampshire.

BUBBLE AND SQUEAK

Melt a little butter in a frying pan, put in some thin slices of cold pork or boiled beef, fry them until lightly browned on both sides. Take them out and keep them hot. Put in one shredded onion, fry it until brown, add some cold mashed potato and greens, season to taste, stir until thoroughly hot. Turn onto a hot dish and place the slices of meat on top.

Mrs. B. M. Russell,
Portslade-by-Sea, Sussex.

STEAK JARRETT

Cut 1$\frac{1}{2}$ lbs. shin beef into pieces 1 inch square and roll them in flour. Put them into a casserole dish or stew jar, add a few sticks of finely cut celery and 6 rolls of streaky bacon. Over this pour 1 cup of water with a tablespoon of Worcester sauce and 2 tablespoons of tomato sauce. The meat should be covered. Put it in the oven and bring it to the boil then allow it to simmer for 2 hours, stirring occasionally. Add more water if too dry.

Mrs. B. Kearvell,
Bosham, near Chichester, Sussex.

TOAD-IN-THE-HOLE

Beat 2 eggs, stir in 2 tablespoons of flour, $\frac{1}{2}$ teaspoon salt, 1$\frac{1}{4}$ pints milk. Beat the batter for 20 minutes. Grease a large pie dish, pour in the mixture and bury in the batter 1$\frac{1}{2}$ lbs. of beef, mutton or sausage meat. Bake in a moderate oven (350 F., Mark 4) for 1$\frac{1}{2}$ hours.

Mrs. N. E. Hodges,
Sittingbourne, Kent.

STUFFED TRIPE IN TOMATO SAUCE

Buy 1 lb. nicely prepared tripe from a good butcher. Put in a pan with cold water, bring to boiling point, cook for 5 minutes, lift out and throw away the water. Scrape off the greasy matter from the underside of the tripe and cut into strips 2 inches wide, 2 inches long. Beat an egg and mix it with ½ lb. boiled potatoes, pepper, salt, 1 teaspoon powdered sage, 2 tablespoons chopped, cooked onion. It should be rather still. Put this onto the strips of tripe and tie them up. Place in a casserole with 1 pint tomato sauce, simmer gently for about 2 hours or until the tripe is tender when pierced with a skewer. Remove the ties, place the tripe on a hot dish, pour round the tomato sauce and serve with sippets of toast and apple sauce.

Mrs. J. Shellier,
Romney Marsh, Kent.

STUFFED SHOULDER OF LAMB

Get the butcher to cut away the bones from the underside of a shoulder of lamb, but leave in the shank bone. At home fill in the part from which the bones have been removed with veal forcemeat and season with pepper, salt and mace. Tie it up, lay a few slices of bacon at the bottom of a stewpan, put in the lamb, cover it with more sliced bacon, add a bunch of sweet herbs, pour in 1 pint veal stock and stew gently for 1½ hours. Take out the lamb and put it on a dish. Have ready some good brown sauce or gravy, add a boiled sweetbread, cut into dice, and 3 or 4 pickled mushrooms. Bring to the boil and simmer for a few minutes, pour this round the lamb and garnish with cut lemon. For 6 – 8 persons, cooking time 1½ hours.

For the veal forcemeat you need 2 ozs. cooked ham and 4 ozs. cold veal minced and pounded with 4 ozs. breadcrumbs, 1 chopped onion, ¼ tablespoon chopped parsley, ½ teaspoon chopped lemon peel and a pinch of cayenne pepper and salt. Bind the mixture with an egg beaten up in ¼ gill of milk. Two eggs may be used in place of the milk if a richer mixture is required.

Mrs. A. Withers,
Dunton Green, Sevenoaks, Kent.

BRAISED SADDLE OF MUTTON (OR LAMB)

Get the butcher to prepare the saddle of mutton or lamb by removing the backbone without injuring the fillets or perforating any of the fat which covers them. Then trim the tail end to a round and cut the flaps square. Well season the inner part of the saddle and roll up each flap piece to make a neat appearance, secure its shape by tying with fine string. In a large saucepan braise 2 or 3 carrots, sliced lengthways and 2 or 3 shallots cut in rings, a few sticks of celery in 1 oz. of butter. Then braise the mutton on these with a little mace and a few cloves, moisten with sufficient good stock to just cover the mutton. Place a piece of buttered paper on top and then put the lid over the pan and leave to braise for 4 hours over a moderate heat. Do not baste too frequently with the liquor. When ready remove from the pan and place on a baking sheet and place in a moderate oven (350 F., Mark 4) for 5 – 10 minutes to just dry off the moisture. Serve with prepared vegetables.

Mrs. R. Dilly,
Carshalton, Surrey.

SHEPHERD'S PIE FROM KENT

Should a shepherd's pie be made of beef or mutton? Some people will tell you with passion that when it's beef it's Cottage and when it's mutton it's Shepherd. Stands to sense, they say. Reheated or fresh mince? Fresh, I say firmly, but some folks have other ideas. Any Man of Kent will tell you that the thing with the mince and mashed potato is a Cottage Pie, and country people anywhere south of Tenterden or Appledore will say that a Shepherd's Pie is quite different and has a suet crust on top.

You put layers of cutlets, then onions and potatoes, then a layer of suet crust in a fireproof dish. Then some cutlets, onion and potato and fill it up with mutton broth before putting on the final lid of suet crust. Bake it for 1½ – 2 hours in a moderate oven (350 F., Mark 4).

"And believe me," Mrs. Mitchell of Hythe told me, "the Romney Marsh shepherd — or looker, as we call him — would indeed think poorly of his pie without the pastry."

ANNIE FUNNELL'S SCRATCHING PIE

Line a deep round tin with pastry, sprinkle 4 ozs. scratchings over the bottom. Mix together ½ lb. parboiled pig's heart, ½ lb. tongue and 4 ozs. liver, a handful of currants, 1 teaspoon mixed herbs, 1 teaspoon brown sugar, 1 teacup brown breadcrumbs, a pinch of caraway seeds, pepper and salt. Spread over the scratchings. Break 2 eggs over whole, prick the egg yolk so that it spreads over the white, but don't mix. Cover with 1 boiled, sliced onion then another 4 ozs. of scratchings, finally the pastry lid. Bake for 1½ hours in a moderate oven (350 F., Mark 4). The meat mixture should be well moistened with stock, not onion water.

Mrs. M. Betchley,
Steyning, Sussex.

KIDNEY IN ROLLS

Cut the tops off 2 crisp rolls. Remove all the dough from inside, line the rolls thickly with 2 ozs. butter. Grate a little onion into each roll. Chop 2 kidneys in small pieces and press them down into the rolls. Put knobs of butter on top and replace the top of the roll. Season with salt and pepper. Put the kidney rolls into a fireproof dish with rolls of bacon and halved tomatoes if liked. Bake for 1½ hours in a very moderate oven (300 F., Mark 2).

Mrs. H. D. Clark,
West Wittering, Sussex.

BOILED BACON WITH CABBAGE

Boil a lean joint of boiling bacon until almost cooked, then add 1 swede and some carrots. After 15 minutes add some potatoes and 1 small flatpole cabbage (whole, after thoroughly washing). A genuine flatpole will not disintegrate. When almost cooked add 2 dumplings per person and boil quickly for 15 minutes, taste and add pepper and salt if necessary. When cooked the bacon is taken out and carved and served with the vegetables and one dumpling per person. The other dumplings are kept hot and served with golden syrup afterwards.

June R. Rea,
San Antonio Abad, Ibiza, Spain.

BOILED PORK HOCK IN PARSLEY SAUCE

Put 1 pork hock in cold water and boil till tender. Test with a fork and when it is getting soft put in 1 or 2 parsnips which have been cut in quarters. Boil them with the hock. When cooked make a parsley sauce with the stock.

E. Brock,
Portslade by Sea, Brighton, Sussex.

FRIED CHITTERLINGS

Fry 1 large sliced onion in a little bacon fat, then fry 4 ozs. streaky bacon, add 1 lb. chitterlings in small pieces. Serve with mashed potatoes and swedes.

F. McClinton,
Hove, Sussex.

Cooked, jellied chitterlings pressed into blocks are still sold in cooked meat shops. In France chitterling sausages — *andouilles* and *andouillettes* — are considered a great delicacy. The andouille de Vire, from Normandy is especially famous.

HAM PÂTÉ IN A PIE CRUST

Line a loaf tin with short crust pastry, keeping some to cover the top. If possible use home cured lard for the pastry. Mix 1 lb. chopped, boiled shoulder bacon or ham with 8 ozs. grated cheese, 1 chopped onion and 3 well beaten eggs (keep a little egg for the glaze). Add pepper and herbs as liked. Put half the mixture into the pastry-lined tin. Shell 3 hard boiled eggs and put them on top of the mixture and cover them with the rest of it. Put the remaining pastry on top, seal and flute the edges. Cut one or two small holes in the top, decorate with pastry leaves etc., Glaze and bake in a slow oven (300 F., Mark 2). Cool in a baking tin and do not cut until the next day.

Mrs. Jean George,
Sheldwick, near Faversham, Kent.

PARSLEY PIE

Line a pie plate, preferably earthenware, with 3 ozs. flaky pastry. Cut up 8 ozs. lean unsmoked streaky bacon and 2 handfuls parsley finely with scissors and put it on the pastry. Break 4 eggs over this and season well. Cover with another 3 ozs. flaky pastry, decorate, crimp and glaze with a beaten egg. Cook in a hot oven (400 F., Mark 5) for approximately 30–45 minutes. This pie is delicious hot with creamed potatoes and diced beetroot or cold with salad.

June R. Rea,
San Antonio Abad, Ibiza, Spain.

HASLET PIE

Cut the pig's heart, tongue and melt into pieces, to this add a piece of salted belly of pork cut in the same way. Add 1 large sliced onion and a small quantity of sage, pepper and salt. Stew this all together slowly for about 2 hours or until tender. Line a pie dish with short crust pastry, add to this the contents of the stew, do not cover the pie with pastry but with the "caul" fat, or veil or flead fat. This can be got from the butchers in small quantities. Bake it in a moderate oven (350 F., Mark 4) until the fat is nicely browned and frizzled.

Mrs. M. Clements,
Deal, Kent.

KILMANY KAIL WITH OATCAKE

Prepare a rabbit by cutting it into 4 pieces. Soak in warm salt water for 30 minutes at least, changing the water once or twice. To blanch it, place the rabbit in a saucepan, cover with cold water and bring to boiling point, then pour off the water. Cover the rabbit and a piece of salt pork with cold water and bring to boiling point. Wash the greens and add to the broth with pepper. Boil for 3 hours. Serve with oatcake.

For this mix together 6 ozs. fine oatmeal, 2 ozs. flour and ½ teaspoon salt. Add 1 oz. melted lard or dripping and enough boiling water to make a firm paste. Roll out very thinly, cut into triangles and bake for 30 minutes at 325 F., Mark 3.

Mrs. Dorothy Newall,
Southsea, Hampshire.

BAKED RABBIT WITH ONIONS

Coat some rabbit joints with flour seasoned with mixed herbs, salt and pepper. Place in a casserole in alternate layers with sliced onions. Top with slices of streaky pork and bake for approximately 3 hours at 350 F., Mark 4. The onion juice and the fat from the pork makes the gravy as it cooks.

Mrs. G. P. Sumner,
Eastbourne, Sussex.

This dish is also suitable for chicken.

ROAST RABBIT

Most people boil, stew or push rabbits into pies here. They do not realise that a rabbit can be roasted, indeed, is most delightful this way. But you give it a slight "treatment" the day before.

All you require is a tender rabbit, skinned and cleaned, some salad oil, a bunch of herbs and a shallow dish that can be used for roasting. The day before cooking the rabbit pour some salad oil, about half inch deep, in the shallow dish. Throw into the oil a sprig of thyme, parsley, bay leaves, a little sage. Bend the rabbit in two and string it, so it stays in this position. Put it in the oil bath and leave it till next day, turning occasionally so that each side gets an opportunity to soak in the oil. After the rabbit has bathed like this for 12 hours pour away the oil from the roasting dish since you have no more use for this. Put the rabbit, now spread out, in the dish, spread some butter on it and roast it in the ordinary way. After the rabbit has been in the oven 15 minutes add a glassful of hot water for the gravy.

This way the rabbit is so delicious that it can be served even at a dinner party.

Mrs. Anita Vulliamy,
Hove, Sussex.

SPICED PORK ROLL

— An old-fashioned economical supper dish which can be eaten with pickles etc.

Spread some spice over a piece of pork rind with 1 oz. fat on it and 10 inches long x 6 inches wide. Sprinkle with salt. Roll up as tightly as possible and tie in three places with fine string. Roll up in a pudding cloth like a roly poly pudding, tie each end. Boil for 4 hours or until really soft and tender. When cold remove the wrappings and cut into slices.

Mrs. E. G. Taylor,
Fareham, Hampshire.

BAKING

GREAT AUNT CLARA'S BIJOU CAKE

— As made by her and sold in the Bijou Café, Bognor before 1914.

Rub 4 ozs. butter into 8 ozs. self raising flour with ½ teaspoon cinnamon and a pinch of salt. Beat an egg well. Add 8 ozs. currants, 8 ozs. raisins, 2 ozs. soft brown sugar, a few chopped almonds and 4 ozs. mixed peel. Add 1 dessertspoon golden syrup and the egg. Mix. Add ½ teaspoon bicarbonate of soda dissolved in ¼ pint of milk. Mix all well. Bake in a large bread tin or a 7-inch cake tin, for 2½ hours (350 F., Mark 4). Reduce to 325 F., Mark 3 after 45 minutes. Reduce again. If using an Aga put it into an Aga Cake Baker, middle size tin, and bake for 1½ – 2 hours on the grid on the floor of the baking oven.

My childhood was chequered with beautiful bijou cakes. Mother made them two at a time and they vanished like smoke, everyone saying: "No wonder Aunt Clara made a great success of her venture into the Bijou Café."

Mrs. Rosemary Lunn,
Henley, Oxfordshire.

TARTE HOLLANDAISE

Sift 4 ozs. flour and 2½ ozs. sugar into a bowl and work in 4 ozs. butter as for pastry. Form into a dough by working in a spoonful or so of apricot jam. Divide into two portions and place in two greased 6-inch flan dishes. Bake in a moderate oven (350 F., Mark 4) until the mixtures have spread themselves over the dishes and become nice and brown. Cool a little before turning out and making a sandwich with a filling of apricot jam.

Ursula Wyndham.
Petworth, Sussex,

SWEETHEARTS

Take some short crust pastry and roll it thinly into a 9-inch square. Mark the pastry into three and slightly dampen the middle third, sprinkle it with sugar and currants. Fold over another third, slightly dampen this and sprinkle it with sugar and currants; now fold on top of this the remaining third pastry. Roll gently so that the currants are embedded in the mixture and cut it into strips about 1½ inches wide. Brush with milk and bake in a moderate oven (350 F., Mark 4) until the pastry is cooked.

Mrs. D. G. Roberson,
Emsworth, Hampshire.

FLEED CAKES

This is an old Sussex recipe. "Fleed" or "flare" fat which it is called in the southern parts of the country, is a white fat, similar to lard. It comes from near the kidneys and is called caul, pronounced *kell*, fat in the north of England. Some recipes call for lamb's "fleed" or "flead". In other parts it is called the veil. It can be bought in small quantities from the butcher.

Sieve 8 ozs. flour into a basin and chop 4 ozs. fleed into it roughly. Add some milk and mix to a soft dough. Beat it with a rolling pin until flat. Fold into a roll and beat again. Repeat this once more, fold again and roll out to about ½ inch thick. Cut into rounds with a scone cutter, fold each over in half, pinch the two edges firmly together where they just meet, but not all round. Lightly brush over with milk and place on a floured baking tin. Bake in a very hot oven (425 F., Mark 7) for 15 minutes. These are delicious hot or cold on their own.

Mrs. D. Weston,
Heston, Hounslow, Middlesex.

SCRAP PIES

In the Surrey town of Guildford prior to and during the First World War, there was a pork butcher and bacon curer who used to make his own lard. When the lard was rendered down by the butcher there was left a golden crispy fat which was sold quite cheaply per lb. and called "scraps". My mother used to make "Scrap Pies".

Line an enamel plate with rough puff pastry, put in the washed currants, raisins and peeled and chopped apples and the scraps. Cover with pastry and bake in a moderate oven (350 F., Mark 4).

Mr. A. H. Harms,
Earlsfield, London.

VARIOUS

TRUFFLES

This is the story of a wild, romantic dream. A magnificent obsession with fungus. *Mr. Assirati* is a quiet, shy man who lays mosaic flooring in Italian cafes in London. At the week-ends he searches for the more recondite fungi, most of which are dismissed in this country as toadstools. "I don't go and pick mushrooms for the money, I get them for the pleasure and as a hobby. And I give them to my friends", he says. Of course you must know what you are doing as some are poisonous, but, though he was born in England, Oreste Assirati's family comes from Central Italy, where they know about these things.

"In the West End they call me the mushroom king; I dream of nothing but mushrooms. Almost every night!"

It was on a wet autumn day in the Home Counties that he found the white truffle. I've seen it, and it weighs at least 4 ozs. A sort of dirty beige, you can just about hold it in the palm of your hand. An English white truffle! Just like the expensive ones that sell for well over £20 per lb. in the Italian shops. We could be sitting on a goldmine. Truffles grow underground, smell awful, taste delicious, and cost a fortune. People usually root them out with the help of pigs and trained dogs.

One day in October *Mr. Assirati* had been searching in woods near London for a kind of mushroom called *boletus* or *porcini*, much used in Italian cooking. He was walking steadily and slowly along the road (there had been a storm), and suddenly by the roadside he saw this thing like a Jersey potato still half-buried in the bank where the earth had fallen. "As soon as I smelt it I knew what it was" he said. "My wife was delighted. We were all delighted. It's a sort of family heirloom." Of course he won't say where he found it for even ordinary mushroom gatherers are secretive. "Truffle hunting runs in the family," he told me. "My boy knows the exact place. All the Italians here are interested in mushrooms but no one has ever found anything like this." He strokes it lovingly, believing he's going to make a fortune by discovering English truffles. He might at that!

"I went to Italy this year" said *Mr. Assirati*, "to buy a dog trained for truffle hunting. But they asked 400,000 lire for it. And then I'd have to get it here, and with the quarantine fees, it would cost about £600. I couldn't afford anything like that" he murmured putting his family heirloom in its bit of brown paper back in his pocket, "though I'm sure if we had one we would find a lot of English truffles. We've got them here under our noses. All this about France and Italy having these wonderful things. They make so much fuss abroad. And we have them here in Britain!"

Mycologists say that quite a lot of truffles can be found in the South of England. There used to be some in the grounds of Bristol University and under the playing fields of Marlborough College.

I was startled to hear from 68-year-old *Mrs. Lillian Moody* of Whiteparish, Wiltshire. Her father, Arthur Newton Collins, and grandfather, Eli Collins, of Winterslow, Wiltshire, were the last of the English truffle hunters. "The English truffle has such a beautiful flavour," she says. "Full and delicious. There are two kinds, the 'garlic' and the 'bud'. The Wiltshire ones are black, marbled inside and very similar to a thunderbolt. As children we washed them, sliced them, and had them with a little vinegar, bread and cheese."

Lord Beaverbrook, who was very interested in English truffle hunting, once asked Mr. Collins to go with him to France. He had made a bet that English dogs made better truffle hounds than Continental ones. The outbreak of the war prevented a result.

Mrs. Moody says the English Kennel Club does not recognise truffle hounds, as some look like terriers and some are quite big. "But I'd have a damn good try to train some now if anyone were interested" she says.

GRATIN OF TOMATOES

This is an old Guernsey recipe.

Skin 1 lb. ripe tomatoes, chop 1 large onion and chop a little ham or slightly cooked bacon. Mix with some chopped parsley and a little thyme and a large pinch of salt, add 8 ozs. cooked chopped potatoes. Stir in 1 beaten egg. Put it all into a greased pie dish. Bake in a moderate oven (350 F., Mark 4) for 1 hour.

Mrs. V. James,
Ville-au-Roi, Guernsey.

MR. STOKES'S CHEESE POTATOES

Mash 1 lb. boiled potatoes and add seasoning, $\frac{1}{4}$ pint of milk and 1 oz. grated cheese. Mix well together. Put the potatoes in a greased dish and sprinkle another 1 oz. of grated cheese on top with 1 oz. butter. Bake in a quick oven (400 F., Mark 6) until brown. Serve very hot.

Mr. C. Stokes,
Totland Bay, Isle of Wight.

TOASTED SWEDES AND CHEESE

Take 1 medium sized swede, peel and cut into 2-inch squares, season with salt and pepper and steam until tender. Drain well, mash and mix in 4 – 6 ozs. grated cheese. Put it in a well greased fireproof dish and sprinkle more cheese on top, finish off with breadcrumbs and dots of butter. Bake in a fairly warm oven (350 F., Mark 4) middle shelf, for 20 – 30 minutes until golden brown.

Mrs. E. M. Hayes,
Bournemouth, Hampshire.

GLAZED TURNIPS

Cut some fresh young turnips into rings or shapes about 2 inches in diameter. Spread a saucepan thickly with butter, put in the turnips and cover with about 2 ozs. sugar. Moisten with about $\frac{1}{2}$ pint of good clear stock and simmer very gently over a moderate heat for 45 minutes. When nearly cooked remove the lid and raise the heat to

boil the moisture down to a glaze. Gently roll the turnips in this with great care to avoid breaking the turnips. Serve on a warm dish, in a neat order and pour the glaze over them.

Mrs. R. Dilly,
Carshalton, Surrey.

POTATO POT

Put a layer of dripping in the bottom of a fireproof dish. Wash and slice some potatoes and onions, but not too thick. Put a layer of potatoes in the dish on top of the dripping, add a layer of onions filling the dish with alternate layers of potatoes and onions, finishing with potatoes. Add a knob of dripping on top then mix some gravy, add salt and pepper, stir and add to the casserole. Bake for 1½ hours in a slow oven (325 F., Mark 3). When it is cooked it eats like roast beef and makes a very good meal.

Mrs. M. Ogg,
Sittingbourne, Kent.

SEAKALE

You know what seakale is? Creamy-white, brittle looking sticks with a tight curl of unopened leaf at the top, they are delicious plain-boiled and eaten with melted butter — something like asparagus. Wash it, trim the root part and boil it in salty water for about 20 minutes — a bit less if you like it crisp. Then serve it in lots of melted butter and the strained juice of half a lemon — very good with underdone beef or a tender joint of lamb. One can also munch it raw with cheese like spring onions.

Most of the seakale on sale used to be grown by nurserymen near Worthing, but you can also find it wild on lonely pebbly shores all round the coast. In spring the shoots push their way up as much as three feet between the smooth round pebbles and come up blanched to perfection, as white as leeks or celery.

I have found it myself at Dungeness, but the wild kind does not normally appear till April. This pale, pretty vegetable is also very nice if it is boiled for only 10 minutes then put in a buttered fireproof dish, well drained, coated thick with cheese sauce, then browned in the oven.

CHEESY BREAD AND BUTTER PUDDING

Sprinkle 6 slices of bread and butter with pepper and salt, spread on some made English mustard. Cut it in neat pieces and arrange in a well buttered pie dish. Sprinkle 6 ozs. grated cheese on the bread. Beat 2 eggs in a basin, stir in 1 pint milk and strain over the bread and butter. Allow to stand for 15 minutes then bake it in a hot oven (400 F., Mark 6) for about 40 minutes.

Mrs. A. M. Holland,
Ventnor, Isle of Wight.

OLD-FASHIONED MACARONI CHEESE

Cook 4 ozs. macaroni in salted boiling water until soft. Drain off the excess water; melt 1½ ozs. butter in a saucepan, add 1½ ozs. flour, ½ pint milk, salt and pepper. Heat, stirring until smooth and thick, add to the boiled macaroni, put a layer in a buttered pie dish, grate some cheese and sprinkle on top. Add more macaroni and finish with grated cheese, about 2 ozs. altogether. Dot with butter. Bake until brown.

Mrs. E. M. Wallcroft,
Walthamstow, London.

QUINCE JELLY

My grandmother lived in a cottage on the Sussex Downs, with a garden full of fruit trees, medlars, plums, apples, crab apples, quinces and a walnut tree. We children were fascinated by the large yellow quinces, with a luscious smell but a flavour to set your teeth on edge if you ever bit into one. Our towny friend had never seen fruit growing and when grandma sent us to pick some for jelly-making we told him the gorgeous looking quinces were used by ancient Druids to make people see in the dark, but you had to eat every bit in the middle of the night. He put one in his pocket and that night my brother and I spent ages giggling outside his bedroom door waiting for him to cry. Though he managed to eat it all and his mouth was very sore, he couldn't see in the dark. When grandma offered him a pot of quince jelly to take home to London he burst into tears and never came to stay again.

Wipe the down off the skins of 5 lbs. ripe quinces and chop them roughly into a large preserving pan. Cover with cold water, bring it to the boil and simmer for 2 – 3 hours till the fruit is pulpy. Strain the pulp and liquid through a jelly bag overnight. Do not squeeze it to extract more juice or the jelly will be cloudy. Measure the juice extracted next morning, returning it to the pan with 1 lb. sugar per 1 pint juice. Heat gently, stirring till the sugar melts. Bring to the boil and boil fast for about 15 minutes. Test for setting. It will set when a little jelly spread on a saucer wrinkles when you touch it with the finger. Pour into warm jars, cover with waxed paper and tie down at once.

The resulting jelly should be a glorious clear orangy-red and it is absolutely delicious with pork, game, goose and duck.

Mrs. E. Gregory,
Daily Express.

In the country, when people have no jelly bag they turn a kitchen chair upside down on another chair so the four chair legs are sticking up like posts. You then place a basin on the reversed chair seat, tie a large clean tea towel by the corners to the chair legs, pour the pulp and juice into it to drip through into the basin. It works perfectly.

APPLE CHUTNEY

Put 4 lbs. apples, 2 lbs. sultanas, 1 lb. onions through a mincer. Boil up in ¾ pint of vinegar with 2 teaspoons cayenne pepper, 1 teaspoon salt and 4 teaspoons ground ginger. Then add the sugar. Boil again until it thickens in about 45 minutes. This quantity makes about 10 lbs.

Mrs. A. E. Miller,
Brighton, Surrey.

PUDDING

CHRISTMAS PIE — CHESTNUT FLAN WITH BRANDY

Put a handful of sultanas in a cup and cover with a little brandy to soak for at least 1 hour. Line a 9-inch flan tin with short crust pastry. Mix 1 cup of caster sugar with 3 lightly beaten eggs, add 1 cup single cream and stir. Add ¼ teaspoon ground ginger and ¼ teaspoon cinnamon. Beat in the contents of a 1 lb. tin of chestnut puree until thoroughly mixed and carefully stir in the brandy-soaked sultanas. Pour into the flan tin and cook in the centre of a medium hot oven (375F., Mark 5) for 40 minutes. Serve warm rather than hot with whipped cream. The chestnut flavour is better as the temperature falls. It may be eaten cold.

Mrs. J. Hiles,
Barming, Maidstone, Kent.

COLD JELLIED CHRISTMAS PUDDING

Put ½ cup currants, ½ cup chopped stoned raisins, ½ cup finely chopped sultanas into a bowl. Cover with boiling water and leave until the fruit is plump and soft. Drain, reserve the water. Add ¼ cup mixed peel, ¼ cup chopped nuts and 2 tablespoons brandy. Mix well and leave to stand for 1 hour. Make up the water from the soaked fruits to 2 cups and dissolve 1 lemon jelly in this. Add 1 cup finely crushed ginger nuts and spices to the fruits. Add the jelly and stir well. Pour into a mould and chill until firm. Turn out to serve with brandy sauce or brandy flavoured whipped cream.

Mrs. E. Platt,
Polegate, Sussex.

GINGER PUDDING

Mix 6 ozs. self raising flour with 3 ozs. butter, 2 ozs. caster sugar and ½ teaspoon bicarbonate of soda. Add 1 tablespoon black treacle, 1 new laid egg and ½ teaspoon ginger and mix all well together.

Boil for 2½ hours in a basin topped with foil. Stand this in a pan of boiling water to come half-way up.

Mrs. J. M. Burchett,
Herstmonceux, Sussex.

SUSSEX WELL PUDDING (in a cloth)

Empty 1 lb. self raising flour into a large basin, thoroughly mix in 1 teaspoon salt, 1 lb. washed and dried currants and 8 ozs. butcher's beef suet, grated. Add enough water to make a soft, easy to roll dough. Roll out a large piece of the dough into a round. Put it on one side while you roll out a smaller round about 3 inches less in circumference than the larger round. Place 8 ozs. dark brown sugar in the centre of the smaller round, place 3 ozs. butter on top of the sugar. Pinch up the dough after sealing the dampened edges. Turn this rounded pudding upside down onto the larger round. Pinch up and also seal the edges of the large round, making the entire dough into a large ball. Tie it up in a floured cloth and steam for 6 hours, after placing it in a pan of boiling water. This pudding can be steamed for 3 hours one day and 3 hours the next. When cooked, place gently on a dish being careful that it does not break. To serve, stick a knife into the pudding and it will become covered with a delicious syrup from the sugar.

Lily Astell,
Hastings, Sussex.

Sometimes called Palm Pudding as it was made on Palm Sunday in Sussex.

BLACK CAP PUDDING

Make a good batter pudding (the same as for a Yorkshire pudding). Pick and wash 4 ozs. of currants and lay them in the bottom of a well-buttered mould. Pour the batter into the mould over the currants. Boil for 2 hours. When turned out the currants will be on top.

Miss Carol Edwards,
Broughton, near Stockbridge, Hampshire.

GRANNY'S GOOD GIRL PUDDING

Peel, core and stew 1 lb. apples with about 1 oz. butter and some sugar to taste. Cut a stale loaf into slices to fit neatly in a pint pie dish. Melt 3 ozs. butter, dip the pieces of bread in it to line the dish. When the apples are cooked mash them well. Add 3 tablespoons jam and 2 ozs. brown sugar. Pour the whole mixture into the bread-lined dish. Arrange some breadcrumbs thickly on top of the mixture.

158

Sprinkle with cinnamon and ginger. Bake in a really hot oven (425 F., Mark 7). Cook either in the top or bottom of the oven. Serve hot.

Mrs. E. E. Burnard,
Bournemouth, Hampshire.

DOWSET — A sort of Custard Pie

Take 1 pint of milk and put ¾ of it into a saucepan to boil. Mix 3 tablespoons of flour well with the rest of the cold milk then add the boiling milk to it, stirring it well and boil over a low heat for 5 minutes, stirring all the time. Turn it into a bowl and when nearly cold add 3 well beaten eggs, 6 ozs. sugar, a little grated nutmeg and some salt. Line a pie dish with puff paste, pour in the dowset, grate a little nutmeg on the top and bake in a moderate oven (350 F., Mark 4).

This can be varied by adding 2 ozs. of currants or a grated lemon rind on top.

Mrs. C. J. Harris,
West Ewell, Epsom, Surrey.

This is also called a Lenten Pie in Kent.

GENERAL SATISFACTION

This recipe is from the year 1885.

Line a pie dish with a rich puff pastry, put a layer of preserve on the bottom, then a layer of ginger sponge cakes, then a layer of the following mixture: take ¼ pint milk, 1 oz. butter, 1 tablespoon flour, the grated peel of 1 lemon and boil until it thickens. When cold add 1 beaten egg yolk, a little nutmeg and sugar to taste.

Bake in a moderate oven (350 F., Mark 4). Whisk 3 egg whites to a stiff froth, lay this over the pudding when cooked. Return to the oven for a few minutes.

Mrs. C. J. Harris,
West Ewell, Epsom, Surrey.

VENUS PUDDING WITH WHIPPED CREAM

This is an old family recipe dating back to early Victorian days — very possibly earlier — we ourselves regard it as late Georgian.

Make a custard with 2 eggs and 2 ozs. caster sugar, ½ teaspoon vanilla essence and 1 pint of milk. Leave to cool. Dissolve ½ oz. gelatine in a little hot water. Cover the bottom of a soufflé dish with strawberry jam. Stir the gelatine into the custard when it is nearly cold, then pour into a dish, leave to set in the refrigerator. Cover with whipped cream — about ½ pint. Decorate with angelica leaves and halved glacé cherries.

Mrs. C. José Berridge,
Pulborough, Sussex.

FOLKESTONE PUDDING PIES

Warm 1 pint of milk with either some grated lemon peel or a bay leaf until it has taken on the flavour. Strain. Add 3 ozs. ground rice and boil for 15 minutes, stirring all the time. Remove from the heat and add 3 ozs. butter, 4 ozs. sugar and 6 well beaten eggs. Put aside to cool. Line some patty pans with puff pastry, fill them with the custard and sprinkle a few currants on top. Bake in a moderate oven (350 F., Mark 4) for 20 – 25 minutes.

Mrs. Agnes Lyon,
Kinver, near Stourbridge, Worcestershire.

This is a famous local dish which used to be eaten during Lent.

PALERMO ICE CREAM WITH PISTACCIO NUTS

"A genuine Edwardian favourite always accepted by the best families". Mrs. Champ prepares this by putting 4 ozs. pistaccio nuts into a mortar with a spoonful of sugar and grinding them almost to a paste. Nowadays we would use an electric mixer. She then makes half a pint of old fashioned egg custard and when nearly cold lets it infuse for 30 minutes with the pistaccio nuts then passes the preparation through a sieve and freezes it. To do this I put it in a plastic box in the ice-making compartment of the refrigerator, turning this to maximum cold and leaving the ice cream 3 or 4 hours to set.

Mrs. Champ,
Milstead, near Sittingbourne, Kent.

DIMPAS DAMPAS GRANDMÈRE

This was grandmother's ideal children's dessert, but perfect for adults with a steaming cup of coffee.

Preheat the oven to 375 F., Mark 5. Beat 3 eggs until light, then sprinkle in 1 tablespoon of sugar and continue to beat well. Add flour and salt alternately with 1 tablespoon of milk. Beat thoroughly till smooth. Peel, core and slice thinly 4 green apples. Fold into batter until well covered. Melt 1 tablespoon of butter in a pre-heated glass pie plate. Pour in the batter and bake for 35 minutes in a heated oven. After the first 20 minutes cover with the inverted pie plate and continue to bake for 15 more minutes when the apples should be soft. Remove from the oven and dot immediately with 1 tablespoon butter broken into bits. As soon as the butter has melted sprinkle generously with cinnamon to taste and lemon juice. Allow to cool slightly, but be sure to serve while still warm.

Mrs. L. Howard,
Walton on Thames, Surrey.

CHERRY STIR-UP PUDDING

Wash 1 lb. – 1½ lbs. "Black Bucks" cherries. Mix 8 ozs. self raising flour with a pinch of salt, 3 ozs. shredded suet, 3 ozs. sugar, ¼ pint of milk and the cherries. Tie in a floured pudding cloth and boil in a saucepan for about 2½ hours.

This is a version of the traditional Buckinghamshire Dumpling.

Mrs. P. Bass,
Redlynch, Salisbury, Wiltshire.

"Stir-up" Pudding which is more usually a plum pudding or Christmas pudding containing dried fruit is traditionally made on "Stir Up Sunday", 21 November when the Collect in church begins with the words "Stir up we beseech thee O Lord . . .".

London and Home Counties

Berkshire, Buckinghamshire, Hertfordshire, Middlesex, parts of Surrey and Essex.

Agricultural Produce

Waltham Abbey Glasshouse Cucumbers, Berkshire Pigs, Black Buckinghamshire Cherries, Aylesbury Duckling.

Gastronomic Specialities

Jellied Eels, Smoked Salmon, Greenwich Whitebait, Whelks, Winkles, Gull's Eggs, Bradenham Hams, Freshwater Crayfish.

Confectionery

Chelsea Buns, Muffins, London Buns, Richmond Maids-of-Honour.

STARTERS

SMOKED SALMON

"It's all coming down", said *Mr. Terence Bird*. "We've got a compulsory purchase order". It seemed to me to be all falling down, not to put too fine a point on it, what with the cottages outside boarded up to stop the children breaking the windows and the temporary roof they've got on the smoke-house after the fire before Christmas. *J. Bird & Sons in Pomeroy Street, New Cross, London*, have been famous for years as fish smokers who specialise in salmon, haddock, trout and bloaters. *Mr. Bird* — a huge, healthy looking man with a fine flow of Cockney rhetoric — is one of the real old craftsmen who still use oak and red sawdust for smoking, although most people now buy deal sawdust or a mixture of the two because of the cost, and the big modern smoke firms now have kilns. Birds had been there since 1850 and his grandfather started it, but haddock smoking in this part of London goes back at least to the eighteenth century and there are lots of small traditional smoke-houses dotted all over East and South-East London. It's a real Cockney speciality and London salmon smokers are often claimed to be the best in Europe.

Mr. Bird was selling his smoked salmon at 16s. a lb. wholesale in Billingsgate fish market and every bit of it was booked the day I visited them, like the delicious smoked trout he was doing for a firm there. I went into a kind of shed with a corrugated iron roof, huge fridge, wooden tubs of brine for salting bloaters, rows of haddocks hanging out to dry and — lots of smoke. He had eight craftsmen left — the last of the few. "How'd you like to work in here, love? It's Dickensian" they said. Well, it is a bit . . .

The fish comes every day in a lorry from Billingsgate. The haddocks are cleaned, split and pickled in brine "the details of that are secret," he said, " as everybody has his own timing for it".

They are then strung on rods to drain and finally put in the smoke-hole for about 6 hours. "But in a couple of months it will all be gone," he said, "they are putting up council flats".

Smoked salmon sliced wafer thin and served just as it is, uncooked, but with a good juicy hunk of lemon to squeeze over it, is a foolproof and always impressive start to a meal.

It also makes delicious brown bread and butter sandwiches especially good if one squeezes a little lemon juice over them at the last moment.

GEHATKEH LEBER

Fry 8 ozs. finely chopped onions in poultry fat and grill 1 lb. chicken livers until all the blood has dropped off (otherwise it is not kosher). Put the liver and onions through the mincer with 3 shelled hard boiled eggs. Add salt and pepper. Serve cold on lettuce leaves.

Mrs. R. Samuelson,
Golders Green, London.

POTTED MEAT

Well soak and scrape an unsmoked ham shank and ½ cow heel. Cut up 1 lb. shin beef and 1 large onion, add 1 pint of water. Put all together and simmer gently for 3 hours. Pour off the liquid, mince all the meat. Season it well with salt, pepper and ½ teaspoon anchovy essence. Add enough of the cooking liquid to make a stiffish mixture and put into wet moulds.

This recipe has been used in my family for over 60 years with great success.

Mrs. H. Mauson,
Bedford Park, London.

KING'S SOUP

Slice 4 large Spanish onions very thinly and simmer them in a little water until soft. Add 4 pints of milk and simmer for another 30 minutes, adding a blade of mace and 4 ozs. butter. Just before serving pour a little of the liquid on 2 beaten egg yolks, stir well and add to the contents of the saucepan. Heat up, but do not boil. Add some chopped parsley and salt to taste. Serve with freshly made diced toast.

Mrs. W. Rapoport,
Croydon, Surrey.

CREAMY CHEESE SOUP

Melt 2 tablespoons of butter and soften in it 1 tablespoon minced onion, over a low heat. Blend in 2 tablespoons flour, gradually add

½ cup of carrot purée, 1 pint chicken stock and 1 pint milk. Cook until the soup is slightly thickened. Stirring well add a cup of grated cheddar cheese, stir away from the heat until the cheese has melted. Season with salt, freshly ground pepper and serve at once. Sprinkle with chopped parsley.

Mrs. W. Rapoport,
Croydon, Surrey.

"SPLOSH" — LEEK SOUP

One of thirteen children I remember eating this soup from basins, around the kitchen range on cold winter nights — the "Splosh" came from the sound of the lengths of leeks, sliding off the spoon back into the basin. I still enjoy this soup, even in a soup plate.

Cut some leeks into strips and some potatoes into cubes. Cook in enough water to cover the vegetables, season well. Cook until the potatoes have gone to a mash and the leeks are cooked (about 30 – 45 minutes). Add ½ pint of milk and a good knob of butter, serve piping hot.

Mrs. J. Wren,
Sunbury-on-Thames, Middlesex.

BAKED SOUP

Cut 1 lb. shin beef into small pieces. Put them in a deep fireproof dish with 1 teacup dried peas (previously soaked for several hours). Add a stick of chopped celery, 1 sliced onion, 2 tablespoons rice, pepper, a little nutmeg and 2 quarts of water. Put the lid on the dish and cook the contents in a moderate oven (350 F., Mark 4) for at least 3 hours. The secret of the success of this soup is in its long slow cooking.

Miss H. Taylor,
Rayleigh, Essex.

STEAK AND KIDNEY BROTH

This recipe is one which has been handed down in my family for well over a hundred years. It is for a most sustaining broth, and I defy anyone to take just one sniff when it is cooking and not to drool! Nothing else to me smells quite so delicious, anything more simple or more aromatic, I have yet to find.

Cut up 12 ozs. steak and kidney, dice 8 ozs. carrots, 8 ozs. turnip, 1 leek and 1 onion. Put all into a large saucepan. Shred 4 ozs. brussel sprouts. Add all to the steak and kidney together with 8 ozs. peas, 1 tablespoon barley, 1 tablespoon lentils, 1 teaspoon marjoram and 1 teaspoon thyme. Cover amply with water. Season well and simmer gently for about 2½ – 3 hours. Serve with suet dumplings simmered in the broth for about 20 minutes.

Mrs. M. Falcon,
Wokingham, Berkshire.

FISH

CRAYFISH

Years ago English people used to have vast crayfish picnics, and eighteenth century cookery books have lots of recipes for them. In Sweden they still think them a greater delicacy than oysters, and from midnight on August 7 when crayfish netting begins, to the end of September everyone has lovely crayfish parties, drinking vodka and eating huge pyramids of these little scarlet prawns with toast and butter in the garden under the moon. Everyone shells his own and the trees are decorated with Chinese lanterns and paper streamers. The crayfish, or *écrevisse*, is a fresh water crustacean, 3 – 4 inches long, brilliant scarlet when cooked, and said to have a finer flavour than even the most exquisite lobster. So great is the French appetite for crayfish that they import them in great aerated tanks from behind the Iron Curtain and now in Lithuania they are opening experimental crayfish farms, hoping to breed them artificially for the French market. One thinks of the exquisite *pain d'écrevisses*, the sauce Nantua, of great Paris restaurants, where they have special crayfish tanks for customers, for they are a classic ingredient for many dishes of the *haute cuisine*. But I have never seen any here. Greedy millionaires would probably have them flown over from France at great cost. They would be wrong. There are masses of crayfish in English trout streams all over the country from Gloucestershire to Yorkshire and beyond.

What started me off on them was a large dedicated-looking French woman I met at a party who says she catches them in the home counties at week-ends. I hated her instantly. "*Ah, ma chère*," she says in a crisp, slightly patronising, voice, "it's far better here than in France — all French streams are over-fished and you English and you didn't even know that!" It nettled me. How do you get them, I said cautiously. "With a *saladier* and an old kipper of course. You just drop it over a bridge." What bridge she was not prepared to say and I am not either. I got a lot last Sunday on the strict understanding that I didn't interfere with the trout fishing and didn't tell you where it is, but it is less than 25 miles from London. We met at 10 a.m. in the yard of the local pub, all got up in trousers and gumboots, though it's a paddling job really. Frank and Florence and me. I can't tell you their other name for security reasons as he is secretary of the trout fishing club. I kept thinking how good they were going to be, boiled in seasoned white wine then drained and served piping hot with parsley, I wouldn't say no skill is required in catching them since before lunch we didn't even see any — we dropped our nets of stinking fish and perforated cocoa tins garnished with kipper temptingly among the water weeds, but caught nothing. But it's full of them, everyone said coldly.

We drove down narrow lanes with trees meeting overhead, peered into limpid water full of minnows, climbed over electrified wire fences dodging cow pats and working our way upstream. Once we turned a corner and came on a huge eighteenth century manor house half asleep in the sunshine at the edge of a lake. Then, after lunch in the shadows under a footbridge, and hiding under the stones in the shade of a bank and an overhanging elder, we at last found them. They crowded excitedly into my prawn gin after the largest, smelliest bit of fish, shoved their heads into the tins, got stuck in our old gooseberry netting. And we pulled them up struggling. But Florence caught the most with a green butterfly net she bought for 1s. 3d. in the village. It's not really *sportif*, it's kitchen fishing. One of the cows named Agnes, with whom Frank and Florence have been on friendly terms when trout fishing, followed us hopefully, sighing from time to time, peering short-sightedly into the bucket, though she never actually drank them. Once home I put them in the bath and they splashed about fighting or making love to one another. I'm not sure which.

Put them into boiling salted water and they turn a brilliant scarlet and die instantly. You boil them for about 10 minutes. If you have done them in white wine you can pour warm brandy over the hot, drained crayfish and set it on fire. Then eat them when the flames die down. If eaten cold, they should be left in the wine in which they were cooked. It will make a basis for a very good fish soup.

OYSTERS

Roll the shelled oysters in some arrowroot. Dip them in egg and then in breadcrumbs. Fry in hot cooking fat until a light, golden brown. They are delicious and unbelievably filling.

Mrs. R. M. Seaber,
Newbury, Berkshire.

TOASTED COD AND SEEMED POTATOES

Skin, bone and mince 1 lb. white fish finely. Mix it with 4 beaten eggs and heat, stirring until the eggs begin to scramble. When the fish has cooked put the mixture into an ovenproof dish. Top with 3 – 4 ozs. grated cheese. Bake in a slow oven (300 F., Mark 2) for 20 – 30 minutes, or until thoroughly cooked and brown on top.

For the seemed potatoes, slice 1½ lbs. potatoes and put them into a fireproof dish with a sprinkling of salt and a small knob of butter. Put them in a slow oven (300 F., Mark 2) until cooked.

Sarah Green,
London S.W.8.

BAKED SOLES

Clean, skin and well wash 2 soles, then dry them thoroughly in a cloth. Brush them with beaten egg, sprinkle with breadcrumbs mixed with a little minced parsley. Lay them in a large flat baking dish with the light side uppermost. They must not be put one on top of the other. Melt 4 ozs. butter and pour it over the fish and bake for 20 minutes in a moderate oven (350 F., Mark 4). Take some of the gravy that flows from the fish, add a glass of sherry, some lemon juice, salt and cayenne pepper. Give it one boil, skim, then pour it under the fish and serve.

Mrs. E. Cook,
South Harrow, Middlesex.

LONDON JELLIED EELS

Nobody knows how old the jellied eel trade is. In Lovatt Lane, Billingsgate, London, outside the wholesale fish market one can see the jellied eel experts cooking them in the traditional wide enamel basins. There are Cockney families who have been in the business, either of cooking or of selling eels, for five generations and it is often said that babies are weaned on jellied eels in the East End of London. Robert Cooke, the Jellied Eel King who had an eel and pie stall years and years ago in the Horseferry Road, left £42,000, a vast fortune in those days. *Mr. Joseph Pegg's* whelk and jellied ell stall is now one of the most famous in London, it has been standing at the top end of Shaftesbury Avenue outside the Marquis of Granby public house for well over 40 years. A lot of the theatricals working locally stop there for a quick saucer of whelks, while they are trying to get a taxi. The eel fanciers have cold jellied eels with a piece of bread and butter for dinner off the stall nearly every other day. Have you ever tried them? It is certainly a real Cockney dish for wherever you get a few Cockneys you find the eel stalls starting up. There are still a few of the old eel and pie shops left in South London. If you go and ask for "pie and liquor" you get a basin with lovely green gravy with parsley in it as well as mashed potatoes.

JELLIED EELS

Clean and skin 2 lbs. eels and cut in 3-inch lengths. Put them in a pan with 2 pints cold water, some salt and pepper and a large sliced Spanish onion, 1 tablespoon vinegar, a bayleaf and some parsley. Simmer for 1 hour or longer until the eel is tender. Strain the liquor and put it in a pan with the slightly whisked white of 2 eggs, simmer it for about 2 minutes then strain it through a cloth. This clears the liquor. Line a basin with bits of eel, pour the liquor over and let it set. Some people add a little sherry to it but my gran never did.

Mr. S. Hayes,
Bermondsey, London.

EEL PIE

Skin and wash the eels, remove the heads and tails. Cut the fish into pieces 3 inches long, season with pepper, salt and nutmeg. Put a rim of puff paste around the dish, put in the eels with 1 chopped onion, a few cloves, add a little stock, a pie funnel and cover with puff paste, brush over the pastry crust with beaten egg. Bake first in a very hot oven (425 F., Mark 7) for about 15 minutes till the pastry is risen. Then reduce the heat to moderate (350 F., Mark 4). Bake until the eel feels tender when tested through a slit in the pie. Lay a piece of greaseproof paper over the pastry to prevent it from becoming too brown. Meanwhile make a stock by simmering the trimmings from the fish etc. Thicken with butter and flour, add lemon juice, strain and pour into the pie through a funnel.

Mrs. G. Allen,
Hambledon, near Godalming, Surrey.

Eel pies used to be a speciality of Richmond, Surrey, where the small Eel Pie Island in the middle of the Thames is called after this once popular delicacy.

CHEESE AND FISH PIE

This recipe was one of my grandmother's favourite supper dishes which was greatly appreciated by her bridge friends on Saturday evenings about 1933.

Bring 1½ lbs. filleted cod to the boil then simmer until flaky. Retaining some of the liquid remove all bones and place the fish in a basin. Add salt and pepper.

To make a cheese sauce: melt 1 oz. of butter in a pan, add 1 tablespoon cornflour then add 8 ozs. grated cheese gradually. Stir in some milk, 1 beaten egg and some of the fish water until a creamy consistency is obtained. Add a large knob of butter.

Line a shallow casserole dish with short crust pastry. Distribute the fish evenly over the pastry then sprinkle with freshly ground pepper. Pour the cheese sauce over the mixture, sprinkle with Parmesan cheese. Cook in a hot oven (400 F., Mark 6) for about 30 minutes until brown and bubbling.

It makes an excellent supper dish on its own, or as starter to a meal, or a savoury to end a meal.

Julia Griffiths,
Catford, London, S.E.6.

A COLD LOBSTER MOULD

Chop up a cooked lobster finely. Bring 1 pint of milk to the boil, stir in 2 ozs. butter. Beat up 2 whole eggs and 2 extra egg yolks, gradually stir in the hot milk. Season with salt, pepper and cayenne pepper. Pour 1 teaspoon cooking oil into a fancy mould or "shape", swill it round to coat it. Arrange the lobster pieces in it, pour the custard mixture over. Stir again. Stand the mould in a tin of hot water to come half-way up. Bake in a very moderate oven (325 F., Mark 3) until the custard is well set. When cold turn it out of the mould, serve plain or garnished with rings of lemon, or cucumber or tomato, with or without a fish sauce. (Tartare sauce etc.)

Mrs. J. M. Munson,
Shoreditch, London.

FRIED HERRING — To be eaten cold.

Cut off the head and open the herring by cutting it down the back (it is then easy to remove the bones). Salt it all over, cover well with flour on both sides and fry in hot fat until it is crisp each side. It is eaten cold and is very good.

Lynette Ashley,
Brentwood, Essex.

LONDON SMOKED HADDOCK IN MILK

Mr. and Mrs. Phillips smoke haddock, cod fillets and bloaters at the back of their sparkling white fish shop in Lower Road, Rotherhithe. People come from all over London for them for the fish is not artificially dyed, just pale and lovely with a superb flavour. You can tell a London smoked haddock because it is split from the head down and has the bone on the left, while a Scottish smoked haddock is split from the tail up and has a bone on the right. It makes lovely kedgeree and is delicious for supper just cooked in milk with a poached egg on top.

Put the fish skin side up under the hot griller for a moment then smack it all over with the palm of your hand and the grey skin will come off easily. Then put the haddock in a frying pan with about ½ pint of milk and 1 teaspoon of dry mustard. Simmer till tender. Keep it warm while you stir a heaped teaspoon of cornflour into 2 tablespoons of cold milk. Add this to the fish liquor, heat, stirring till you have a creamy sauce to pour over the fish. Top with poached eggs.

Mrs. Constance Phillips says fresh haddock roes are lovely, rolled in flour and fried to eat piping hot with sliced pickled cucumbers. Skate knobs are another London delicacy in which *Mrs. Phillips* specialises. Luscious hunks of fish which are delicious egged and crumbed and fried. Or stewed with lots of parsley, rather as they do hot eels and mash in the old eel and pie shops. There are still some left in Bermondsey and Rotherhithe.

ARNOLD BENNETT'S OMELETTE

One of the gastronomic specialities of the Savoy Hotel is its smoked haddock omelette, a real London dish created for Arnold Bennett in 1937 by the chef of the Savoy Grill, Jean-Baptiste Virlogeux. He was known as "Rocco" in Arnold Bennett's novel "Imperial Palace". This is the original recipe.

Mix 3 eggs with a tablespoon of Gruyère cheese in $\frac{1}{4}$ inch cubes. Flavour with a little salt and some freshly ground pepper. Add 2 tablespoons of smoked haddock cut in small cubes, a little more pepper but no salt. Beat it with a fork. Melt a little butter in the frying pan. Tip in the mixture, lifting the edges with a fork so the runny top flows underneath and begins to set. If you don't know how to turn it over whole, then brown the runny top lightly under the grill. It should still be rather fluid when served on a dish. Cover it with cheese sauce. Sprinkle grated cheese on top. Brown it once more under the grill.

The Savoy Grill,
London.

MEAT, POULTRY AND GAME

BUTCHERS' BACKSLANG

How about a nice *Birerof*, or a *Niolris of Feeb* for dinner on Sunday, as London butchers say in the old Cockney backslang, when they don't want customers to know what they are talking about? Or, in plain English, a forerib or sirloin of beef.

A lot of London butchers still use backslang and at Smithfield and Spitalfields wholesale markets they still talk about a *delo woc* — or an old cow — and a *tib o' the delo*, or a bit of the old. I know one South London butcher who speaks it fluently. *Erf yennep* or three-pence used to be a common expression, like *toggams* for maggots. Inverted numbers, *eno*, *owt* and *erth* and so on are normal, but *yob*, for an uncouth boy, seems to be the only backslang which has become part of common speech.

ROAST BEEF

To get a good Sunday joint you have to have a good butcher. And for my palate — if I were pushing the boat out a bit — it would be sirloin on the bone — a joint that looks like a giant cutlet — and not topside, which eats dry and is really better casseroled or pot roasted. Eaten with fresh-made English mustard, cooked rather rare and still pink and juicy in the middle it would be better than duck or chicken — and much more expensive.

Roast it 15 minutes per lb., in a preheated hot oven (425 F., Mark 7). Joints under 4 lb. slightly longer. Add salt only after it is cooked and roast the meat on a rack for about the last half hour so you can slip your dish of Yorkshire pudding under it and allow the meat to drip on this in cooking. Serve with roast potatoes and the traditional mashed buttered parsnips, horseradish sauce and hot gravy. When it is done put it on a warm dish and let it stand 15 minutes on the edge of the warm oven to set and become easier to carve. You can drink almost anything with roast beef — the most exquisite claret or Burgundy you can afford. Connoisseurs say that its plain simple flavour sets off an expensive wine to perfection.

In Ireland they mix the gravy with strong cold tea — a startling but excellent idea, for it gives a good colour to the gravy. Pour the fat out of the tin without disturbing the sediment. Sprinkle in a little flour, mix well, when it has coloured, gradually add some strong cold tea (obviously without milk). Cook it 5 minutes, stirring. Strain and season.

Of the sirloin, the chump end sold with the undercut is the best of all, but the price will probably be astronomical. If you want a really large joint the aitchbone (known as the Mouse Buttock in some parts of England) is a huge piece which makes a good family roast. Whole roasted onions are delicious with roast beef — and said to cure a cold. You want one of those huge Spanish onions per person. Leave the skin on but cut the whiskers off. Put them in a roasting tin with no more than an inch of water. Bake them with the joint in the oven. They are done if they are soft when you squeeze them. To eat them pull back the skin and eat the hot onion with salt, pepper and a pat of butter.

For Horseradish Sauce: beat up $\frac{1}{4}$ pint double cream with 2 tablespoons milk. Add pepper and salt and gradually stir in 3 teaspoons lemon juice and 2 level teaspoons grated horseradish. Add $\frac{1}{2}$ teaspoon icing sugar.

MY MOTHER'S OXTAIL SHAPE

I make this dish every holiday time including Christmas as it is such a change from the other cold meats. It keeps like a dream for ages without drying out if the basin it has been "shaped" and cooled in is replaced on top of it after each use.

Wash an oxtail and $1\frac{1}{2}$ lbs. shin beef. Cut the beef into 2-inch cubes and put it all into an appropriate sized saucepan, an iron bottomed one if possible and only just cover it with water, bring to the boil and simmer until half done in about forty-five minutes to one hour. Add some sea salt (Essex Maldon salt) and coarse ground black pepper to taste. It is done when the meat pulls easily off the bone with a fork and finger. Put the broken up meat into a fireproof glass dish, strain enough of the stock over this just to cover. When cool put it in the refrigerator and next day you have a lovely fine "shape".

Mrs. Dickie Foster Kemp,
London, N.W.8.

ROASTED MINCE

This makes a delicious meal for four people if served with creamed or whole potatoes and creamed turnips. A nice sweet to follow would be apple dumplings, which can be baked while the oven is being used.

Grease a meat tin. Put 1½ lbs. lean minced beef, 8 ozs. chopped lean bacon, 6 ozs. breadcrumbs, with salt and pepper, 1 teaspoon of chopped parsley and a few drops of Worcester sauce into a bowl. Add a beaten egg and if necessary a little milk. Mix well together. Put the mixture in the prepared tin, cover with greaseproof paper and bake for two hours in a hot oven (400 F., Mark 6).

Mrs. V. V. Courtenay,
Walthamstow, London.

TURNIPS IN MILK

Peel 1½ lbs. turnips and slice very thinly. Place in a small fireproof dish with pepper, salt and enough milk to cover the turnips. Bring to boiling point and cover the pan with a lid before placing it in the oven.

Ian Smith,
Colliers Wood, London.

HAM CAKE

Line a shallow fireproof dish with pastry. Mince some ham trimmings and mix with 1 grated onion. Lay them in the bottom of the dish. Make four wells in the mixture and crack into each one a raw egg. Cover the dish with pastry, brush over with a little milk and bake in a moderate oven (350 F., Mark 4) until golden brown. Eat hot or cold.

Mrs. F. E. Norris,
Edmonton, London.

One can sometimes buy a ham bone cheaply from good grocers, the trimmings from the bone are usually plenty for a ham pie or cake.

VEAL CASSEROLE WITH FORCEMEAT BALLS

For the forcemeat balls mix some soft white breadcrumbs, some chopped parsley, salt, pepper, a pinch of garlic salt, some finely chopped onion with a beaten egg and milk to bind. Shape it into balls which roll lightly in flour and put them to one side until the meat is prepared.

Cut 1½ lbs. veal fillets into pieces, roll in seasoned flour, remove the rind from 12 ozs. bacon, lightly fry the bacon on both sides and remove. Place the veal in the bacon fat (more dripping may be necessary) brown on both sides, remove, now fry 1 large onion lightly and place in a casserole dish in layers with the veal and bacon. Season to taste. Thicken the residue in the frying pan with a little cornflour, adding stock or water as required (meatcubes may be added for flavour), also a little browning. When slightly thickened pour over the contents in the casserole. Place in a hot oven (375 F., Mark 5). Turn down to 350 F., Mark 4 after 1½ hours. Leave for a further hour. Add the forcemeat balls, return to the oven for another 20 minutes. Serve with creamed or roast potatoes and green vegetables. Sufficient for four persons.

Julia Griffiths,
Catford, London, S.E.6.

AYLESBURY DUCK

There's a pair of white duckboots in the County Museum in Aylesbury. These have nothing to do with poultry, are ankle high white canvas (or "duck") slippers which were worn by ladies some hundred years ago with a crinoline. What is an Aylesbury duck? It is that delicious white Jemima Puddleduck breed with pale yellow feet that gets so fat in early youth. At the Experimental Poultry Feeding Station 2 miles outside Aylesbury, at Stoke Mandeville, they say the bird is perfect killed and eaten at exactly 8 weeks old. "You have only about three days to work on for full flavour" they told me "earlier they are immature, wait any longer and they begin casting their 'stubby' feathers and are full of pens and uneatable then till 14 weeks". The amateur must rely on a good retailer to tell the age of a duck since a 1 or 2 year old bird is often the same size as a duckling.

They have roasted duckling with the traditional apple sauce, green peas and sage and onion stuffing every day at the Bull's Head in Aylesbury, this being the speciality of the house. For the Bull's Head is the scene of Aylesbury's annual Duck Dinner when the mayor and corporation solemnly partake of roast duckling to the accompaniment of pipe and drums and a troop of Morris Dancers from the nearby village of Whitchurch.

ROAST GOOSE WITH APRICOT STUFFING

Also suitable for an Aylesbury Duckling.

Cut 4 ozs. dried apricots into small pieces, soak overnight. Drain and stir in 2 ozs. breadcrumbs, a pinch of mixed spice, ½ oz. melted butter, the grated rind of a lemon. Lastly add a beaten egg. Having removed the grated rind and pith from the lemon put it in from the other end of the bird against the apricot stuffing. Roast the goose as usual for 30 minutes and pour off the excess fat. Then pour a breakfast cup of cider over the crop. Continue to roast and baste in a moderate oven (350 F., Mark 4). Cooking time, 25 minutes per lb. stuffed weight.

Mrs. L. S. Wills,
Knightsbridge, London.

See page 68 North of England for Roast Goose.

MASHED POTATOES WITH CHESTNUTS

Cut a slit in the flat side of each chestnut, put them in a meat tin and bake for 10 minutes with enough water to cover the bottom. Take off the shells and the brown skin while hot. Now put the chestnuts in enough slightly salted water to cover and cook gently for 20 minutes. Cook some potatoes, mash them with a knob of butter and a little pepper and salt and then mix them with the chestnuts. Nice with brussels sprouts.

Mrs. I. Stewart,
Chelmsford, Essex.

GROUSE STUFFED WITH BANANAS

Peel and mash 2 bananas and mix in 1 teaspoon black pepper, $\frac{1}{2}$ teaspoon salt and $\frac{1}{2}$ teaspoon lemon juice. Stuff the grouse with the mixture and roast in the usual way.

Mrs. S. L. Wills,
Knightsbridge, London.

See page 68 North of England for Roast Grouse.

JUGGED PIGEONS

Boil 4 pigeon livers for about 10 minutes then mince. Mix with 1 teaspoon chopped parsley, the yolks of 2 hard boiled eggs, the chopped peel of 1 lemon, 1 oz. suet, some breadcrumbs, pepper, salt and grated nutmeg. Mix in a little butter and 1 raw egg. With this stuff 4 pigeons, including their crops, dip them in warm water, dredge with pepper and salt. Put them in a jar with 1 head of celery, a bunch of sweet herbs, 4 cloves, some mace and a glass of white wine. Cover the jar closely and set it in a pan of boiling water for 3 hours, or in a dish of water in a very moderate oven (325 F., Mark 3). When cooked strain the gravy into a stew pan, stir in a knob of butter rolled in flour. Cook until thick and pour over the pigeons. Garnish with slices of lemon.

Mrs. I. Smith,
Swindon, Wiltshire.

ROOK PIE (an Old Essex dish)

Order 12 young rooks from the local rook catcher. With a sharp knife remove the breasts only. Coat these with seasoned flour, slice a large onion and fry them together till golden brown. Cut 1 lb. fat streaky bacon into strips. Arrange with the breast meat and the fried onions in layers in a pie dish. Add ½ pint port wine, the grated rind of a lemon and a bunch of savoury herbs to ½ pint stock, pour it over the contents and cover the dish with puff pastry, brushing the top with egg or milk. Decorate with 4 washed feet sticking out of the centre of the pie to show the contents and bake for 1 hour. Sufficient for six portions.

Mrs. Whitehouse,
Bursledon, Hampshire.

JUGGED HARE WITH FORCEMEAT BALLS

Make 8 ozs. good forcemeat.* Divide the hare into joints and put it in a deep earthenware jar with ½ lb. beef steak and ½ lb. fat bacon. Hare and beef in layers, and the bacon between. Season with mixed herbs and the rind of half a lemon, pepper and salt. Pour over some water or stock. Cover the jar and bake in a moderate oven (350 F., Mark 4) for 3½ hours. Put the forcemeat balls in during the last 30 minutes. Ten minutes before the hare is served add a glass of port. Be careful to lift the balls out carefully so as not to break them. Send red currant jelly to the table.

* For the forcemeat:—If the liver of the hare is perfectly sound, boil it gently for 6 minutes, mince it finely and mix with 4 tablespoons of flour and mixed herbs, 2 teaspoons grated lemon rind. Mix the dry ingredients together then work in 2 ozs. butter and 2 egg yolks. Everything used in this forcemeat must be perfectly fresh or a very unpleasant flavour may be given to the dish.

I used to look forward to this dish coming in from school before the First World War.

Mrs. D. Stubbs,
Reading, Berkshire.

BOILED PORK

The most outrageous and lovely hat I have ever seen in my life belonged to *Becca Matthews*, the Pearly Queen of Hampstead, and was in blue velvet with 15 enormous ostrich feathers on it in orange, green, blue, purple and peuce. I have never tried on anything more becoming.

It was some years ago when I found her sitting behind the lace curtains of her nice little cottage sewing the pearl buttons on her shoes. She and *Bert*, her husband, the Pearly King, were going to the donkey races. *Mrs. Matthews* told me she thought that donkeys were coming back, for the races at any rate. A most charming old lady I fell completely for her even before I tried on her gorgeous hat.

She told me she had to be careful when it rains as the feathers come out of curl and have to be re-twiddled with a knife.

Mrs. Matthews told me she favoured a bit of boiling bacon for dinner or a nice piece of hand and spring of pork, something you can have a go at, eaten hot the first day with pease pudding "and then I've got a bit cold next day to take to the donkey races".

A hand or front leg of pork can be boiled 30 minutes per lb. It usually takes about 2½ hours and should be put into boiling water then, after bringing it to the boil again, the liquid should be skimmed. When it is clear again add some carrots, leeks, onions, 2 cloves and a pinch of herbs and boil till tender. It is usually served with carrots cooked with the meat and covered in parsley sauce. Pease pudding can be bought in tins but if you want to make your own there's a recipe in the North of England section. You can buy the pork either fresh or slightly salted in which case it will be pink like ham when cooked.

BONED STUFFED LEG OF PORK

Get the butcher to open a 8–9 lb. leg on the inside and take out the bone. The leg should not be too boney. Fill the space with a stuffing made from 1 lb. minced beef, 1 chopped onion, 8 ozs. chopped mushrooms and breadcrumbs. Bind the stuffing together with 2 eggs. Make the stuffing in a roll as big as a rolling pin and place it right down the inside leg. This will help soak the inside which is often raw. Tie up with several pieces of string. Bake for 2½–3 hours in a moderate oven (350 F., Mark 4). Cover the leg with foil. For the last 30 minutes uncover the leg and turn down the heat so as to let the leg brown.

Mrs. A. Payne,
Trowbridge, Wiltshire.

APRICOT STUFFING FOR A HOT ROASTED HAM

Wash and drain 1 lb. dried apricots, clip them with scissors into small pieces. Melt 4 tablespoons of butter in a saucepan, add to this ½ cup chopped celery, ½ cup chopped parsley and a finely chopped onion. Cook for a few minutes. Then add 4 cupfuls of fine dry white breadcrumbs, salt and the apricots. Stir together for some minutes till well mixed. With this mixture stuff a boned, partly cooked and skinned ham. Then put it in a meat tin and bake the roast first in a very hot oven (450 F., Mark 8) then reduce the heat and continue baking in a moderately slow oven (325 F., Mark 3).

Mrs. W. Cooper,
East Sheen, London.

The ham or gammon should be soaked for 12 hours — or longer if very salty, then put in a pan with fresh cold water to cover. Bring to the boil, simmer 10 minutes per lb. and 10 minutes over. Remove the string, strip off the rind, stuff the ham or gammon as above. The fat should be coated thickly with brown sugar, or have some honey poured over it before roasting. It may be basted with stout or cider.

Black Bradenham Hams were once a speciality of the Buckinghamshire village of that name, though nowadays they are really prepared elsewhere, it is an expensive delicacy, coal black on the outside and dark red inside, and pickled in treacle.

LENTILS WITH BACON RASHERS

Having lived in the south for over forty years I have never heard of Londoners say they have heard of "Lentils and Bacon". We always had them in the north of England and still do today.

Boil 8 ozs. lentils for 30 minutes and when cooked strain them and season well with salt and pepper. Serve them with bacon rashers, pouring a little of the bacon fat onto the lentils.

Mrs. M. Garralty,
Kensington, London.

BERKSHIRE STUFFED MELT

This recipe was used by my great grandmother, and would be over 100 years old, and comes from Berkshire. With other cooked vegetables it made a main meal in the old days.

Mix together some diced potato, some pieces of bacon chopped into small pieces, 2 chopped onions, sage or parsley, salt and pepper. Stuff a pig's "melt" with this mixture and sew it around with cotton. Put it into a moderate oven on a flat tin greased with pork dripping and bake for 30–40 minutes. Turn onto a warm plate to serve and remove the cotton.

Mrs. F. M. Stevens,
Windlesheen, Surrey.

PAIL DINNERS

At Leighton Buzzard I recently found a man who still paints those brightly coloured roses and castles on the narrow boats. There are still a few left carrying coal to the paper mills and to a jam factory in London from the village of Croxley, near Coventry. The whole round trip takes about a week. Several boats passed while I was there, linked in loaded pairs with long-haired men at the tiller and sometimes with a lean, shaggy dog following them along the towpath. There are no horses now — they use diesel engines — but the boats' cratches which support the long planks and sheeting are still brilliantly painted. Some of the cabins still have lace edged plates hung thick around the walls and are all decorated with fairytale castles. *Joe Harrison*, who works for the Wyvern Shipping Company, a small firm on the canal bank, does them with a free hand and uses ordinary gutsy marine paints in the traditional manner. I bought one of his painted buckets for my own kitchen, it is grass green with a scarlet base and handle and there are big blue, yellow and red roses done thick all over it. But there aren't many working boats left now and when I got there he had just finished doing the two back panels of somebody's Mini estate van with two large bunches of yellow roses.

The great gastronomic favourite of the old narrow boatmen was the "Pail Dinner". It is very practical if space is limited for the entire dinner could be cooked in one dinner pail or bucket. The cook used to stand a can or an old 7 lb. jam jar in the bottom of the pail, filling it with a layer of turnips and cut rabbit or bacon hock, then fingers of carrots and parsnip. She filled it and the bucket with water and brought it all gently to the boil while she made a lid of suet pastry which was laid across the simmering meat and vegetables. By the time the pastry had risen the peeled potatoes could be put on top, then more pastry. On top finally she put some peeled apples, tied a cloth on top and left it for about 2 hours to cook. It was delicious. Hot broth, then meat and vegetables in suet pastry and finally a hot apple pudding all ready at once.

Pot pies done in a heavy iron saucepan were another old favourite on the inland waterways. And they used to be dab hands at the old bag puddings. These are boiled suet puddings, often filled with beefsteak and mushrooms, made in a floured cloth instead of a basin. The cloth was hung from a wooden spoon in boiling water or a broth to cook.

Sixty or seventy years ago in most Buckinghamshire villages at pig killing time people used also to make Bucks. Backbone Pie. As *Mr. J. S. Macer Wright* of Chesham, Buckinghamshire writes, "the day after the pig was killed it was cut into joints. Some were given to neighbours; the hams were put to be cured, and the chunky pieces of the backbone, with quite a lot of meat left on, were saved for the pie which was flavoured with sage and decorated with pastry leaves". Buckinghamshire dumplings made from liver, suet pastry, bacon and sage and onions, are still popular. They are not unlike the Bishops Stortford Pork Pluggers, Bedfordshire Clangers and the Buckinghamshire Bacon Badgers for which we have had so many recipes from this part of the country.

BUCKINGHAMSHIRE BACON BADGER

I often make a "Bacon Badger" and think back to one of my grandmother's favourites, which she steamed in a large saucepan on the old black cooking range.

Wash and chop a leek and some raw or cooked bacon, mix with pepper and chopped herbs. Spread it over some suet pastry and roll it up in a Swiss roll. Tie in greaseproof paper and a pudding cloth. If there was any left over it was sliced, when cold, and fried.

Mrs. J. Payne,
High Wycombe, Buckinghamshire.

BERKHAMSTED BACON DUMPLING

Mix 1 lb. flour with 8 ozs. suet and salt and pepper. Peel and chop 1 large onion and ¾ lb. cooked bacon and mix it all together — meat, vegetables and pastry — with a little water. Make into a roll, like you would for a plum duff. Put in a floured cloth, boil gently for 1 hour.

Mrs. L. A. Meads,
Berkhamsted, Hertfordshire.

"SAVOURY DUCKS"

Mince or chop 1 lb. pig's liver not too finely together with 8 ozs. onions and 2 ozs. streaky bacon or pork. Add 1 tablespoon chopped fresh sage and 8 ozs. breadcrumbs or soaked bread squeezed dry. Mix together in a bowl, then add 1 heaped tablespoon flour, some pepper and salt and 1 egg. Just a sprinkle of salt should be added or none at all if bacon is used. Mould the mixture into balls and place into a roasting tin in which you have melted some lard. Bake for 1 hour in a fairly hot oven (375 F., Mark 5).

My mother used to tell a tale of the Irishman who came over here and wrote home to say "This is a wonderful country, ducks a penny each". The reply was "Send us some" he sent some and got the reply, "The muck's arrived when can we expect the ducks?".

Mrs. Amwegg,
Silchester, Reading, Berkshire.

PUDDING

GRANDMOTHER STATHAM'S DELICIOUS PUDDING WITH RICH SHERRY SAUCE

I am a fifth generation Australian who has lived over here for 35 years, a prized possession, that has literally gone through fire and water with me is an old hand-written book of recipes that I presume came down from my great-great-grandmother.

Beat 3 egg yolks well, stir in alternatively 1½ tablespoons flour and ½ pint milk and 1 level tablespoon melted butter and 1 teaspoon salt. Stir in the stiffly beaten egg whites. Pour it in a buttered dish, bake in a hot oven for 20 minutes (400 F., Mark 6). Serve with rich

179

sherry sauce:— Boil to a thin syrup 8 ozs. sugar with ½ pint water. Stir into this syrup 4 ozs. butter and 1 tablespoon flour. Cook to thicken. Season with wine or sherry. Cream can be eaten with it too. This must be served at once.

Mary Patchett,
London.

BUCKINGHAMSHIRE CHERRY TURNOVERS OR BUMPERS

Buckinghamshire used to be famous for its large black juicy cherries. The trees once grew all along the roads as well as in orchards but there are not many left now. When they were in full season at the end of July a lot of pubs used to make a feature of Cherry Turnovers or Bumpers (which are the same thing only larger). You had these with a glass of beer and you ate them in your fingers. Stone 12 ozs. of black Buckinghamshire cherries and sprinkle them with sugar. Make some short crust pastry from 8 ozs. flour and 4 ozs. lard and roll it into rounds 3–4 inches across and ¼ inch thick. Heap the centre with tightly packed cherries. Damp the pastry, fold it over and pinch it together to seal it. Brush with milk, bake them in a hot oven (400 F., Mark 6) for 20–30 minutes. Dredge them with sugar and eat them hot or cold.

WINDSOR PUDDING

Pare and core and boil a dozen baking apples. When soft beat them to a smooth pulp and beat with 1 oz. of best rice boiled in milk till it is tender, 1 oz. of sugar, a teaspoon of lemon juice and a pinch of grated lemon rind. Whisk the whites of 4 eggs to snow, stir them into the pudding mixture and beat it again until it is very light. Dip a pudding mould into boiling water, take it out and whilst it is still hot pour the mixture into it. Leave room for the mixture to swell. Cover the top with foil and put the pudding mould in a pan with boiling water to come half-way up it. Cook for 1½ hours or until the mixture sets. If the water boils away always refill with *boiling* water. Turn it out and pour round it a custard made with the yolks of the eggs. Serve at once.

To make the custard: Beat up the 4 egg yolks with a dessert-spoon of sugar. Bring ½ pint of milk to the boil either with a piece of lemon peel or 2 bay leaves in it to give it flavour. Stir the boiling milk gradually into the egg yolks and tip it all into the top of a double saucepan, the lower half containing not quite boiling water. Heat, stirring all the time till the custard thickens. If it boils, however, it will curdle.

Mrs. Ruth Jones,
Aberdaron, Caernarvonshire.

BAKED COOKHAM PUDDING

Cream 1½ ozs. butter and lard, mixed with 2 ozs. caster sugar, add 2 whipped eggs, stir in 2 ozs. flour. Add ½ pint milk gradually. Bake in a well-greased pie dish for ¾ – 1 hour in a moderate oven (350 F., Mark 4). This may be eaten with golden syrup.

Mrs. P. Hannen,
Wargrave, Berkshire.

BAKED LEMON PUDDING

Break up 2 ozs. stale cake and pass it through a wire sieve. Mix in a basin with 3 ozs. caster sugar and the grated rind of 2 lemons. Squeeze the juice of the lemons and add it to the dry ingredients. Beat 3 egg yolks and add ¼ pint of milk to them and stir into the mixture. Whip 2 whites of eggs very stiffly and stir in lightly. Roll out 4 ozs. short crust pastry, line a pie dish with it, decorate round the edge with pieces of pastry cut out with a star cutter. Turn the mixture into the prepared dish, and bake in a moderate oven (350 F., Mark 4) for about 20–25 minutes. Whip 2 more egg whites very stiffly and when the pudding is done cover the top with the beaten whites. Dredge with sugar, place in the oven for a few minutes (350 F., Mark 4).

Miss L. Stanley,
London.

APPLE CHARLOTTE

Butter a deep pie dish and line it with 4 slices of bread and butter. Fill up the dish with 1 lb. peeled, cored and sliced apples, sprinkle each layer with a little cinnamon. Warm ½ cup golden syrup with ½ cup water, pour it over the apples and sprinkle it with 1 tablespoon demerara sugar. Place a layer of buttered bread on top, sprinkle another tablespoon of sugar on top with a few knobs of butter. Bake in a moderate oven (350 F., Mark 4). Turn the pudding out to serve, sprinkle with caster sugar.

Miss H. Taylor,
Rayleigh, Essex.

GRANDMA'S BAKED PLUM PUDDING

Soak a loaf of bread overnight in water. Squeeze out the water, mix the bread with 8 ozs. currants, 8 ozs. raisins, 4 ozs. sugar, 2 ozs. lemon peel, 4 ozs. suet, 3 eggs and a pinch of nutmeg. Cook in a deep tin in a very slow oven (300 F., Mark 2).

As children we used to eat this pudding on the way to school in the winter. It's full of goodness.

Mr. J. Brown,
London, N.W. 8.

FRUIT BATTER

Put 4 ozs. flour in a basin and a pinch of salt. Make a well in the centre, break in 2 eggs, beat well, adding ½ pint milk to make a thin batter. Allow this to stand. Peel and core 2 lbs. apples. Melt a small piece of lard in a pie dish and when smoking hot pour in the batter. Put in the apples, add 2 ozs. sugar and, lastly, sprinkle 1 oz. freshly chopped suet over the top. Place this dish on the fifth grid-runner from the top of the coal range oven.

Ian Smith,
Colliers Wood, London.

ALDERMAN HUMPHREY PUDDING

This is a recipe my mother always used at Christmas, it was so different from the ordinary pudding and was delicious. Custard was served with it made from milk, eggs and sugar.

Chop 8 ozs. suet into lumps, mix with 2 eggs and 8 ozs. raisins, 2 tablespoons flour, 2 ozs. peel, 2 tablespoons sugar, 1 tablespoon currants, some salt and nutmeg. *Milk* must not be added. When the ingredients have been well mixed, put into a greased basin and steam for 6 hours.

Mrs. M. Harwood,
Kingsbury, London.

STEAMED CHESTNUT SOUFFLÉ

Put 3 ozs. butter and 3 tablespoons plain flour in a saucepan over a gentle heat and stir. When blended add ½ pint milk, cook, stirring until thick. Add 2 tablespoons sugar and 4 egg yolks, 4 ozs. cooked and mashed chestnuts then lightly fold in 4 stiffly whipped egg whites. Steam in a foil covered basin for 1 hour. Turn out to serve with hot chocolate sauce or whipped cream.

Mrs. J. Fowler,
Hockley, Essex.

BLINTZES

Both my grandmothers, or "bubba" to give them their Jewish name, cooked in the traditional manner. They used to make the most delicious blintzes, sometimes filled with curd cheese and topped with soured cream or honey. We had them fried in oil at the Chanucah festival, sometimes with apple sauce or with sugar and cinnamon. They were also served at Shavuot to celebrate the time of the giving of the law on Mount Sinai. For the batter beat up 2 large eggs with a pinch of salt and 4 ozs. of plain flour and ½ pint of milk and water mixed. Make the batter, leave it to stand for an hour and pour it into a jug. For the filling mix 1 lb. of curd cheese, 2 tablespoons of soured cream, 2 egg yolks, 3 tablespoons of sugar, a pinch of salt and a dash of vanilla essence. Oil an omelette pan lightly, heat it, pour in a little batter tilting to spread it evenly. Cook over a medium heat. When the bottom side is brown the top will be just set. Turn the blintzes out bottom side up onto a clean towel or a sheet of grease-proof paper. Repeat until all the pancakes have been made. Now lay the pancake brown side up on a board, spread a tablespoon of the filling thinly over one half, turn in the sides and roll it up into a long thin roll. Repeat with each pancake. Blintzes can be heated on a hot dish for 10 minutes in a moderate oven (350 F., Mark 4) then be served with plain or soured cream or honey poured over them. Some cooks brown them again in butter just before serving.

Miss Helen Berke,
Daily Express

PANCAKES

English people have been eating pancakes on Shrove Tuesday since the days of Edward II. It marked the beginning of the Lenten fast and a "pancake" or Shriving Bell used to be rung from the church steeple at noon on Shrove Tuesday. The Westminster pancake Greaze is an ancient ceremony taking place on the same day at Westminster School, London, they toss a pancake over a bar which separates the Lower school from the Higher. Boys scramble after it and he who gets the biggest piece is paid one guinea. The cook gets 50p.

At Olney in Buckinghamshire they have a centuries-old pancake race to the church. The women competitors run a course of 515 yards carrying a frying pan with a hot pancake in it and they have to toss it three times as they run. At the church the winner receives a prayer book from the vicar and is kissed by the sexton. A shriving service then takes place with all the pancakes and frying pans piled up before the font.

In the south of England Shrove Tuesday pancakes are often eaten with lemon juice and sugar sprinkled over them. In Lancashire they have them with hot golden syrup.

BAKING

MUFFINS

When I was a boy we lived at Tottenham and every Sunday afternoon the muffin man would come round covered in flour and ringing a little bell. He carried trays of muffins on his head. One Sunday he did not come and my granny found out he had hurt his foot. She took them round for him and in return he gave her the recipe. It was so good we stopped buying his and had granny's.

Sift 1 lb. plain flour and a large teaspoon of salt. Mix 1 oz. of fresh yeast to a smooth liquid with a little luke-warm milk. Blend in 6 tablespoons of lukewarm water and the rest of the lukewarm milk, ¼ pint altogether. Add it to the flour with 1 oz. of melted butter and a beaten egg, mixing it to a fairly stiff dough. Knead it for 10 minutes on a well floured board until the dough is no longer sticky. Leave it covered to rise until double in size. Knead it again. Lightly roll it out to ½ inch thick. Cut it into 12 rounds with a 3½ inch biscuit cutter. Put the muffins on a floured baking tray and dust them with flour. Let them rise again, covered, until double in size. Bake for 5 minutes in the top of a hot oven (450 F., Mark 8). Take them out, turn them over and bake another 5 minutes.

Muffins are eaten hot after being toasted on both sides. Pull them apart with your fingers, put thick slices of butter inside. Don't try to spread it, put the muffins back together again.

Mr. J. Scott,
Palmers Green, London.

PINEAPPLE CAKE (very good and easy)

Mix 14 digestive biscuits and 2 ozs. butter together. Drain a 1 lb. can crushed pineapple well. Line a greased cake tin with the biscuits. Put the pineapple, 2 cartons of soured cream and 1 tablespoon caster sugar in a basin and mix together. Pour onto the biscuits. Bake for 45 minutes at 325 F., Mark 3.

G. W. Davis,
Wembley, Middlesex.

LIGHTER-THAN-A-FEATHER-SPONGE

Beat 1 teacup caster sugar, 5 eggs and the grated rind of a lemon together until the mixture is thick and holds a trail (about 20 minutes with a rotary beater). Lightly fold in ¾ cup of sieved flour and a pinch of salt with a wooden spoon. Pour into a prepared 8 x 9 inch tin, shake a little caster sugar on top. Bake for about 1½ hours in a very slow oven (275 F., Mark 1).

Mrs. T. Poole,
Bushey, Watford, Hertfordshire.

COCONUT CAKES

It was one August Bank Holiday when I went up to the fairground on Hampstead Heath, there I found Mrs. Abalon Edwards just washing up in a showman's caravan with a gold painted ceiling and Nottingham lace curtains. Mrs. Edwards was born in a caravan in Glastonbury. She told me she had lived in one all her life and that she travelled round mostly in Wiltshire and looked after the juvenile ride when the fair is working. "We don't have much time" she said to me "the fair gets bigger, too, every year."

All her cooking is done on cylinder gas she said, adding that she always tried to make some cakes for Bank Holidays. For Mrs. Edwards' Coconut Cakes: melt or soften 8 ozs. butter until almost liquid. Add 8 ozs. sugar, beating them up well together until fluffy. Then beat in 2 eggs, 4 ozs. of sifted self raising flour, 4 ozs. of desiccated coconut. Three-quarters fill greased patty tins with this mixture, put a glacé cherry on each, bake in a moderately hot oven (375 F., Mark 5) for about 20 minutes.

GRANNY'S SEED CAKE

Cream 4 ozs. butter and 4 ozs. caster sugar in a basin, add 4 drops of vanilla essence, add 2 eggs and beat well. Sieve 8 ozs. self raising flour and mix, add some milk to make a soft mixture. Then add 2 teaspoons caraway seeds, mix. Bake in a greased oblong tin lined with buttered paper for $1\frac{1}{4}$ hours (350 F., Mark 4). Baking in an oblong tin makes the outside crispy, if a softer outside is preferred, bake in a 6-inch round tin.

Mrs. E. Wallace,
Leighton Buzzard, Bedfordshire.

GREAT GRANNY'S CHRISTMAS CAKE

Crumble 5 ozs. yeast into 1 pint of cold milk and leave on the oven top or in a warm place to be warmed gradually. The yeast dissolves and rises in the milk and is then ready for use.

Line a large cake tin with 2 – 3 layers of greaseproof paper. Butter the layer of paper next to the cake. Rub $1\frac{1}{2}$ lbs. butter and 8 ozs. lard into 3 lbs. plain flour (as for pastry). Then add 1 teaspoon bicarbonate of soda, $2\frac{1}{2}$ lbs. sugar, $2\frac{1}{2}$ lbs. currants, 1 lb. candied peel, 2 ozs. glacé cherries, 2 ozs. ground almonds, 2 ozs. chopped almonds and the peel of a grated orange and a grated lemon. Then add a quarter, or more, of a grated nutmeg. Finally add 8 beaten eggs, then the yeast gently stirred in the milk and, if liked, 1 small wineglass of brandy. Mix well and smooth evenly into a cake tin. Pre-heat the oven to a hot temperature whilst preparing the cake, then turn down to (300 F., Mark 2). Bake for 4 hours. A piece of foil laid lightly over the tin for the second half of the cooking time keeps the top a nice light colour. Test the cake with a warm skewer after 4 hours.

Joan Carmichael,
Totteridge, London.

POTATO CAKE

This recipe was an old favourite in our family about 60 years ago. It is nicer eaten hot, sliced through and spread with butter though it can be eaten cold.

Mix 4 ozs. mashed potato, 1 egg or the whites of 2 eggs, 4 ozs. self raising flour, 4 ozs. mixed fruit, 4 ozs. creamed butter, 1 oz. chopped peel, 4 ozs. caster sugar and 1 teaspoon nutmeg well together and beat thoroughly. Put into a greased 8-inch tart tin sprinkle with brown sugar and bake for 15 minutes at 400 F., Mark 6 or until browned.

Mrs. D. Fuller,
Ruislip.

CHELSEA BUNS

It was fashionable in the eighteenth and nineteenth centuries to go to Chelsea to taste the buns in the well-known Bun House. Even King George II and Queen Caroline used to patronise it. A sort of one storey kiosk with a colonnade in front, it was pulled down in 1838.

Roll out 1 lb. bun dough into a rectangle 10 inches x 16 inches and brush this with melted butter. Sprinkle the buttered dough with some small fruit, some mixed peel, some brown or nib sugar, the grated rind of a lemon, and a little mixed spice. Wash the four edges with egg, roll into a fairly tight cylinder and divide into 16 pieces and while still together brush with melted butter. Place them, face down, on a lightly greased 1 inch deep four sided tray fairly close together. Egg wash the tops and prove in a warm place until double the size. All the buns should be touching each other. Bake at 425 – 450 F., Mark 7 – 8 for approximately 15 minutes. Remove from the oven when cooked, and while still hot, brush with bun wash and dust with caster sugar.

This recipe is from the late Maria Floris who was the Queen's baker. It is from her "*Bakery, Cakes and Simple Confectionery*" Wine & Food Society, Michael Joseph (£3.00).

London buns are plain, long, finger-shaped buns with soft white sugar icing on top.

Scotland

Agricultural Products
Aberdeen Angus Cattle

Dairy Products
Dunlop Cheese, Highland Double Cream Cheese, Caboc Cream Cheese, Hramsa, Ayrshire Cream Cheese, Islay Cheese.

Gastronomic Specialities
Spiced beef, jugged hare, grouse stuffed with wild raspberries and with skirlie, grouse in port, pheasant in burgundy, gigot steaks, salmon, Partan bree, bawd bree, Scotch broth, cock-a-leekie, mussel brose, venison soup, Cullen skink, cabbage and bacon, kail or kale, Fife broth, Cabbie claw, Arbroath smokies, Finnan haddies, potted hough, herrings fried in oatmeal, rizzared haddies, venison, ptarmigan, Scotch collops (mince), Scotch eggs, porridge, haggis, Isle of Arran venison pâté, Isle of Arran hare pâté, venison pasties, little mutton pies.

Pastry
Almond Shortbread, Petticoat Tails, Dundee Cake, Black Bun, Balmoral Shortbread, Forfar Bridies, Oatcakes, Aberdeen Crullers, Ballater Scones, Bannocks, Scots Currant Bun, Barley Bannocks, Barm Loaves, Girdle Scones, Morayshire Gingerbread.

Confectionery
Edinburgh Rock, Jethart Snails, Dundee Marmalade, Dark Arran Marmalade, Thick and thin peel marmalade, Heather Honey, Vintage Marmalade matured in whisky casks.

Liqueur Whiskies: Chivas Regal, Old Rarity Islay Mist. Malt Whiskies: Macallan Glenlivet, Glen Grant Glenlivet, Dufftown Glenlivet, Smith's Glenlivet (The Glenlivet), Glenmorangie, Blair Atholl, Tomatin, Talisker, Cardhu, Laphroaig, Glenfiddish Highland Park (Kirkwall Orkney).

SOUP

FATHER'S BROTH
My father made this to feed seven children and himself. He made it in a huge cast-iron pot and even though we had two helpings each, it lasted two days and tasted better the second day. It was so filling that we just had milk pudding after it and had the meat sliced for tea. We always had high tea (we lived in Glasgow).

3 lbs. boiling beef   marrow bone (essential)
½ lb. barley   1 lb. butter beans
1 lb. dried peas   about 1 lb. carrots
swede, turnips about 1 lb.   2 leeks
celery when available   parsley and ½ cabbage

Boil the beef, bone and barley for about 2 hours. Take out the beef, add the beans and peas, which should have been steeped in cold water for 24 hours, while this is boiling. Cut up the carrots and turnips and add. Boil for 2 or 3 hours until the beans and peas are soft, then add the celery, leeks and cabbage cut up. Boil for about half an hour. Add the parsley just before serving.

Mrs. A. Brown,
Norwich, Norfolk.

HARE SOUP

Take one undamaged (not badly shot) young hare. Skin and cut it up, be careful not to break the inside. Put in your hand and remove the lungs, hold the hare over a basin to catch the blood, cut the hare in pieces. Put aside the pieces in a large stock pan, cover well with water, add pieces of turnip, carrot, stalk of celery, a few small chopped onions and bring to the boil. Simmer for 1½ hours. Pour the blood through a hair sieve. Add some cold water and put in a stewpan then stir *one* way till it boils. Put hare meat and vegetables through the coarsest plate of the mincer, return strained liquor, boiled blood, meat and minced vegetable to the large pan. Simmer a further hour.

Then add the following:— 1 tablespoon plain flour, 2 tablespoons Worcester sauce, pepper and salt to taste and a little browning. Mix with a little cold water, blend well then add to soup. Stir till it comes to the boil again.

Just before serving add a glass of port to make it just right.

Mrs. Mary Gifford,
Ford, Midlothian.

POTATO SOUP

Place 1 lb. roast beef bones in a pan, add 4 pints of water and simmer for 1 hour. Add 2 chopped onions, 10 medium sized peeled, sliced potatoes and 2 large peeled tomatoes. Grate and add 1 large scraped carrot. Cover and simmer slowly for 1½ hours. Remove the bones and season to taste.

Mrs. H. Stewart,
Edinburgh 12.

PARTAN BREE (Crab Soup)

Crabs, rice, white stock, salt, pepper, anchovy and cream.

Pick all the meat from 2 crabs and set aside that from the large claws. Boil 5 or 6 ozs. of rice in milk till tender and soft and pass it with the crab meat through a tammy.* Stir this with a wooden spoon till perfectly smooth and add to it, very gradually, sufficient white stock for 12 or 14 people. Season with salt, white pepper and anchovy. Put it all into a pan and stir it over the fire until quite hot, do not let it boil. Add pieces of meat from the claws and just before serving, stir in half a pint of cream.

* The rice and crab meat could alternatively be puréed in an electric mixer.

Mrs. J. Thomson,
Leven, Fife.

SHEEP'S HEED (HEAD) BROTH — POWSOWDIE

Up here in the cold north-east we use a lot of fish, also we are famous for our beef (Aberdeen Angus). World wide famous. We are only a working class family and can't brag about whole pigs or sheep and lambs.

My grandma used to make sheep's heed (head) broth and here is her recipe.

1 sheep's head	1 onion
1 leek	1 large carrot
1 small turnip	2 ozs. pearl barley
chopped parsley	salt and pepper
2 – 3 quarts of water.	

Wash the head well and split it in half. Remove the brains (to be cooked later, stewed or fried) and soak the head for 30 minutes in cold water. Put the head in a pot, cover with cold water and bring it to the boil slowly. Skim. Cut the vegetables into dice, add to the water and boil for 3 hours. 30 minutes before cooking is completed add the barley. Remove the head, skim the soup, add 2 tablespoons chopped parsley and serve.

Mrs. J. Fraser,
Woodside, Aberdeen.

In Scotland chopped parsley is usually sprinkled on top of the broth just before serving whereas in Wales they always put the chopped parsley into the soup tureen first and then pour the broth on top.

SHEEP'S HEAD BROTH AND BRAIN CAKES

One can hardly get a sheep's head from a butcher now, but if you can, get him to split it in half. Remove the brains and soak them in cold water and vinegar to blanch them. Make the head into broth.

When the broth is cooked add the chopped meat to it. Bring to the boil for a few minutes again.

The brain was used for brain cakes which made another dish. Remove from the vinegary water and boil gently for 15 minutes. Strain from the water and chop the brains. Mix with 2 tablespoons breadcrumbs, 1 dessertspoon chopped parsley, pepper and salt and the small yolk of 1 egg. Mix all together and form into small cakes on a floured board. Fry in butter until brown. All this from a sheep's head long ago. The cakes used to be eaten with the broth as bread was not procurable.

Mrs. Margaret Turnbull,
Fortrose, Ross-shire.

FISH

HERRINGS

Mallaig is a desolate Scottish village seven and a half hours by train north of Glasgow — very desolate in November — but with Ullapool and Oban almost the only place in Europe with herrings coming in at this season. Most of them are kippered or quick frozen, and a few are salted down in barrels. Mallaig is also the old centre for salt herrings, which, boiled with jacket potatoes, were the staple food of the Highlands and Islands for generations. They used to export them to Russia, gutted and preserved in wooden casks between layers of salt, but the trade has almost died out. "Each home in this hospitable place" it says in Gaelic (pronounced garlic) over the railway ticket office, "is giving you a hearty welcome".

Three sheep live in the station, grazing along the track and apparently belonging to nobody, like warehouse cats, for this is the end of the line, as well as the end of the road, from anywhere. The only place you can go from Mallaig is over the sea to Skye, five miles off (too rough), or to Rum and Eigg, large islands way off in the mist (even rougher).

I went out well before dawn to watch the herrings auctioned in a hut on the harbour. The quays are thick with spilt fish, the gulls so fat they can hardly walk, and most of them won't look at a herring. People say the fishermen are making a fortune, and that when they tell you they don't want their sons to go into fishing it isn't really serious. I heard it said (and denied) that one skipper was making £9,000 a year.

But the story of the herring is an extremely complicated one, fraught with conflicting interests, not to say passions. A bell rings when the boats are coming in, and as I ran down the dark street in the driving rain they told me that there are gales here in winter when you can only go out on your hands and knees. Fishermen get blown off the quays onto the boats below, landing with broken skulls. Nowadays they wear fluorescent orange or yellow oilskins which glow under the arc lamps in the black harbour like something on a film set. The men who wore the first lot crept out shame-faced, trying not to be seen in them. But they are obviously necessary here for picking a man out if, for instance, he is washed overboard.

"The best way to eat herring," said *Mr. Alec McCleod*, manager of the quick freezing plant, "is when you catch them at sea. Tear off the head, rip out the guts, and put them in a bucket of hot water for a few minutes. Then eat them in your fingers while they are still warm . . . It's an old way. Local fishermen eat them like this regularly. I have done it every time I've been out".

But the way I had them for breakfast, I am thankful to say, was plain fried in oatmeal. They were absolutely delicious, all hot and crunchy and only rivalled next day by a luscious pair of juicy grilled local kippers. For breakfast is the great Scottish invention, their gastronomic gift to humanity — what with hot fresh baps and Dundee marmalade, the oatcakes and heather honey, the kippers and porridge and cream. There's nothing like it anywhere on earth.

KIPPERS

Most of the cooking is plain boiled and wholesome like the people. I've eaten haggis and bashed neeps (mashed turnips), masses of boiled potatoes, Scotch broth, suet pudding. Squelching through a peat bog in my gumboots, I've heard of recipes handed down from mother to daughter. Some unusual ones like the Krappin, traditional to the Isle of Skye, an improbable mixture of cod's livers mashed with oatmeal to make dumplings for soup and said to be quite delicious.

All the local kippers are dyed and oak-smoked over the shavings from whisky barrels. "People won't eat pale, undyed ones today," *Angus Ewen Craig* told me. "They have to be smoked much harder and English people don't like so much salt in the kippers as we do for ourselves. I personally like a pale kipper, it has more flavour, but most don't." *Mr. Craig*, or "Ginge" as they call him, works through the night at the smoking kilns until four or five in the morning, when the girls come in to pack the kippers.

A kiln is a great black hole two storeys high with smoking heaps of sawdust down below, and hundreds of kippers hung up in rows on tenterhooks. I saw 10 cran (more than 11,000 kippers) in one kiln and it was not a full day. "At night" *Ginge* told me, "I get a sheet of white paper, roll up a kipper tight in it, dip it in water and shove it straight into the fire. When it comes out in 10 to 15 minutes, it's lovely".

They are marvellous too rolled in foil and done in the oven to eat hot with brown bread and butter. The whole place smelled lusciously of kippers, warm and smokey; and the doors in front of the kiln, hinged like a loose-box are inches thick with tar from the oak shavings which are never scraped off, for that is what gives the flavour.

The ones I took home with me were delicious. I had one lot fried in butter and ate them with a plate of plain boiled spaghetti which I tossed in the buttery juices of the kippers. The others I grilled, first covering the grill pan with foil to stop it smelling. They too were exquisite. I've never believed in people who didn't like food which smelled of . . . well . . . food. Taste is akin to smell and if you have ever tried to eat grilled gammon rashers with a cold in the nose you will know how much the pong contributes to the gastronomic picture.

EILEEN MACGREGOR'S BAKED STUFFED HERRINGS WITH BOILED POTATOES as served at the Marine Hotel, Mallaig

Scrape, bone and season young washed herrings. Fold them over a stuffing of breadcrumbs, salt, pepper, shredded suet, lemon juice, chopped onion and chopped parsley if you can get it. Pack them in a pie dish with salt, pepper and melted butter on top. Cover with foil and bake for about 30 minutes in a moderate oven (350 F., Mark 4), removing the foil towards the end to brown the herrings.

Eileen MacGregor,
Mallaig, Inverness-shire.

Eileen Macgregor serves boiled potatoes with them but one could also serve piping hot buttery jacket potato with the herrings.

SKIRLIED HERRING

Take 4 large herrings. *Filling:*— 1 lb. mashed potatoes, 2 ozs. butter, 2 ozs. pinhead oatmeal, 1 large chopped onion and a good teaspoon of mustard. Clean the herrings and remove the bones. Make the stuffing by mixing together mashed potato, oatmeal, butter, onion and mustard. Lay a little on each herring, roll it up and secure with a stick. Place on a greased fireproof dish. Dot with butter and cover with greaseproof paper. Bake in a hot oven (400 F., Mark 6) for 30 minutes or so.

Mrs. A. Hutchison,
Killearn, by Glasgow.

FRIED HERRING

Scottish cooks never wash a fresh herring as it spoils the flavour, they just scrape off the scales towards the head, split the fish down the back then wipe, bone and season them. As they should be very dry leave the herrings for an hour or so wrapped in a clean tea towel. Then dip them in seasoned oatmeal and fry, skin side first, for 5–10 minutes. Serve on a hot ashet (dish) for breakfast or high tea with vinegar and oatcakes. And sometimes a glass of buttermilk.

TATTIES AND HERRING

Almost fill a pan with unpeeled potatoes. Boil until half cooked, then pour off most of the water. Put the split, clean herrings carefully over the potatoes, cover closely, steam until done. Lift the herrings on a hot dish. Steam the potatoes till dry and mealy.

CROFTERS' HOT POT

Fillet 4 herrings, season well and place half in a well buttered casserole dish. Slice 2 large onions and 4 potatoes thinly, cover the fillets with onion slices then with potato slices, season and dot with butter. Repeat the layers finishing with potatoes, season again and dot with 2 ozs. of butter. Put a lid on the casserole and bake for 50 minutes at 425 F., Mark 7. Remove the lid and bake for 10 minutes longer until the potatoes are nicely browned.

Mrs. H. Stewart,
Edinburgh.

COD

Boil some cod, skin and bone it. Put it into a big dish with a liberal sprinkling of pepper. Place 8 ozs. of butter on top of the fish and when it melts flake the whole lot together. Serve with potatoes mashed with a little butter and some milk and pepper. Also have a glass of buttermilk.

Mrs. M. Morrison,
Port of Ness, Isle of Lewis.

SMOKED HADDOCK

Smoked haddocks belong more to the east coast than to the west of Scotland. Moray Firths are very pale smoked haddocks, Glasgow Pales are small split smoked haddocks while Finnan Haddocks are darker and more nutty. Traditionally at the fishing town of Finnan the haddocks are cured by smoking them over burning seaweed. Like whiting and herrings (for kippers) they are cold smoked at under 85°F. and so are not cooked during the smoking. Finnan haddocks with the bones removed are delicious cooked on a griddle or in an iron frying pan, then filled with butter which has not quite melted when they come to table. A spoonful of whipped cream or a poached egg may be served on each portion.

Hot smoked fish like Auchmithie or Arbroath smokies are lightly cooked in curing and have a much smokier flavour.

ARBROATH SMOKIES

The very name brings back memories of my old friend, Mrs. Betsy Swankie, for many years queen of the Arbroath fish merchants, bidding for boxes of line-caught smokies auctioned on the wind-

(and often spray-) swept quay as the small boats landed their catches at Arbroath harbour.

Then admiring her skill as she deftly gutted and beheaded the fish and tied them in pairs by the tail ready for "cooking" in the smoking pit.

They can be eaten without any further cooking, or simmered for 10 minutes in a pie dish.

But best of all, remove the two "fillets" of flesh from skin and bone and fry them lightly in butter with some bacon and mushrooms.

Mr. Jim Nicoll,
Daily Express.

OLD FASHIONED SAVOURY SMOKED HADDOCK

Fry a minced onion and 4 small tomatoes in 2 ozs. butter. Add 1 cooked and skinned sliced smoked haddock and simmer all together very gently for 15–20 minutes, adding pepper to taste. Boil some rice, put it on a serving dish. Pour on the savoury haddock and sprinkle with chopped parsley.

Mrs. A. MacDonald,
Waternish, Isle of Skye.

A very similar dish was once a speciality of the old Cavendish Hotel in Jermyn Street, London, in the days when it was run by the celebrated and much loved Rosa Lewis.

BLAWN OR WIND-BLOWN WHITING

The whiting should, if possible, be line caught and very fresh. Clean and wipe them, take out the eyes, cover the fish over with salt, immediately after which take them out and shake off the superfluous salt, pass a string through the eyeholes and hang them up to dry in a passage, or some place where there is a current of air. The next morning take them off if small but leave them till the third morning if large. Grill them gently over a slow fire and serve very hot with a small piece of fresh butter rubbed over each, or serve quite dry if preferred. These should be eaten with oatcakes and butter.

Aberdeen Fish Market Association.

WHITING IN ANOTHER SCOTS WAY

Choose small, perfectly fresh fish, rub them in flour till it adheres, lay them in a frying pan with a good bit of butter, fry them very slowly. They should not be dry or coloured. Mince some parsley and green onions or chives very finely, put them into some stock (or milk) with a little salt and about 2 tablespoons of cream, mix it well together and pour it over the whiting before they are quite finished cooking. Move them about very gently, not to break them, till they are done. They are very delicate and excellent done this way, which, though simple, requires great care. No butter should be used but what is required to fry them.

Small fresh haddocks may be prepared in either of these ways, but require a little more salt and a little longer cooking.

Aberdeen Fish Market Association.

RIZZARED HADDIES

These are similar to the wind-blown whiting and are generally served hot for breakfast in a folded napkin. Choose fairly big fish otherwise they get very dry. Gut and wipe the fresh haddock and leave them in salt all night, next string them on a wire through the eyeholes, hang them on a wall in the open air in a fresh cool breeze, but not in the sunshine. Take them down after three days, skin, bone and grill them like a blawn whiting. Serve a nice jug of melted butter with them.

Jimmie Cameron,
Stonehaven, Kincardineshire.

HOT PARTAN "PIE"

Take all the meat from a large boiled partan, or crab as they call them in England, taking it from both the body and the claws. Throw away the gills and apron but keep the small claws for garnish. Chop up and season the crab meat with salt, pepper and grated nutmeg and a teaspoon of made mustard. Add a tablespoon of soft white breadcrumbs, the juice of a large lemon and some pieces of butter. Stir it up well together, wash the shell, brush it over with salad oil, fill it with the crab meat. Brown it under the grill and serve hot garnished with the small claws. I allow one small crab per person but we generally share the very big ones between us.

When I was a girl the old cottage way used to be to heat a shovel in the parlour fire and hold it over the "pie" to brown the top.

Mrs. M. Buchanan,
Edinburgh.

BOILED SALMON—plain Scots style

My father was a ghillie on one of the salmon rivers and he always said that whether salmon is caught in some famous river such as the Spey, Tweed or Tay or elsewhere, they should always be simply cooked, and served. This is how I used to prepare it for the summer visitors before the First World War.

We always served the boiled salmon with fresh green peas, mealy potatoes, pepper and vinegar and no sauce, just a little of the salmon bree and a jug of melted butter. Skin and scale it without unnecessary handling. Put the fish on a rack in the fish kettle, cover with cold water, bring slowly to the boil and skim adding ½ oz. of salt per quart of water. Simmer gently for the required time, about 10 minutes per lb., but it is often overcooked. When done lift it on the rack and rest this across the pan to drain it throwing a folded tea towel over the salmon to keep it warm. If it is to be served cold leave it in the bree or liquor till cold and drain it before serving. The carver should give a slice of thick with a slice of thin.

Mrs. Fiona Cameron,
Stirling.

As it is so rich, 1½ lbs. salmon is enough for 4 people, but it is cheaper per lb. when sold whole. Of the pieces of salmon middle cut is costliest. An adult salmon may weigh 8–20 lbs., a salmon grilse or young fish (in season in June and July) weighs 3½–7 lbs.

CUCUMBER SAUCE — sometimes served with cold salmon

Grate a cucumber, whip ¼ pint double cream, add a dessertspoon of fresh chopped tarragon, a little salt and pepper and stir in the grated cucumber before serving the sauce with cold salmon.

"SOLE UPPERS"

In the days of my childhood here in the Shetland Isles fish was both plentiful and cheap, and the small sole or plaice was much used. Here is how my late mother used to cook them. It made a very tasty and cheap main dish, and didn't take long to cook.

One fish was usually enough per person and the following recipe is sufficient for 6 people.

Required:— 2 or 3 cloves, ½ cupful milk, ½ cupful water, 1 tablespoonful cream (this came from the top of the milk).

Wash and fillet 6 small sole or plaice, season with salt, pepper and lemon juice. Roll up each piece of fish and set close together on end in a deep baking dish, well greased. Next take the bones and trimmings of the fish and put them into a pan with ½ cupful milk and ½ cupful water, 1 bay leaf, some parsley stalks and shallot or small onion, cut small. Season lightly with salt and pepper. Simmer for some minutes. Next melt 1 oz. butter in a saucepan, add 1 oz. flour and cook for a few minutes, stirring all the time, then add the fish stock previously strained and stir until this comes to the boil. Bake the fillets in the oven for 10 minutes then strain the fish stock over them and sprinkle a little parsley on top and lastly spoon a little cream – about 1 tablespoon – over. This was much enjoyed by both the young and old members of the family.

Miss M. A. Johnstone,
Lerwick, Shetland Isles.

HAIRY TATTIES or HAIRY WILLIES

Take a packet of salt fish, put it in a basin, pour boiling water over the fish and let it stand overnight. Pour off this water which helps to take some of the salt out, then put the fish in a pan and cover with cold water, put on to boil. When it comes to the boil, pour water off. Do this three times, on the last boil, boil for fifteen minutes, when the fish will be ready to flake. Flake the fish into a bowl, grate a couple of raw onions, and let stand until ready to use it. Peel a pot of potatoes, and put onto boil with salt to taste, pour the potatoes when cooked and dried, put in the flaked fish and raw onion and a good lump of butter, mash together until a fine creamy consistency, but not too wet. You can add chopped chives, or parsley. Keep hot till ready for serving. This served with melted butter or mustard sauce, is really a perfect delight with a quarter of Scotch oatcakes and a glass of milk. If any left over, make into fish cakes.

Kirty Jarrod,
Malvern, Worcestershire.

FRIED BROWN TROUT

There is plenty of brown trout from the burns, in season from March to September. I salt the trout slightly, leave it overnight, and next morning I wipe the fish, split it down the back and take out the bones. Then wipe it, dip it in milk, coat it thick in coarse oatmeal and fry it in a pan of smoking hot lard for a few minutes, turning it until it is brown on both sides. Drain, and serve it with butter and lemon for breakfast.

Mrs. F. Mackay,
Wick, Caithness.

MEAT, POULTRY AND GAME

BEEF

Scottish beef is world-famous and perhaps even better than the whisky. Angus, one of the most beautiful counties in Scotland, is the home of black, hornless cattle, the Aberdeen Angus which give the best beef on earth. The pedigree bulls fetch tens of thousands of pounds in the show ring and are exported all over the world.

Now, for the first time in 150 years, they have a new breed in Scotland, the Luings, shaggy looking animals specially bred to thrive in the wet climate of the Western Highlands. Herds of Luings are growing and the Queen, an early supporter of the breed, recently showed a white Luing bull from Sandringham at the Smithfield Show in London.

At Dumbarton, *William Sloan*, master butcher, has a small shop just down the road from the nuclear submarines, which are full of

H-bombs and more nuclear power than all the explosives of the Second World War put together. *Mr. Sloan* is a former President of the *Scottish Federation of Meat Traders*, does his own slaughtering and has no time for what he calls commercial beef. I watched them cutting up some superb Aberdeen Angus baby beef, traditionally fed and only 16–17 months old. There was some luscious rolled sirloin with the undercut, as well as the less fashionable cuts such as nine-hole barley beef, nowadays sold well below cost for making soup. Though even in Scotland, *Mr. Sloan* told me, not nearly so much soup is made at home as formerly and housewives are taking far too little interest in the cheap flavoursome cuts.

In the Glasgow area many of the cuts of meat are different, not only from England, but from those around Aberdeen. I saw gigots (or legs) of lamb — they cut delicious gigot steaks across the top of these then sell the shank cheaply for broth. Boned and rolled shoulders of lamb — so popular in Scotland and so easy to carve — and there were many more stewing cuts than we have.

Shetland lambs, like Shetland ponies, are tiny, about half the size of an ordinary one. The whole carcase weighs 20–25 lbs., they have almost no fat, like venison, and there are not many of them. They cannot be produced on the mainland, but *Mr. Tony Anderson*, farmer and butcher of Weisdale, Shetland (Tel: Weisdale 214) can sometimes supply them. The lambing season is in late summer, much later than in England.

Pork is not so popular in Scotland as it is over the Border and was rarely seen until the end of the last century.

Venison has always been plentiful in Scotland, but there are now more wild red deer than ever before, with some danger of over-stocking. They export a lot of venison to Germany.

SUTHERLAND VENISON

This is a very old way — and one of the best — of cooking venison in the North of Scotland. The juices are retained in the suet crust. The best part to get is a solid bone-free piece from the haunch; the only other requirements are some standard suet paste and about 2 ozs. of butter. Roll out the paste to a thickness of about $\frac{1}{2}$ inch and completely encase the meat in it, carefully sealing up all joins in the paste. Melt the butter in a baking dish with a grid to lift the joint off the bottom; place the encased joint on the grid and bake in a moderately hot oven, allowing about 30 minutes over. Baste with the butter from time to time and especially towards the end of the cooking period so that the crust becomes richly brown. Serve pieces of the deliciously savoury crust with the meat and accompany the dish with crab-apple jelly — or rowan berry jelly.

Mrs. E. Borland,
Kirkcolm, Stranraer.

HIGHLAND HARE PATTIES

Being a Scot I love good food and the older the recipe the better. Here is one my mother used to make in Perthshire many years ago, and I still do it here.

Mince 8 ozs. cooked hare and about 4 ozs. cooked pork and mix with 1 tablespoon of fried minced onion, an egg and a few chopped fried mushrooms. Add 2 ozs. stale bread having softened it beforehand in either water or milk. Shape into cakes, coat with crumbs and fry in hot fat till well browned on both sides. Garnish with seasoned butter, this is 2 ozs. butter creamed with salt, pepper and parsley, and placed on top of the patties. Serve with creamed potatoes and a green vegetable, also redcurrant jelly.

Mrs. K. E. Flint,
Little Baddow, Essex.

STEAK WITH OYSTER STUFFING OR CARPETBAG STEAK

This recipe was taken from an old handwritten cookery book, the original owner of which died in about 1912. The recipes date from 1898–1911. In those days, of course, steak and oysters were not the exorbitant prices they are today. I can remember when I was a little girl, about 1913, we used to get new laid eggs from local farms at 16 for 1s. Boiling fowls 1s. and roasters 1s. 6d. Skim milk and butter milk were 3d. or 4d. for half a gallon. Those were the days! Fresh milk was 2d. a pint and we got it within an hour or two of it being taken from the cow. Such a thick cream came on it, that during the 1914–18 war, we used to shake it up in a 2 lb. treacle tin till it turned to butter. It was a somewhat tiring chore which we children were not fond of doing, though we liked the end product well enough. It was the only butter we got in the war period. I well remember the green mouldy meat, maggoty flour and other horrors. I am glad that during the last war the rationing was better organised, though I now wonder however we managed on the meagre quantities we were allowed. Still we did.

Take about 2 lbs. of rump steak in one thick piece. Cut a slit horizontally across it, not quite severing the edges. In this put one score of oysters and sew it up. Dredge with a mixture of flour, pepper and salt. Fry in boiling fat until nicely browned then pour off the fat and cover the meat with stock. Stew gently for 2 hours and, just before dishing, add the liquor of the oysters and one wineglass of sherry.

Mrs. D. Seddon,
Laide, Achnasheen, Ross-shire.

POTTED HOUGH

Choose a large piece of shin bone from the shiny knobbly end. Wash it and put it in a pan with enough water to cover. When the water is warm, add 1 lb. of shin of beef, 1 carrot, 1 onion, salt, pepper and a bayleaf. Bring slowly to the boil. Simmer for 3—4 hours until the meat is so tender that it will separate when you put a fork into it. This requires long, slow cooking. When ready remove the meat into a basin and break it up roughly with a fork into small pieces. Do not put the meat through a mincer, as it will make it too fine. Return the meat to a saucepan and just cover with the stock. Boil briskly for 10 minutes. Rinse out some glass dishes, or a pie dish, with cold water and divide the mixture into the prepared dishes. The best method is to pour off all the liquor equally in the dishes and then spoon out the meat evenly. Leave until cold and set. This is a delicious jellied meat. It can be served with a salad or hot with vegetables.

Miss M. McQuarrie,
Inveraray, Argyll.

HOUGH PIE

Cut 1 lb. hough (shin beef) into cubes into a pie dish, add pepper, salt and cover with cold water. Don't be tempted to use a more expensive cut of meat; it is the hough that supplies the special flavour. The secret of the lovely flavour is in the slow cooking of the hough. Don't add onions, they detract from the flavour. Bake the meat for 2 hours in a moderate oven (350 F., Mark 4). Remove the pie dish and add 1 tablespoon flour mixed to a smooth paste and return the dish to the oven until boiling again. Cut some potatoes into dice and put them into the gravy, completely filling the pie dish. Return the dish to the oven and bake until the potatoes are nearly done. Cover it with 8 ozs. short crust pastry, making a hole in the centre. Bake for another 20 to 30 minutes. Serve with peas or sprouts.

Mrs. M. Morrison,
Port of Ness, Isle of Lewis.

Hough—pronounced Hock—is in Scotland the joint of meat off the part of the hind leg between the knee and the fetlock—Shinbeef.

HIGHLAND CHICKEN STOVIES

Cut your chicken in pieces, chop 2 lbs. peeled potatoes, peel and slice 2 nice onions. Arrange all these in a deep fireproof dish in layers, sprinkling each layer with salt and pepper and dotting it well with butter. The top layer must be potatoes. Pour in ¾ pint of water and cover tightly. Cook 3–4 hours in a fairly slow oven (325 F., Mark 3).

My granny always used to cook it in an iron pot over an open fire.

Mrs. Alison Maclaren,
Dingwall, Ross and Cromarty.

Bread sauce is usually served in Scotland with roast chicken, turkey and game birds. A thick egg sauce is poured over a boiled fowl, with the yolks grated over the top of it. Minced parsley or chives are stirred into the sauce, and, if wanted very rich, eggs and cream may be stirred in just before serving. Howtowdie is a traditional dish of boiled fowl with oatmeal stuffing, which was once served with eggs poached in the chicken broth.

FARMHOUSE GLAZED SAUSAGE

This old recipe handed down several generations, and originally made for hungry farm workers, still produces a wonderful family week-end standby. It was originally "a method for using up the end of a ham" and tastes best if even a few minced fragments from a knuckle end can be included.

Mince 1 lb. smoked streaky bacon, 8 ozs. lean pork scraps, 8 ozs. stewing steak without gristle or skin. Put in into a large mixing bowl and blend very thoroughly with some minced ham scraps, 2 large cups fine white breadcrumbs, 1 teaspoon salt, ½ teaspoon freshly ground black pepper, a pinch of nutmeg, 4 or 5 finely snipped leaves of rosemary, a pinch of dried herbs and 6 chopped leaves of fresh sage. Add 1 large egg and when this is completely combined with the whole bulk cover the bowl and leave it in a very cool place for at least 3 hours. The different flavours will permeate the whole, even better if left a few hours longer.

Turn onto a board, and having rinsed the hands in cold water, shape the mixture into a big sausage. Cover it completely with lightly buttered greaseproof paper. Roll up in an old piece of clean linen cloth scalded and floured and tie the ends (not the middle) to preserve the shape. Put it into a pan of boiling water, it is best to use a covered roasting tin with an old plate in the bottom to prevent sticking. Boil steadily for fully 3 hours, refilling with boiling water as needed. Lift out, drain off the surplus water and put on a dish until cold. Next day unwrap the sausage and glaze it with aspic flavoured with Marmite. Two coats are best for a good finish. Sprinkle with some toasted crumbs in a line down the centre and serve with a salad.

Mrs. R. Bruce,
Killin, Perthshire.

This is very good served cold with hot potatoes baked in their jackets and is sometimes known as an Aberdeen sausage. If the mixture is too dry after the egg is added some cooks moisten it with a little milk or brandy, or add another egg.

HASH

Slice 2 lbs. cold mutton neatly, remove the skin and gristle. Put the meat on a plate, mix together 1 glass mushroom ketchup, 1 glass port or sherry, 2 tablespoons red currant jelly, 1 tablespoon lemon juice, 3 cloves, 1 finely grated onion and salt and pepper and pour over the meat. Leave it until 1 hour before the hash is required. While the meat soaks, make the brown sauce. For this chop 1 small carrot and 1 small onion, dry well. Melt ½ oz. dripping and fry them slightly, then add ½ oz. flour and stir carefully on a low heat till a good brown colour. Add ½ pint second stock by degrees, also a pinch of salt, some pepper and 1 dessertspoon ketchup. Boil up and skim thoroughly. Put on a lid and simmer the sauce steadily for 30–40 minutes, stirring and skimming when necessary. Strain and re-heat.

Now strain the liquid from the meat into the brown sauce, season it, place the meat in an earthenware casserole, or pan, cover, cook very very slowly for 1 hour. Serve hot with potato croquettes, or, if liked, snippets of crisp fried bread.

Mrs. V. Boyle,
Clackmannan, Clackmannanshire.

POTTED HEID

Clean 1 pig's head, 4 feet and 1 cowheel by soaking in warm water and rubbing salt well in to extract any blood etc. When cleaned put in a saucepan with as much water as will cover. Add a little cayenne, 6 pounded cloves, 1 blade mace, 1 bayleaf, a few peppercorns, a sprig of parsley, some allspice and 1 teaspoon of salt. Simmer gently at the side of the stove or on the cooker at a low heat for about 6 hours. When ready the bones will have separated. Remove them, cut up the meat into small pieces, add more seasoning as required. Mix with the strained stock, put it into moulds to set overnight, or into a meat loaf tin and press it well down with a weight.

Mrs. Kennedy,
Inverness.

If put to set in small moulds or tins the potted heid is delicious served like a pâté for starters with hot toast and butter.

MUTTON PIES

People talk with nostalgia about mutton pies — a purely Scottish speciality that they buy from the baker. It is difficult to find good ones in London and they seem to be getting rarer in Scotland too. A Saturday night treat for many Scottish children used to be a hot mutton pie, full of juicy meat and gravy, which they supped with a teaspoon sitting in front of the fire in their "nicht goons." In Glasgow all the men tell you that a mutton pie and a glass of beer make a perfect match. Even Queen Victoria seems to have got a taste for them at Balmoral (probably without the glass of beer), for little mutton pies have been served at receptions both there and at Buckingham Palace for the last 100 years and are still popular.

For the traditional ones: Have a pan containing ½ pint of boiling water. Add 4 ozs. of beef dripping and 1 teaspoon of salt. Pour it onto 1 lb. of flour. Mix. When cool form it into a lump. Knead this on a floured board. Divide two-thirds of the dough into six to line small straight sided tins. Fill these with 12 ozs. of lean lamb or mutton, chopped small. Add salt, pepper and nutmeg and then moisten with gravy. Make the rest of the pastry into lids. Damp the edges, put them on, make a little hole in each, brush with milk. Bake in a moderate oven (350 F., Mark 4) for 40 minutes. Fill up each pie with gravy before serving.

BENALTY (BATTER) PIE

Melt a little butter in a pan, put in 1 lb. raw mince and brown it well, until all appearances of red have vanished, stirring all the time with a fork. Add 1 gill of water and season to taste. Cook for 5 minutes then put it into a deep pie dish. Sift 4 ozs. plain flour with ½ teaspoon baking powder and a pinch of salt. Rub in 2 ozs. of butter with your finger-tips, stir in a beaten egg and 1 gill milk and mix well. Pour this batter over the mince and bake in a moderate oven (350 F., Mark 4) for 45 minutes or until firm and nicely browned.

This is an excellent dish for luncheon, high tea or supper.

Mrs. Duncan,
Stranraer, Wigtownshire.

SPATCH-COCK

Wash, dry and split a young rabbit its entire length. Make a stuffing of 1 cup of fresh white breadcrumbs, 1 dessertspoon of finely chopped parsley, 1 dessertspoon of finely grated carrot, a pinch of powdered sage, a little finely chopped onion. Add salt and pepper, bind with an egg and stuff the rabbit lengthways. Place it in a roasting tin, brush with the remaining egg, dust with flour, add a generous supply of dripping, bake in a moderate oven, basting frequently till golden brown. Half fill the dish with Yorkshire pudding batter, bake in a very moderate oven (325 F., Mark 3) for 1½ hours.

Mrs. Kennedy,
Inverness.

SCOTCH COLLOPS

Scotch collops are an excellent dish when properly prepared with good beef as in Scotland. The better the steak the better the mince. Brown 1 lb. of fresh minced beef, preferably from the topside or shoulder with a large finely chopped onion in 1 oz. of butter or beef dripping, stirring it to stop it lumping. Add salt, pepper, a big cup of water and 1 tablespoon of oatmeal. Let it simmer with the lid on for a good 30 minutes. Pour it onto a hot ashet (meat dish) in a circle of creamy mashed potato. Some cooks add a dash of Worcester sauce at the end, others put a poached egg on top.

VEAL OLIVES

Cut some veal in thin, rather wide slices of 3 to 4 inches long. On each slice lay a rasher of bacon, a layer of forcemeat, a little very thinly sliced shallot, some pepper, salt and cayenne pepper. Roll them round and fasten each with a small skewer. Brush with egg. Fry the veal olives a nice brown and pour round the mushrooms boiled in gravy. Simmer till tender. Delicious with mashed potatoes creamed in buttermilk.

Flora Macdonald,
Duns, Berwickshire.

SWEETBREAD PIE

Bake a pastry shell "blind". Parboil 8 ozs. lambs' or calves' sweetbreads in water for 10 minutes. Skin them. Then simmer them with 2 ozs. sliced mushrooms, a little salt and pepper in enough milk to cover for 30 minutes. Drain, thicken the liquor with cornflour. Slice 2 hard boiled eggs onto the pastry shell. Add the sweetbreads and mushrooms and pour the thickened sauce over.

Mrs. Graham,
Hawick, Roxburghshire.

LEG OR GIGOT OF MUTTON IN MILK

Place a leg of mutton or lamb in a large container, pour 1 pint of milk over this. Add 1 onion and 1 carrot, chopped small, add a bouquet garni, pepper and salt to taste. Bring it to the boil and simmer with a lid on for 2 hours. Remove the meat from the pan and place it in a flat dish, either whole, or sliced to save carving later.

Make the sauce as follows:— Melt 2 ozs. of butter in a smaller pan, stir in 2 tablespoons of flour and 1 chopped onion, if desired. Gradually stir in the liquid in which the meat was cooked, after removing the bouquet garni. When the sauce thickens, add 2 tablespoons of capers, if desired. Pour over the meat and serve the dish hot or cold.

Mrs. J. Baird-Smith,
Drymen, by Glasgow.

STUFFED BREAST OF LAMB

Remove the bones from a breast of lamb and simmer them for 30 minutes. Strain, then reserve the stock. Mix 1 gill of soft white breadcrumbs, 2 slices of lean chopped bacon and 3 mushrooms with a little pepper and salt, then mix with an egg, mix well, using enough milk to moisten. Spread the mixture on the meat, roll and tie it up, cut 2 peeled onions, 2 scraped carrots and 1 small turnip into thin slices. Melt 2 tablespoons butter in a casserole and add the vegetables. Now put the meat onto the vegetables. Pour the bone stock over and cook the whole thing in a slow oven (300 F., Mark 2) for 2½ hours.

Mrs. M. Morrison,
Port of Ness, Isle of Lewis.

BARLEY MUTTON

Put a piece of rolled mutton in a large covered dish in the oven. Add 1 small teacup of barley and cook very slowly for 1 hour with enough water to come up one-third of the dish. Add 1 teacup diced carrots, 1 teacup diced turnip, 1 small diced onion, the diced white of 1 leek, salt and pepper and, if desired, 1 dessertspoon of Worcester sauce. Allow to cook for another hour. Serve the mutton whole surrounded by the diced vegetables and then add some of the barley stock in which the meat has been cooked.

Mrs. J. Anderson,
Canonbie, Dumfriesshire.

SCOTCH HAGGIS

1 sheeps pluck and stomach bag	1 lb. oatmeal
½ lb. suet	2 or 3 onions
seasoning	

Take the stomach bag and wash it perfectly clean in cold water, then turn it inside out, scald it, and scrape it with a knife quickly. Put in salt and water till needed. Parboil the liver, lights and heart of one sheep, grate the liver and mince the other parts quite fine. Mince also the suet and toast the oatmeal thoroughly before the fire. Mix all these ingredients together, season them well with salt and pepper, then fill the bag. Before sewing it up put in a little of the water in which the onions were boiled, which will give sufficient flavour. Sew up the bag which must not be full, as the oatmeal swells considerably. Prick all over with a needle to prevent bursting. Put in a saucepan with enough boiling water to cover, having placed a small plate under. Boil for 4–5 hours, keeping haggis constantly covered with boiling water.

Mrs. M. W. S. Thom,
Hoddesdon, Hertfordshire.

PORK HOUGH

Soak sufficient butter beans and dried peas overnight, enough for 4 people. Wash 1 pickled pork hough and put it in cold water. Bring to the boil and pour off this water. Return the hough to the soup pot and cover with boiling water. Cook for 30 minutes. Tie the beans and peas in muslin bags and insert into the pot with 1 turnip cut in slices and some carrots cut lengthways. Cook until tender then add 1 cabbage cut in quarters. When the hough is tender remove, cover with oatmeal and put it in the oven to brown and crisp. Season if necessary before removing the hough, the pickling may make salt unnecessary. This meal is served with Golden Wonder potatoes in their jackets. A delicious meal served with five colourful vegetables and plenty of stock for soup the next day.

These houghs usually come from Ireland, and being pickled may only be obtained in certain shops.

Margaret Soutar,
Greenock, Renfrewshire.

WHITE MEALIE PUDDING, BACON AND TOMATOES

Allow half a white or mealie pudding per person and three rashers of bacon (preferably back) and half a tomato.

Put the white or mealie puddings on to boil in cold water. Bring them to the boil slowly, in order not to burst them. Then take them off the heat immediately the water boils and allow them to get cold in the water. When cold, take them out and dry them. Cut them in half and split each half down the middle. Put these in the foot of the grill pan, along with half a tomato. Place the rack (toaster) over them, and lay the bacon on top. Grill it, not too quickly, in order to allow the bacon fat to drip down onto the puddings and the tomatoes.

Dr. Janet Fraser,
Inverness.

VARIOUS

WHISKY

The single malt Scottish whiskies are the unblended ones they drink in the Highlands and Islands of Scotland. For years they were thought too heavy and liverish for urban tastes and have only recently become generally popular. They are quite different from the nationally famous blended whiskies and also older and more expensive. Glenfiddich is the one most widely sold and most easily obtainable in the south. They are distilled from a mash of malted barley in a pot still. The malting floor where the grain is spread out is warmed by a peat fire which gives them a special smoky flavour. And they are all different; indeed, a malt whisky still on one side of the road can produce quite a differently flavoured whisky from one a hundred yards away on the other side, and no one seems to know why.

In Dufftown, Banffshire, for instance, they have two distilleries almost side by side using the same water, for Glenfiddich malt and Balvenie malt, and the characteristics are utterly different.

Strathisla (you don't pronounce the second "s") is as pale as a Rhine wine, almost greenish and has such a delicate bouquet that you could well drink it from a brandy glass, or a whisky nosing glass, with your after-dinner coffee. Laphroaig, on the other hand, is very dark and peaty, the colour of cold tea, and tastes almost like drinking liquid kippers.

Don't dream of having soda, much less ice, in these whiskies. Drink them neat or with a little water. Scotsmen swear they never give you a headache. There are about 130 of these malt whisky distilleries and four distinct areas with local characteristics, just as in French vineyards. Some of the famous names are worth ranking with the great Cognacs of France.

Whisky only became known south of the border during the Napoleonic Wars when brandy was difficult to get. Then came the patent still, invented in 1830, which made it possible to make grain whisky on a large scale from imported maize. It has little flavour and is blended half and half with the malt whiskies, and makes the famous commercial brands, which are exported in vast quantities. The conventional whisky-and-soda only became really fashionable in London in the 1920s and some aristocratic drinkers never really took to it. Sir Winston Churchill, for instance, always had a brandy and soda as a nightcap. Drinking either whisky or brandy with soda is a habit which has only been known for about 100 years.

There are many single malt whiskies, all with their own characteristics, some of which are hard to get south of the border. Recently, in Scotland, I tasted some Macallan-Glenlivet which is more than 100 deg. proof. This is more than 15 years old, bottled in bond out of sherry wood by a distillery at Craigallachie on Speyside. You can also get 100 deg. proof Glen Grant-Glenlivet in Scotland though I have never seen any as strong as this on sale here. You could probably get it by post from *Gordon and Macphail*, 58-60 *South Street, Elgin, Scotland.*

Sometimes two identical malts differ in colour because one has been matured in white wood casks, the other in sherry casks.

Smiths Glenlivet (70 deg. proof), 12 years old and bottled in bond in sherry wood, is a superb whisky and the only one allowed to call itself "The Glenlivet", after a High Court decision in 1880. Dufftown Glenlivet (70 deg. proof) on the other hand, is 8 years old and a typical Speyside malt from one of Bell's distilleries. Though miles from the parish of Glenlivet, Speyside distillers are allowed to use the name if hyphenated with theirs. Highland Park (70 deg. proof), is made in Kirkwall in the Orkneys. The distillery was founded in 1789 and is still making one of the best malts. Talisker (80 deg. proof) comes from the Isle of Skye and is out of sherry wood. It is less peaty and lighter than Laphroaig. Tomatin (70 deg. proof) is 10 years old and made in a distillery 1,020 feet up 20 miles south of Inverness. It is more peaty than the Glenlivets. Glenmorangie (70 deg. proof) is over 10 years old, a delicate, mild whisky made in Ross and Cromarty, the distillery is owned by Macdonald and Muir of Leith. Cardhu (75 deg. proof) is over 12 years old, a Speyside malt from the Cardow distillery which has been owned by Johnnie Walker since 1893. Blair Atholl (70 deg. proof) is an 8 years old Glenlivet style whisky from Perthshire, made by one of the three distilleries owned by Bell's of Perth and nearer to Pitlochry than to Blair Atholl.

LIQUEUR WHISKY

Liqueur whiskies are blended ones which have been matured longer in wood than the standard blends, seven years and more instead of three to five years; whiskies such as Chivas Regal, 12 years old, 75 deg. proof, Red Hackle, Antiquary, Old Rarity (75 deg. proof) and Islay Mist, which is blended Laphroaig.

Drambuie (70 deg. proof) is a best selling liqueur in the United States. It was in 1906 that a 25-year-old Edinburgh wine merchant from Skye, Malcolm Mackinnon, determined that the family liqueur should become famous. First experiments with jelly bags and pans led slowly to success by the twenties.

"Whisky Mac" is half whisky and half green ginger wine, with soda water added if liked. Green ginger wine is as Scottish as kilts, whisky and ship's engineers. It has been made in Leith by Crabbies since 1801 and perhaps earlier. Some of the family were known as wine makers in Queen Anne's day. It is a grape wine, fermented in Leith, with herbs and spices and ginger added to it, then left about 2 years in oak casks.

The Aberdeen Mineral Water Company of Inverness is now exporting bottles of Highland water and ice cubes to the United States, to go with the whisky. Of course, in Scotland, ice is not normally put into the glass with it.

AMBROSIA

This is a simple old Scottish recipe for a cold winter's night. Take 1 cup of made porridge, add 1 tablespoon of honey and 1 of cream, add 2 or 3 tablespoons of whisky. Stir into a smooth cream and drink it. Hot or cold.

Countess Dorothy Di Montegnacco,
London W.1.

ATHOLE BROSE OR ATHOLL BROSE

Mix 3 ozs. oatmeal with cold water to a thick paste. Let it stand 30 minutes. Strain and use the creamy liquor for the brose mixing it with 2 tablespoons heather honey with a silver spoon. Put it into a quart bottle, fill up with whisky. Shake well before serving. (If it is to be kept the bottle must be corked tightly.)

Mrs. McMurray,
Brechin, Angus.

KOUMISS MILK WINE

Mix 1 quart of buttermilk and 2 quarts sweet milk (fresh milk) together, add 4 teaspoons sugar and stir until it melts; let it stand in a warm place for 12 hours, covered with a cloth, then bottle. As it is an effervescing drink the corks must be tied down then the bottles kept on their sides. When the Koumiss is opened use straight away.

Mrs. Mary Gifford,
Ford, Midlothian.

This is called Blaand in the Shetland Isles.

BEEF TEA

Remove the fat and shred finely 1 lb. of gravy beef, or pass it twice through a mincing machine. Place it in an earthenware jar and add 1 pint of cold water and 1½ teaspoons of salt. Cover closely. Place the jar in a saucepan of boiling water, or in a slow oven and cook slowly for 3 hours, stirring occasionally. Strain, remove carefully all traces of grease and serve.

Mrs. Jessie Hislop,
Glasgow, W.3.

PORRIDGE

As a matter of fact the last time I was in Edinburgh I could only find one person who had actually eaten porridge for breakfast. Me! Porridge is dying out. Everybody says so, the modern Scot has corn flakes. Not because they don't all believe deeply in porridge, it makes you healthy they say and deepens the intellect. Everybody talks about fresh ground oatmeal the way some people go on about coffee. "Porridge is like a guid rice pudding, it should really be cooked all night". Nowadays this is too much trouble and so most people have a light breakfast. I can't blame them really. After all the baps, bannocks and what-do-you-call-its are heaven and the Scots did invent marmalade. Some Scotsmen habitually refer to porridge in the plural and say "they" should be served with cream but "they" may be eaten with sugar or honey, or syrup if you like. Some people have beer or stout with them. The hot porridge should be ladled into deep white porringers, wooden bowls, soup plates or huge cups and served with a jug of cream, or milk, or buttermilk to pour over, though this is sometimes served in separate bowls for each person. You then dip a spoonful of porridge into it before

209

swallowing. It is thought best to sup the porridge with a horn spoon, as porridge can overheat a metal one. There are many ways of making porridge. "They" can be thick or thin. Porridge can also be spoiled by steeping the oatmeal too long and by cooking it too long and by serving hot milk with it.

PORRIDGE I Thick

For 4 people. Into 2 pints of boiling water sift a handful of oats through the fingers of the left hand stirring all the time with a porridge stick, thible or spurtle (or, of course, a wooden spoon). Repeat this operation until the porridge is fairly thick adding 4 to 5 handfuls of oats. Either draw the pan to the side of the stove and put a lid on, cook it steadily for about an hour, stirring it at intervals energetically, or cook it in the top of a double boiler stirring it from time to time with a spurtle or wooden spoon. Add salt just before serving or sprinkle it on it.

PORRIDGE II Thin

Have 1 pint boiling water in a deep pan. Add a level teaspoon of salt, add the oatmeal, medium oatmeal, sprinkling it in as before and stirring all the time to avoid lumps — 2 tablespoons of oatmeal. Boil for 5 or 6 minutes, stirring till the oatmeal is swollen, then reduce the heat and simmer covered for at least 30 minutes, stirring frequently. It may need more boiling water as it is meant to be thin. Some people stir the oatmeal into cold water the night before, then boil it for 30 minutes before breakfast. Adding salt before the oatmeal makes the meal harder.

Serve with cream, buttermilk or sweet milk.

SCOTS BREAKFAST MARMALADE

This is particularly good with hot baps. Scrub 4 lbs. of Seville oranges, 2 lemons and 1 sweet orange. Cut them into halves. Squeeze the juice out of them and strain it. Tie the pips and pulp into a muslin bag or clean handkerchief and cut the skin into thick or thin strips according to your family's taste. If you like the thick, bitter kind of marmalade leave on all the pith, if not quite so bitter cut it off and put it in the bag with the pips and pulp.

Put the juice, 4 quarts of water, the muslin bag and the strips of peel into a large bowl or crock and let it soak for 12 hours. Next day pour it in the jam pan, bring to the boil and reduce the heat. Simmer until the pieces of orange peel are tender. If the peel is not cooked long enough it will be tough and the colour poor and you will not get a good set. Remove the bag of pips etc., add 8 lbs. of sugar, brown sugar if you like and cook gently, stirring till the sugar melts, Bring to the boil and boil for 20 — 30 minutes till setting point is reached. Let the marmalade stand for about 15 minutes before bottling so the peel is evenly distributed. Bottle in warm jars and cover with wax discs while still warm. Tie down the jars when cold.

Don't overcook the marmalade or it will be very dark and the flavour spoiled. When set it should be 22°F. on the sugar thermometer.

Mrs. Fraser,
Perth.

RODDEN (OR ROWAN) JELLY

This jelly has a pleasantly tart taste and goes very well with saddle of mutton, venison or grouse. It is made from mountain ash berries picked in early November when almost ripe. Allow 2 lbs. apples to 3 lbs. of rodden berries without their stalks. Wash and drain them, chop the apples roughly leaving on the skin and cores which help the jelly to set. Put all the fruit in a jam pan with water just to cover and bring to the boil and simmer for about an hour. Strain the juice through a jelly bag (see Quince Jelly, South Coast), don't press the fruit, it makes the jelly cloudy. Measure the juice, put it in the rinsed out, dried and lightly buttered jam pan with 1 lb. sugar per pint of juice. Bring gently to the boil, stirring until the sugar melts then boil till setting point is reached in 30 minutes or so. Bottled in small warmed jars.

Mrs. Joyce,
Dunfermline, Fifeshire.

CRAB APPLE AND ROSE HIP JELLY FROM FIFE

You want 1 lb. of cooking apples, cut in quarters but neither peeled nor cored, to every breakfast cup of wild rose hips. These are the scarlet seed pods. They should be measured after they have had the seeds removed. Put both fruits in a jam pan with water to cover (rose hips should not be cooked in an aluminium pan, an enamel one is best), simmer till soft, strain the liquid through a jelly bag without squeezing the fruit (see Quince Jelly, South Coast). Having buttered the pan a little with unsalted butter pour in the juice. Add 1 lb. of sugar to every pint of liquid. Gently stir till all the sugar melts then boil the resulting syrup for about 10 minutes or until setting point is reached. Bottle in warmed jars and cover when cold.

Mrs. Murray,
Kirkcaldy, Fifeshire.

Dr. Samuel Johnson's definition of oats was "A grain which in England is generally given to horses but in Scotland supports the people." To which somebody replied "Yes, sir. But where will you find such horses or such people?"

Oatmeal, which is used so much for broths, skirlie, oatcakes, porridge and so on is oats with the husks removed, after the grain has been separated from the chaff the oats are ground, but because

211

of its low gluten content oatmeal does not make a workable dough when mixed with water and so cannot be used for bread. Freshly roasted oat grains have a smell not unlike vanilla.

SKIRLY

Heat 8 ozs. lard in a frying pan till so hot it stops sizzling. Add 1 large chopped onion, fry lightly then add 3 handfuls of oatmeal, let it fry for 2 minutes, add salt and pepper and lastly add about 1 cupful of boiling water which thickens the skirly ready to serve.

Mrs. W. Forbes,
Kincardine O Neil, Aberdeenshire.

Pan Haggis is a very similar dish to Skirly. Skirly is sometimes served as a garnish for roast grouse and other game, but often as a main supper dish with mashed potato and vegetables.

SCULLIGALEE

Fry lightly 2 ozs. of roasting fat (or dripping), add 1 finely cut onion and 4 ozs. coarse oatmeal. Cook until the fat is absorbed. Add $\frac{1}{2}$ pint of milk, some salt and pepper; put on a lid and cook slowly for 20 to 30 minutes. Serve with mashed turnip and mashed potatoes.

Mary Lunsden,
Rutherglen, Lanarkshire.

"DONKEY" FROM FIFE

Finely chop a large onion and mix it well with 1 cup of oatmeal, 3 ozs. suet and a little salt. Mix in $\frac{1}{4}$ pint of cold water. Grease the top pan of a double boiler and turn the mixture into this. Steam it for 3 hours, turn out and serve with cold roast beef (if you have no double boiler, this may be steamed in a bowl in a pan of water, but make sure it has plenty of room to swell).

Mrs. I. P. Froy,
Hitchin, Hertfordshire.

SCOTS STUFFING FOR TURKEY

Rub 2 ozs. of dripping from beef or home cured fat bacon into 8 ozs. of oatmeal. Chop 1 large onion very finely and add it to the mixture with salt, pepper and, if liked, 1 teaspoon of made English mustard. Stuff the fowl with this in the usual way.

This is an old recipe my gran used to make. If she had lived she would be 97 years of age.

Mrs. D. Millard,
Bishopbriggs, near Glasgow.

KALE

Wash and strip and boil one head of fairly green kale in 1 pint of water for about 45 minutes. Remove the kale from the pan and chop it finely. Return it to the pan and add 2 tablespoons of fine oatmeal, 1 oz. butter, stirring it to a paste with 1 gill of milk. Add pepper and salt to taste. Simmer for 15 minutes. This can also be made with stock from a bone, omitting the butter and milk, or it can be made with boiling meat, adding turnip, carrot and an onion.

Mrs. A. M. Hay,
Dyke, Forres, Morayshire.

KAIL OR KALE

Kail is a kind of dark green curly cabbage very popular in Scotland. From this comes Kail Yard, a back garden where cabbages and vegetables are grown. (The strictly Scottish form is Kail-Yaird) a word also used to describe a school of Scottish writers of stories about everyday life in Scotland, which are mostly in dialect. The writers and poets got the name from a Scottish Jacobite song "There grows a bonnie brier bush in our kail-yard". From this Ian MacClaren took the title for a series of short stories published in 1894 "Beside the bonnie brier bush" which were an early and popular example of this school of writing.

STOVIES

My granny always made this on the top of the old kitchen range where it could sit slowly cooking all day. The secret is in the *protracted* gentle heat, but I do it in a good, strong pan on a very low gas. This is a traditional Scots recipe when meat was scarce.

You need 3 fair sized potatoes sliced rather thinly, 2 onions sliced up and some dripping. Melt the dripping and lightly brown the onions, then add the sliced potatoes and keep stirring them around, gradually pour in sufficient water to keep the mixture from burning but not enough to make it too soggy. Put the lid on the pan and leave to cook for about 2 hours on a very low heat. It should never be mushy.

Mrs. Ivy Ross,
Westcliffe-on-Sea, Essex.

STOVIES (Another Way)

Peel a few potatoes and cut into small pieces walnut size. Place in a saucepan with chopped onion and about an inch and a half of water. Add some small pieces of left-over (cooked) meat, preferably roast, and mix all together. Add salt and pepper and top with 2 ozs. of roast beef dripping. Place a lid on the saucepan and cook until the water has evaporated and the contents are nice and "mushy".

Very savoury and a good method of using up the remains of a joint.

Mrs. E. Cairns,
Edinburgh.

213

CLAPSHOT (from Orkney)

to eat with sausages.

Put 12 ozs. sliced turnip (or what in England are called swedes) into boiling salted water and cook for 15 minutes. Add 1 lb. peeled quartered potatoes and boil together till soft. Drain, add salt and pepper, 1 oz. butter and 1 finely chopped raw onion. Mash all together and serve with sausages.

Mrs. I. P. Froy,
Hitchin, Hertfordshire.

STOVED CHEESE AND POTATOES

Slice 6 cooked potatoes, grate 2 ozs. cheese. Put a layer of potatoes with 1 large sliced onion in a pie dish then sprinkle on the cheese. Fill the pie dish, add pepper, then add enough milk to come to the rim of the dish — about ½ pint. Bake for 30 minutes then sprinkle thickly with grated cheese. Allow to brown and serve very hot.

Mrs. A. R. Scott,
Crail, Fife.

POTATOES

In Scotland they have several breeds of excellent potatoes which you scarcely ever find south of the border. Golden Wonder is a pear-shaped, russet-skinned, very floury potato with a slightly nutty flavour. It is particularly good for baking in its jacket. Then Kerr's Pink is a round pink potato with deep red eyes. It is popular for mashing and making scones and potato cakes.

Arran Chief is one of the first early potatoes, available from May to August. It has a white soft flesh but is not floury and makes delicious potato salads.

AFTERS

AVERNS OR WILD STRAWBERRIES

These are found in some parts of Scotland in August. Cover the strawberries with port, leave them well sugared to marinate for several hours before serving with thick (unwhipped) cream and Highland Crowdie.

S. Burrowes,
Pitlochry, Perthshire.

STRAWBERRY HYDROPATHIC PUDDING

Although instructions are given for making this pudding with strawberries only, any other fruit or any mixture of fruits will do.

Take a basin the size that the pudding should be. Put at the bottom a round piece of stale crumb of bread about the size of a five shilling piece. Place round this in an upright position and about an inch apart from one another, fingers of bread, three to four inches long, according to the depth of the basin. Pick some strawberries and boil them with a spoonful or two of water and as much sugar as will be required to sweeten them pleasantly until they are reduced to pulp. Put the hot fruit gently into the basin with a spoon so as to disturb the bread as little as possible; cover the surface of the fruit with little odds and ends of bread cut up into small dice, and press the pudding by putting a plate upon it with a weight on the top. Leave it in a cold place for three or four hours, or all night if convenient. When wanted, remove the weight and the plate, turn the pudding upon a dish and serve. It will come out in a shape. A little custard or cream served with it will be a great improvement.

Mrs. J. K. Mackay,
Dornoch, Sutherland.

BAKED TOFFEE APPLE PUDDING

Take 8 ozs. of short crust pastry, 1½ ozs. butter, 4 ozs. brown sugar, 1 lb. apples cored, peeled and sliced fairly thickly. Grease a pudding basin thickly with butter, sprinkle about ⅓ of the sugar in, line the basin with pastry, trim the edges, half fill it with the apples, add the remain ng sugar and the rest of the apples. Wet the edge of the pastry, roll the pastry trimmings into a round to fit the top of the basin. Bake in a moderate oven (350 F., Mark 4) for about 2 hours. Turn out and serve alone or with a sweet sauce.

Mrs. A. R. Houston,
Glengarnock, Ayrshire.

CLOOTIE DUMPLING

A Clootie Dumpling is a very old favourite in Scotland. It is often made for birthdays, parties, and usually one graces the table at Hogmanay. In case you are at sea with the word "Clootie" — it means "cloth" i.e. a dumpling cooked in a cloot (? or clout).

1 cup of fine breadcrumbs	2 cupfuls of self raising flour
1 cupful suet	1 cupful sugar
2 teaspoonfuls of cinnamon	2 teaspoonfuls of mixed spice
pinch salt	1 cupful raisins
1 cupful sultanas	1 cup of warmed treacle
¼ cup of warmed syrup	1 cup of milk with 1 egg beaten into it

Put all the dry ingredients into a baking bowl and add warmed treacle, syrup, milk and egg. Mix thoroughly. Turn into a cloth which has been dipped in hot water and lightly floured.

Tie end firmly, and put into a pan of boiling water (having put a plate in the bottom of the pan) and boil for at least four hours.

Make sure the pan does not go off the boil, and add boiling water if the water boils away.

When the dumpling is ready, it can be served with custard or brandy sauce; or it may be left until cold and then sliced. It is also delicious fried with bacon and egg.

(If desired more fruit can be added, but I find the above measure of fruit quite adequate).

Mrs. M. McGathan,
Cairniehill, Bankfoot, Perthshire.

CHEESE SOUFFLE

Mix 1 dessertspoon of cornflour with $\frac{1}{2}$ pint of milk and heat, stirring until it boils for a few minutes. Stir in 2 ozs. finely grated cheese and a little salt and pepper. Leave aside. Beat 3 egg yolks slightly, stir the warm mixture into them. Whip the whites firm enough to stand in peaks and then fold them into the mixture and turn this at once into a deep, straight sided, ovenproof pottery soufflé dish. Bake at once in a fairly hot oven (375 F., Mark 5) for about 30 minutes. The dish should be served immediately it is cooked and eaten at once.

Mrs. M. Wilson,
Kirkton, Dumfriesshire.

SCOTTISH CHEESE

Caboc, an ancient Highland cheese made from pure thick cream rolled in pinhead oatmeal — very small and very rich — is made by *Mrs. Stone* of Tain, and is beginning to be widely available in the better grocers. It dates from the 15th century, and *Mrs. Stone* had the recipe from her mother who was a direct descendant of Macdonald of the Isles. It goes well with a full bodied red wine, and matures in flavour even in the refrigerator.

Hramsa is a fresh double cream cheese mixed with the wild garlic or ramson leaves you find growing in the woods in May all over Britain. And there is a new one called Lammermoor, made like a *Coulommiers* but instead of being allowed to ripen it is smoked over a peat fire.

Caithness and Morven cheese both come from Lybster near Wick. They are both something like a *Port Salut* but with a character of their own which is most enjoyable.

Then there is Highland Crowdie, from Tain on the Dornoch Firth, a low fat soft cheese which is delicious to eat with thick cream and home made strawberry jam. There is also a smoked cheese from the Orkneys with a pleasant peaty flavour which is excellent with small thick oatcakes.

The Dunlop is an old Scottish cheese similar to Cheddar. It was first made in 1688 by Barbara Gilmore, a dairywoman in the Dunlop district of Ayrshire.

BAKING

BLACK BUNS

In Bothwell, Lanarkshire, at the Cottage Bakery in Hamilton Road, I saw *Mr. Douglas Sommerville*, who is a Master Baker, making the famous Scottish Black Bun which is square and rather like a Christmas Pudding rolled in pastry. It is very spicy and some of the best have rum in them. Bun is the Scottish name for plum cake, black buns are always eaten at Hogmanay (New Year's Eve) and are usually made months, sometimes a year, beforehand and left to mature. They keep very well wrapped in greaseproof paper in an air-tight tin.

Mr. Sommerville was also cooking crusty brown loaves with a cross on top, and pan loaves, with no wasteful crust on either end, in a long bread pan. When I arrived he was flourishing a thing like an old fashioned carpet beater with a 12 inch handle. This is used for putting bread into a Scotch oven, which is a huge thing about 12 foot square with an oil heated side flue. The bread is baked on the hot flagstones which line the floor and any connoisseur of bread will tell you that it is delicious. There is a great selection of bread and cakes in Scottish tea shops. Fancy buns and cakes are called tea bread, and brown and white baps are what you have in Scotland for breakfast eaten with plenty of farmhouse butter. There are also Butteries and Softies, indeed there are all kinds of morning rolls in Scotland with different names, according to where they are made and varying from town to town and shop to shop. There are round flat baps cut in two, spread with butter filled with bacon and fried egg as a sandwich, and floury baps which should be eaten warm or re-warmed from the oven.

SCOTCH BLACK BUN

Mix 8 ozs. of flour with ½ teaspoon of baking powder. Rub in 4 ozs. of butter, mix this into a firm pastry dough with a little water and roll it out into a thin sheet. Grease the inside of a large square cake tin and line it with the pastry keeping back a piece for the top of the bun, trim the edges. Into a large basin put 1 lb. of flour, 1 lb. of raisins, 2 ozs. of currants washed in cold water and dried, 6 ozs. of chopped blanched almonds (not ground almonds), ½ oz. of ginger, ½ oz. of powdered cinnamon, ½ teaspoon of black pepper, 1 small teaspoon of baking soda, ½ oz. of cayenne pepper, 1 small teaspoon of cream of tartar. Add 8 ozs. of sugar, 4 ozs. of chopped candied peel and then add a breakfast cup of milk. Mix the ingredients with your hands and put them into the lined pastry tin. Wet the edges with water, put on a pastry lid, pinch it over and mark it with a fork. Brush with a little egg. With a skewer make 4 holes right down to the bottom of the cake and bake it in a moderate oven (350 F., Mark 4) for about 4 hours. It improves with keeping.

Mrs. W. B. Macfarlane,
Glasgow.

SCOTCH PANCAKE, TEA PANCAKE OR DROP SCONES

Mix 4 ozs. of flour, $\frac{1}{2}$ teaspoon of bicarbonate of soda, $\frac{1}{2}$ teaspoon of cream of tartar and 2 ozs. of sugar. Beat in an egg and add 1 oz. of melted butter then enough soured milk to make a thin smooth batter the consistency of thick cream. Lightly brush the griddle with melted butter, heat and get it really hot. Drop a spoonful of the batter on it. This should be brown underneath in less than a minute if the griddle is hot enough. Now drop spoonfuls of the batter on it well apart. Cook till little bubbles rise to the surface. The underneath is then done. Turn your Scotch pancakes carefully with a palette knife and cook the other side. When the second side is golden brown and the edges are dry they are cooked. Wrap them in a warm napkin, take them straight to table. They are eaten hot with butter for high tea and sometimes with jam or honey as well. Stale drop scones are very good fried up with the breakfast bacon.

Mrs. A. M. Andrews,
Fort William, Inverness-shire.

SCONES

The name is perhaps taken from the ancient town of Scone where the kings of Scotland were crowned or from the gaelic Sgonn — a large mouthful. They are most often baked on a griddle or hot plate or girdle or a frying pan but sometimes in the oven. In Scotland they are generally made without sugar, but they are made with variations all over the English speaking world. They are very quick to make and usually the quicker you make them the better they are.

SODA SCONES

Sift together 8 ozs. flour, $\frac{1}{2}$ teaspoon bicarbonate of soda, $\frac{1}{2}$ teaspoon cream of tartar, $\frac{1}{2}$ teaspoon salt. Add enough sour milk or buttermilk to make a soft dough. Turn it onto a floured board. Halve. Knead each half into a round. Roll it out $\frac{1}{4}$ inch thick, cut in four triangles. Bake till a pale brown first one side then the other on a hot griddle. Cool them in a towel to keep them soft. Serve hot, sliced lengthways and spread them with butter.

Mrs. J. M. Grant,
Aboyne, Aberdeenshire.

SCALDED SCONES

Put a small bowl of self raising flour into a basin, add a teaspoon of sugar, a little salt and a piece of butter the size of a walnut. Over

these pour the same measure of boiling milk as you have of flour. Mix well with a knife, then turn it onto a well floured board. Knead lightly adding as little flour as possible. Roll out very thinly and cook on a hot plate or griddle till brown, turn over and cook the other side. The hot plate should not be too hot.

Mrs. W. Brownlie,
Carnwath, Lanarkshire.

POTATO SCONES

This is how granny made the potato scones in Scotland. They can be eaten for tea rolled up with butter, or, next day, fried with bacon and egg. Oat or wheaten meal may be used instead of flour if you wish.

Heat the girdle, mash 8 ozs. of cooked potatoes smoothly adding 1 oz. of melted butter and ¼ teaspoon salt. Fold in 1 oz. of flour. Turn the mixture onto a floured board and knead in another 1 oz. of flour. Cut the mixture in two and shape each piece into a round. Roll this out thinly and cut them in four. Prick them with a fork and cook them on a high girdle for about 2 minutes each side. Cool in a clean towel.

Mr. James McMillan,
Daily Express.

BANNOCKS

These are the same as scones but as large as a meat plate. They are mostly made with buttermilk and baked on a hot griddle, but in practice there are several kinds of bannocks. A Pitcaithy Bannock is a kind of shortbread with candied peel and almonds in it. A Selkirk Bannock is more like a fruit loaf. St. Bride's Bannocks are eaten on the first day of spring, Hallomass Bannocks on the first day of winter. There are bannocks, too, for Shrove Tuesday or Brozeday. In parts of Angus they make a thick oatcake which is called a bannock. Ordinary bannocks, however, are made with flour or flour mixed with barley or potatoes.

PITCAITHY BANNOCKS

Put 1 lb. of flour, 10 ozs. of butter, 4½ ozs. of caster sugar, 2 ozs. of blanched chopped almonds, 2 ozs. of chopped candied peel into a bowl. Knead them well until the butter absorbs the flour and so on. Don't use any water. Make them into two round flat cakes or bannocks, pinch them round the edges and bake them slowly in a moderate oven (350 F., Mark 4) for about 30 minutes.

Mrs. McLeish,
Edinburgh.

COCONUT GINGERBREAD

Put 1 lb. golden syrup, 4 ozs. butter, 4 ozs. moist brown sugar into a saucepan. Let them heat very slowly until the butter is quite melted, when it will be well mixed with the syrup, then pour the mixture into a bowl containing 8 ozs. ground rice, 8 ozs. of the best flour, 1 oz. of ground ginger, a pinch of salt, 1 dessertspoon of baking powder, the rind of half a lemon cut into small pieces and 1 oz. of chopped candied lemon. Mix thoroughly. Put the paste on one side and when it is quite cold stir into it the finely grated white part of a large coconut. When it is well beaten drop the paste upon a well buttered tin in small cakes and bake these in a moderate oven (350 F., Mark 4) for about 30 minutes.

Mrs. J. Mackay,
Dornoch, Sutherland.

DATE AND WALNUT LOAF
— To serve sliced and buttered for High Tea.

Grease a 9 inch x 2¾ inch loaf tin. Sift 12 ozs. of plain flour into a bowl with 6 cubes of sugar and 1 level teaspoon of salt. Add 2 ozs. shelled chopped walnuts, 8 ozs. stoned chopped dates. Whisk 2 tablespoons of corn oil with an egg and add this to the dry ingredients. Dissolve 2 level teaspoons of baking soda in ½ pint of boiled water and stir this into the dry ingredients. Beat it well to form a slack mixture and pour it into the greased loaf tin. Bake in a moderate oven (350 F., Mark 4) for about 75 minutes. Serve sliced and spread with butter.

Mrs. J. Taylor,
Coatbridge, Lanarkshire.

SELKIRK BANNOCKS

Sift 8 ozs. warm plain flour into a warm bowl with a pinch of salt. Melt 2 ozs. lard in a pan adding ¼ pint of milk which bring to blood heat. Cream ½ oz. yeast with 1 teaspoon sugar and pour the warm lard and milk over it. Having made a well in the middle of the warm flour, pour in the yeast mixture and with it work the flour to a fairly soft dough, stirring from the middle. Then knead it about 5 minutes on a floured board, before putting it back in a greased basin in a warm place to rise to double its size. It should be covered with a damp cloth and will take an hour or more. Knead in 1¾ ozs. sugar and 4 ozs. currants into the dough on a floured board, forming it into a large round. Let this stand for a good 10 minutes on a greased baking tray near the heat till it rises a little and goes puffy, before baking it in a really hot oven (475 F., Mark 7) for 15 minutes. Reduce the heat to fairly moderate (375 F., Mark 5) and bake till a golden brown, in about 25 minutes. It should then be brushed on top with glaze — made by melting a dessertspoon of caster sugar in a dessertspoon of boiling water. Cool on a wire rack.

Mrs. Fortescue,
Galashiels, Selkirkshire.

Selkirk, a pleasant Scottish border town in the midst of some very good scenery, has been famous for years for its superlative bannocks. A Selkirk Bannock is a yeasted fruit loaf very like the Bara Brith so popular in Wales, a delicious mixture of best butter, flour, dried fruit and yeast, flat underneath and with a shiny brown top speckled with sultanas. You can have it sliced thick or thin, buttered or unbuttered, for tea, supper or to take on a journey. Nowadays it is sent all over the world, it was a favourite of Queen Victoria and has been supplied to several Prime Ministers, even Sir Walter Scott mentioned it in "The Bride of Lammermuir".

Robert Douglas's original baker's shop which was opened in 1859 is in a corner of Selkirk Market Square just by Sir Walter Scott's statue. When he first started up in business Robbie Douglas introduced several features which improved the flavour of the local bannock and so made them widely known; his original recipe is still followed, though the shop now belongs to a firm of bakers. Their Mr. Guthrie, who has been with the firm for over 50 years, supervises the despatch of some 20,000 parcels of bannocks every Christmas.

SHORTBREAD

At Robert Cresser's small shop in the Corn Market, Edinburgh, one can not only find the old wooden porridge spurtles or thibles (pronounced thievel) for stirring porridge, but the shop is also famous for its hand carved shortbread moulds. The 7 inch size is the best for cooking. "To make perfect shortbread," Robert Cresser says, "mix 8 ozs. of plain flour, 2 ozs. of sugar and knead in 6 ozs. of butter. Add no moisture, but just knead it till you get a dough. Press it by hand into two round cakes about ¾ inch thick pressing them into the mould." He says, however, with Scottish honesty, that you can mould your own shortbread just as well in an ordinary tin but should crimp the edges with your fingers and prick the middle with a fork so it won't rise too much. Bake it till pale golden brown in a very slow oven, the slower the better.

Robert Cresser,
Edinburgh.

OATCAKES

There are several kinds, thick and thin. They are very good buttered for breakfast with honey or marmalade and with hot fried herrings. They are also very good with cheese.

Heat the griddle. Mix 1 teacup of oatmeal with a pinch of salt, a pinch of bicarbonate of soda. Melt 1 teaspoon dripping with ¼ teacup of hot water. Mix it with the meal to make a smooth paste. Turn it onto a board sprinkled with oatmeal. Knead well and when smooth shape it into a round and roll it out very thin, Brush off the meal. Cut it into *six*. Brush the meal from the underside. Bake them on the hot griddle till the edges are beginning to curl. Finish the second side.

Wales

Agricultural Products
Mountain Lamb and Marsh Lamb, New Potatoes from Pembrokeshire. Market Gardening.

Dairy
Caerphilly Cheese, Shir Gar (Salty yellow farmhouse butter).

Gastronomic Specialities
Salmon, Sewin or Sea Trout, Crabs, Lobsters and Crawfish (*Langoustes*), Radnor Mutton with Onion Sauce, Laver Bread and Bacon, Oyster Soup (Gower), Welsh Rabbit, Sir Watkin Williams-Wynne's Pudding, Boiled Salt Duckling, Leek and Bacon Pie, Welsh Broth, Char, Gwyniad and Vendace in Lakes Bala and Vrynwy, Brown Trout.

Pastry
Teisen Lap, Bara Brith, Aberfraw Cakes.

SOUP

WELSH MUTTON CAWL — OR BROTH — OR CIG DAFAO
This soup should be made the day before, then when it is cold the fat can be skimmed off.

Trim off any excess fat from 1½ lbs. scrag end and breast of mutton or lamb and put the meat and bones into a saucepan with some bacon rinds. Put in 2 sliced onions, add 1 turnip, 2 medium carrots, all chopped fairly small, then a little pepper and 1 teaspoon mixed herbs. Pour 2½ pints water in, bring to the boil, take off the scum. Cover closely with a lid and leave to simmer slowly for about 4 hours. Strain into a large bowl. Discard all the bones, add meat and vegetables to the stock. Leave overnight. Next day skim off the fat. Put in 1 tablespoon of pearl barley and reheat until the barley is cooked.

Mrs. D. Crossman,
Grangetown, Cardiff, Glamorgan.

ONION SOUP (2 persons)
Slice 12 ozs. onions as thin as possible. Boil to a pulp. Add 4 ozs. grated cheese with ½ oz. butter. Mix thoroughly adding ½ pint milk and stirring to boiling point. Add salt and pepper to your taste.

Mr. Rosser,
Llansamlet, Swansea, Glamorgan.

WELSH SALMON SOUP

Very nice if you have got a salmon or a sea trout. This is the way to use the bones. If not get some salmon bones, heads and skin from your fishmonger and one or two whiting trimmings or sole bones. Put them all in a pan, add the usual soup vegetables, 1 sliced turnip, 1 sliced carrot, 1 onion, a stick of celery, cover with water and simmer for an hour. Off the fire remove the fat and oil with a paper. Strain the soup and then thicken it by stirring in some mashed potato. Add, if possible, a little fresh raw salmon perhaps from the tail and a handful of fresh brown breadcrumbs. Bring to the boil and simmer till the salmon is cooked, the soup is then ready. Put a tablespoon of chopped parsley in the bottom of the soup tureen and pour the soup over.

Mrs. B. Thomas,
Machynlleth, Montgomeryshire.

FISH

"The meals I most clearly remember are those suppers on Saturday nights in my grandfather's farmhouse in Carmarthenshire when I was a schoolboy. I shall never forget sitting there in the dark kitchen with the smoked hams hanging from the rafters. They usually started with a dish of steaming cockles bought that morning in Carmarthen market. They were followed by trout my father caught in our brook, fried in butter with the skin crisp. And there would be potatoes roasted in the bakers' oven next to the main fireplace.

My grandfather's housekeeper used to make pancakes, 20 or 30 at a time, on a griddle in the wash-house. We ended the meal with a cheese, something between a strong Caerphilly and the French Cantal which was made by my aunt. To drink? Buttermilk or tea".

Dr. Glyn Daniel,
St. John's College, Cambridge.

TEISEN GOCOS

When we have plenty of fresh cockles we usually make them into cockle cakes. You need about 2 pints of them. If there is time let them stand overnight in water sprinkled with oatmeal to make them plump, but in any case they must be well rinsed in a colander in plenty of cold running water and then in a basin in several changes of cold water to get the sand out of their shells.

Put them in a pan with a little boiling water, cook them over a fierce heat, stirring, until the shells open in about 5 minutes. Take them from their shells and put them in a thick pancake batter and fry them, a spoonful at a time, in a pan of hot oil.

Mr. Clive Gammon,
Daily Express.

LAVER BREAD AND COCKLES

Coat 8 ozs. laver bread liberally with seasoned flour and fry it in some bacon fat in one half of a frying pan. In the other half fry 4 ozs. of freshly cooked and shelled cockles. Serve garnished with sprigs of parsley.

Mrs. Vera Griffiths,
Llanelli, Carmarthenshire.

The women of Penclawdd, in South Wales, have been going out with a sieve and a basket and a donkey for generations to reap the vast cockle harvest of Llanrhidian Sands. The laver is a kind of seaweed which also grows at Penclawdd. (See note in the meat section, page 226). You can nearly always buy both laver "bread" and fresh cockles in Swansea Market. Some people are very fond of hot laver mixed with orange juice as a vegetable to go with lobsters. Others mix the laver with oil, lemon juice, salt and pepper and serve it for starters, with hot dry toast — as Caviar Cymreig.

COCKLE PIE — PASTAI GOCOS

How times have changed! When we were small children we used to go and collect cockles along the beach on the Gower Peninsular and, dreadful to relate, we did this on Sunday mornings despite the warnings from our neighbours that we would die for such wickedness!

But still we always enjoyed our Sunday tea and cockles. My mum used to make a pie with them.

Rinse about 1 quart of fresh cockles in cold running water scraping off any weed etc. Put them in a basin of cold water and change it several times to get rid of the sand inside them. Cook them in about ¼ pint of hot water just till the shells open in about 4 minutes. Line the sides of your pie dish with thick short crust pastry. Put a layer of shelled cockles on the bottom. Sprinkle them with chopped spring onions then with diced streaky bacon. Go on in layers till the dish is full. Strain the liquor in which the cockles were cooked through a clean fine cloth, pour it into the dish. Add pepper, no salt. Lay a trellis of pastry strips over the pie. Bake it in a moderate oven (350 F., Mark 4).

Mr. Wilfred Davies,
Glamorgan.

DABS AND SHALLOTS IN A MUSHROOM SAUCE

Coat 1 lb. of dabs with seasoned flour and then shallow fry them in oil. Meanwhile chop up 1 lb. of shallots very finely and make a mushroom sauce using 4 ozs. mushrooms.

Serve the dabs covered with finely chopped shallots and the mushroom sauce.

Mrs. Vera Griffiths,
Llanelli, Carmarthenshire.

SMALL BROOK TROUT OR BROWN TROUT THE FARM-HOUSE WAY FOR BREAKFAST

We get them from the brook at the end of the paddock. I clean and wipe them dry, I fry them either side in a pan lightly greased with bacon dip and we have fried bacon with them. Perfect.

Mrs. Gwynneth ap-Jones,
Dolgellau, Merionethshire.

GRILLED HADDOCK

It was at Criccieth, near Lloyd George's home at Llanystumdwy, that I first tasted the delights of the Welsh kitchen. Criccieth overlooks Tremadoc Bay and you can see the Lleyn Peninsular from the castle and to the south the eerie outline of Harlech Castle. Here too I learned of the Welshman's love for singing. I often helped my mother prepare the grilled haddock, gaily singing "My Hen laid a haddock on top of a tree" — my interpretation of "Mae hen wlad fy nhadau yn anwyl i mi" — as the fish sizzled in the grill pan. It wasn't until a few years later that I came to realize haddocks don't live in trees . . .

For four people you will need four haddock fillets and a few thinly sliced mushrooms. Turn the grill right up and in the bottom of the grill pan melt 1 tablespoon each of butter and olive oil. When this is sizzling put in the haddock cutlets. Turn them over quickly to sear. Season with salt and freshly ground black pepper, then reduce the heat and cook the fish, basting it frequently with the juices to prevent dryness. When it is half cooked scatter the thinly sliced mushrooms on top. Dot with more butter and finish the cooking. Remove the fish and mushrooms with a fish slice and keep hot. Turn the griller right up again and add either a dash of white wine vinegar or the juice of half a lemon to the juices in the bottom of the grill pan. Heat, then pour over the fish.

We always had this with hunks of bread to mop up the juices and a green salad tossed in olive oil and lemon juice.

This is particularly good done with hake though any white fish can be used.

Miss Jill Walker,
Daily Express.

TEIFI SALMON SAUCE

In summer when I have been fishing we sometimes have so much salmon and sea trout I do not know what to do with it, I send some to a firm in London who smoke it for me at about £1·50 a fish and then tell me which train they are putting it on so I can collect it at Swansea station.

This however is an old Welsh way of cooking salmon which we enjoy very much.

Wash the salmon in salted water, dry it well and cut it in slices. You will also need ¾ pint of melted butter, stir a glass of port and a little ketchup into it together with a boned, chopped anchovy in a saucepan over a low heat. Put the salmon slices in a fireproof dish and pour the sauce over them, cover the dish with foil. Bake it in a fairly hot oven (375 F., Mark 5) for about 40 minutes.

Mr. Clive Gammon,
Daily Express.

MEAT AND POULTRY

LAMB

In Britain a roast leg of lamb is perhaps most often served with mint sauce, brown gravy, roast potatoes, peas and sometimes red currant jelly as well, though it is sometimes treated differently in different parts of the country. In Radnorshire, in Central Wales, a county famous for its small delicious and very lean legs of mountain lamb, they sometimes wrap them completely in flour and water dough or "huff paste" then bake them in a moderate oven (350 F., Mark 4) for about 2 hours and serve them with a thick onion sauce and rowan jelly. Some butchers on the Welsh border sell these small lean Welsh joints skewered into a large lacey apron of caul fat. The joint is then roasted in the fat to keep it moist and succulent (but of course without the huff paste).

In South Wales the local salt marsh mutton, similar to the luscious *pré-salé* of the north of France, though not nearly so well known, is served with laver sauce, either plain or mixed with Seville orange juice. Laver (*porphya lacinate* or *porphyra vulgaris*) is a seaweed, rich in iodine — the sauce is made from "laver bread", a delicacy which is usually on sale in Swansea market. Laver bread is made, however, by rinsing the seaweed thoroughly in seawater and wringing it dry, then cooking it in boiling seawater with a dash of vinegar. Then drain it. It should not be cooked in an iron pot.

For the laver sauce: mix the thick gravy from the meat with 2 ozs. butter and about 1 lb. laver bread. Serve very hot, stir with a silver spoon.

WELSH DINNER

I am going 73 years of age, but when I was a child my mother used to make us a marvellous Welsh dinner.

Its ingredients were, a neck of lean lamb, 1 lb. of carrots, 1 lb. of parsnips, 1 lb. onions, small swede, 2 lbs. potatoes, 1 leek and a bunch of parsley. This is enough for a family of 6. (You boiled the potatoes separately.) You boiled all these, less the leek and parsley as you would a stew, putting the vegetables in large slices. When cooked you added the leek about 10 minutes before serving.

You served the clear soup as a first course. You boil the potatoes separately. You also make a parsley sauce with ½ pint milk and ½ pint water, thicken with plain flour or cornflour, add a dollop of butter and a pinch of salt; when ready add chopped parsley. You now serve a dinner with the lamb and all the slices of vegetables, fresh boiled potatoes and parsley sauce.

Mrs. G. Mosford,
Swansea, Glamorgan.

"MAMS FRESH GREEN PEA STEW" — Lamb Stew with Spring Vegetables

Buy about 1½ lbs. of best end neck of Welsh lamb, 3 lbs. of fresh peas and 1½ lbs. of small new potatoes. Wash the meat well and see to it that you have no small splinters of bone after the meat has been chopped but left in one piece. Put it in 1½ pints cold water and bring to the boil. Let it simmer, adding salt and pepper and a tablespoon of sugar and a good sprig of fresh mint. Add the shelled peas and the potatoes about 20 minutes before you dish up.

I have now tried this recipe with 4 to 5 chops in a piece, a large bag of frozen peas and a sprig of mint and 4 small potatoes, and the condiments, of course.

Mrs. B. Bucknall Jones,
Portmadoc, Caernarvonshire.

BEEF OLIVES

You need about 1½ lbs. beef steak cut in rather thin slices. Make a forcemeat with 1 teacup of fine white breadcrumbs, 1 tablespoon chopped bacon, ½ teaspoon thyme, 1 dessertspoon chopped parsley and 2 eggs. Flatten the pieces of steak, put a layer of forcemeat in the centre of each piece, roll up and tie with string. Fry them a nice brown in a little butter then place in a stew jar. Brown a tablespoon of flour in the pan in which you browned the steaks, add ¾ pint of gravy and stir till it boils. Pour over the olives. Allow to simmer for a good 2 hours. When ready dish the olives and gravy. Remove the strings.

Mrs. E. Thomas,
Colwyn Bay, Caernarvonshire.

227

PORK SPARE RIB AND PIG'S TAILS CASSEROLE

Soak 2 lbs. spare rib and pig's tails in salted water for a few hours then wash and place in a casserole. Cover with water, add a little salt, 1 lb. small cleaned carrots and 1 lb. small sliced onions and a small quantity of herbs. Cook for 2 hours or more in the oven. When done thicken with cornflour mixed with milk.

Boil 2 lbs. or more potatoes together with 1 lb. swedes (the potatoes in large pieces, swede cut thin, salt). When done drain and add some butter and milk then beat them together until creamy. Serve with the spare rib and tails. Lovely.

Mrs. G. M. Pegler,
Llanfyllin, Montgomery.

In Britain a spare rib of pork is a relatively inexpensive cut from near the shoulders. It roasts well and should not be confused with the American cut of the same name which is just the pared down ends of the cutlet bones — often served here in Chinese restaurants in a spicy sauce.

FFAGOD

Pig-killing week in the country was a gourmet's dream when I was a child. Here is one of the recipes for a good family meal; it can, of course, be reduced if necessary.

Take 1 lb. each of pig's liver, cooking apples, onions and bread-crumbs. Mince together with 4 ozs. of good suet. Add some chopped sage, pepper and salt according to taste. When thoroughly mixed form into balls and place in a well greased tin and add a little water. Ideally each ffagod should wear a neat cap of caul,* but failing this a small knob of butter will serve. Bake slowly in a moderate oven (350 F., Mark 4).

*Caul is the lacey apron of fat from near the kidneys variously called flead fat or flare in other parts of the country.

Mrs. S. P. Barrett,
Cardiff, Glamorgan.

CHICKLINGS

Pig's intestines cleaned and all the fat taken off then turned inside out and thoroughly washed under running water. The small intestines were cut into lengths and each three plaited. Put all in a crock with salted water and a little bicarbonate of soda, leave overnight. Take out and wash. Then boil until cooked. When cold cut into chunks and fry adding salt and pepper to taste.

Mrs. Frances Thomas,
Ammanford, Carmarthenshire.

They are called Chitterlings in some parts of the country.

KATT PIE

A traditional dish made on Templeton Fair day, 12th of November, for at least 200 years.

Make a hot water pastry by boiling 8 ozs. suet in water then add to 1 lb. of flour and some salt, stirring well with a wooden spoon. When cool shape into pies about 4 inches in diameter. Arrange the filling in layers — mutton, currants and sugar, salt and pepper. Cover with a round of thin pastry. Bake in a moderate oven (350 F., Mark 4) 20 to 30 minutes. Eat hot.

Mrs. R. MacGregor,
Maesteg, Glamorgan.

HWYADER HALLT FERWEDIG
WELSH SALT DUCKLING

This ancient dish is of the same family as the delicious *confits de canard* and *confits d'oie* of South West France, but it is boiled after salting and served with a hot onion sauce instead of being preserved in poultry fat.

Rub the duck or duckling with a handful of salt all over, and leave it for 24 hours. Rinse it next day and leave it to soak in fresh cold water for about 40 minutes. Put it in a pan with hot water to cover, adding some pepper or 12 peppercorns and if liked a few fresh sage leaves. No salt. Bring to the boil and simmer, gently bubbling, till tender in about 2 hours or longer. Some cooks tie it in a cloth to keep it together.

For the sauce, simmer 1 lb. peeled sliced onions in 1 pint of milk till tender, adding pepper but no salt. Melt 1 oz. butter in another pan. Stir in 2 tablespoons of flour and gradually stir in the strained hot milk from the onions, heating and stirring till the sauce is smooth and thick, add the cooked onions. Cut the duck in 4 portions in the kitchen with poultry or dressmaking scissors and serve it covered with the onion sauce.

Freshly made cold horse-radish sauce may be served as well, but in Wales a hot laver and orange sauce sometimes accompanies it as well as the onion one. For this about half a pint of laver bread should be heated with the juice and the grated rind of an orange in a covered pan over a low heat. The laver will stick if it is too fiercely heated. Use a silver fork or spoon, or a wooden spoon to stir it and an aluminium, not an iron saucepan.

FFOWLIN CYMREIG

This is a very good way of cooking an old boiling fowl which is popular in Wales.

Leave the bird whole, but peel and chop 8 ozs. carrots fairly small, dice 8 ozs. bacon and chop up 2 large well washed leeks with some

229

of the green part. Put the vegetables and bacon in a large fireproof dish with 1 oz. butter and cook them gently with a lid on the dish for a short time so as to soften rather than fry the vegetables. Stir in 1 oz. flour, let it colour lightly then stir in $\frac{1}{2}$ pint of stock. Add the chicken, a small washed and chopped cabbage, a bunch of mixed herbs, some salt and pepper. Put a few knobs of butter or dripping on top of the bird and cook it, closely covered for 2 to 3 hours in a moderate oven (350 F., Mark 4).

The old hen should be served on a bed of cooked cabbage and garnished with carrot. Pour the rich chicken stock over the cabbage.

Mr. Clive Gammon,
Daily Express.

VARIOUS

If I shut my eyes and say *"Mrs. Williams-by-the-post-office,"* I can see her now. It is, of course, the physical surroundings, the smell of half-dried seaweed in the porch, and the feel of lots of sand in the toes of old, frayed tennis shoes that I think of first. And then the glass cabinet full of thin Japanese teacups, dried grass and peacock's feathers, with the pot doll in the black hat labelled "A Present from Llanfairfechan". They were in the front parlour where we had tea in the Welsh village where I used to stay at the seaside when I was a child. It was a prim, ossified room in which nothing ever seems to have happened. Except the tea, of course.

Mrs. Williams must have been a good cook. It's all coming back to me, and it's not only that she had old-fashioned back laced corsets and a figure like an egg boiler, but a lot of old-fashioned sayings as well. "It isn't the hen that cackles the most that lays the biggest egg," she used to say, standing back and watching us munching seed cake or bread and butter. Or: "There's nothing certain in this life, as I cried when the turbot eloped with the cat." She would have "no nonsense" and her strength was in good plain cooking: fried eggs and potted meat. Most of the delicious dishes she produced had an appropriate saying to go with them: "In love and sausages," she would remark at dinner time, "only one thing is required — perfect confidence."

TREACLE TOFFEE PUDDING

There was her treacle toffee pudding which we used to have afterwards at home and that I make occasionally now. Put 4 ozs. of brown sugar and 8 ozs. of golden syrup together in a frying pan with 4 ozs. of butter. Stir it over a gentle heat until everything has melted, then bring it gently to the boil. Cut about three slices of bread from a sandwich loaf. Half an inch thick. Real doorsteps. Remove the crusts and cut the rest into 2-inch squares which soak in milk. Then fry them in the toffee-like mixture in the frying pan for about 5 minutes. Put them in a hot dish and pour the remaining toffee over them. If you have a sweet tooth this is delicious served with whipped cream.

Mrs. Williams used to slam it down on the table then stand back with her arms folded defiantly to see if we were enjoying it.

WELSH FISH CAKES

Then there were the Welsh fish cakes which we had hot for supper — or was it high tea? — with toast and watercress. You just plunge 3 nice Manx kippers in a jug of hot water, leave them for 2 or 3 minutes till soft. Then flake up the flesh without any of the skin or bones and mix it with 3 or 4 large mashed potatoes, a chopped hard-boiled egg, and 1 tablespoon of butter. No salt because of the kippers, but you can add a little cayenne pepper if you like. Grease a frying pan or bakestone and get it hot. Spread the mixture on it as though for a pancake. Fry it till brown underneath. Turn it over with two fish slices and brown the other side and serve it with grated cheese on top.

We used to have shrimp sandwiches in brown bread and butter. Another of her triumphs was a glass bowl of sponge fingers set in jelly and topped with raspberry jam. These are what are now known as boudoir biscuits in grocers' shops. The only thing was that *Mrs. Williams* always said they were funeral fingers. I had never known what she was talking about until recently when somebody told me these biscuits were often served with a glass of sherry to mourners in Wales in the nineteenth century. And that Welsh children often got a little bundle of them tied up with black tape to eat in the carriage on the long drive to the cemetery.

There was nothing lugubrious about her rich seed cake however, and if you make it according to my recipe I think you will find it delicious.

SEED CAKE

Sift 1 lb. of flour and see that it's very dry. Crush and sift 1 lb. of lump sugar, cream 1 lb. of butter and then beat the sugar into it. Whip the whites of 8 eggs until they are so stiff you can turn the basin upside down without them falling out. Fold them into the creamed butter and sugar, then add the 8 egg yolks well beaten. Stir in 2 ozs. of caraway seeds, 1 teaspoon powdered cinnamon, 1 grated nutmeg. Stir well and add the flour lightly. Put it into a buttered cake tin and bake for 2 hours in a quick oven (375 F., Mark 5) and let it stand for 2 hours when you have taken it out. I do hope you enjoy it.

"A rolling stone gathers no moss, but look at the excitement it has," she used to say sadly when I jumped up and ran off to the beach without waiting for pudding.

CAERPHILLY CHEESE

Caerphilly Cheese is a fresh skimmed milk cheese only ten days old and lightly pressed. It takes its name from the Glamorganshire village of that name, and was once very popular with Welsh miners for taking down the pits. It is now mostly made in Somerset.

BAKED PARSNIP AND CHEESE

Fill a pie dish with alternate layers of cooked, sliced parsnips, grated cheese and breadcrumbs. Cover with a tomato sauce. Top with a thick layer of breadcrumbs mixed with grated cheese. Pour a little melted fat over the top and bake for about 15 minutes.

Miss Audrey Maxfield,
Cardiff, Glamorgan.

WELSH RABBIT — CAWS TOAST

Grate 6 ozs. Cheddar into a pan, stir it till it melts, gradually stirring in 2 tablespoons of ale and a teaspoon of mustard. Heat gently, stirring till smooth and thick. Add pepper. Pour over hot buttered toast. Brown the top under the grill and serve at once.

Miss Megan Thomas,
Rhyl, Flintshire.

TOASTED CHEESE — CAWS CYMRU

Have some slabs of cheese toasted before an open fire with a toasting fork, spread them on buttered toast, smear with freshly mixed mustard and sprinkle with a little cayenne pepper. Eat at once, really hot.

Mrs. Mair Edwards,
Conway, Caernarvonshire.

REAL WELSH RABBIT

Slice 4 large onions thinly, put them on a large plate with salt, pepper, a lump of butter and 2 tablespoons of water. Put it into a hot oven (400 F., Mark 6) and cover. When half cooked place 2 slices of bacon on top, then 8 ozs. grated cheese, make the cheese into a hollow. Break an egg in the hollow, bake for 10 minutes. Very tasty.

Mrs. W. H. Jones,
Wrexham, Denbighshire.

Andrewe Boorde, a man of witty and cheerful disposition who wrote the first English book of diet and health cooking (*Compendyous*

Regyment or A Dyetary of Health, published in 1562), had an amusing story about how heaven was once full of Welshmen all talking and shouting at once, so that Saint Peter wanted to get rid of them. Saint Peter went outside the gates and began shouting "Roasted Cheese! Roasted Cheese!". The Welshmen, believing they were being offered some Welsh Rabbit, all rushed outside, whereupon Saint Peter slammed the gates shut. That's why, he wrote, there are no Welshmen in heaven.

TATWS pym mynud (Five minute potatoes)

Peel a few potatoes, cut them in slices, put them in a frying pan. Add 1 sliced onion and put a slice or two of bacon on top. Sprinkle with flour and water, salt and pepper and put it on the stove to cook until the potatoes are soft.

Miss Myfi Jones,
Daily Express.

POTATO PANCAKES OR LUTKAS

Potato pancakes to be eaten with meat or fish are prepared as follows: Grate 1 lb. large peeled potatoes into a bowl, allow the bowl to rest in a slanting position for a few minutes then spoon and drain out most of the liquid which is mainly starch. Add to the potatoes grated onion, pepper and salt and mix to a nice consistency with 1 tablespoon flour and fry in a tablespoon of oil, corn oil is preferable. Heat the oil and drop a spoonful of the potato mixture into the frying pan. Brown and turn. Drain on absorbent paper. They must be eaten very hot. No eggs are required, in fact they spoil the pancakes. These pancakes are a very popular German, Russian, Polish and Jewish dish and are truly delicious eaten hot.

Mrs. K. Levinson,
Riverside, Cardiff, Glamorgan.

You can buy ready-made Lutkas powder in most delicatessen shops. Expert opinion is divided on whether or not you should add an egg. Some Jewish cooks say it improves potato pancakes.

SALAD DRESSING

When preparing a green salad I like to make the following salad cream, which has a delicious flavour.

Put 1 small teaspoon of mustard into a small cup, mix with 1 teaspoon of vinegar, then add 2 teaspoons of cream. Pour over the salad.

Mrs. A. Rees,
Porthcawl, Glamorgan.

PUDDING

SIR WATKIN WILLIAMS-WYNN'S PUDDING

Surely, I said to myself, very few people in this country have actually got an ancestral pudding. Family crest, yes. Ancestral seats, sometimes. Pudding, no. *Sir Watkin Williams-Wynn* agreed with me. "I have never heard of another family pudding in the whole country," he said. They have one. They also have a family pack of foxhounds. The Watkin Williams-Wynn Hunt has been famous on the Welsh border for generations. The Watkin Williams-Wynn name is all over the place in North Wales and every second pub seems to be the Wynnstay Arms after the family home in Ruabon, now a school. The present *Sir Watkin* is Lord Lieutenant of Denbigh and has been a Master of Hounds since 1946.

The family pudding is still served regularly with hot jam sauce at his table and at that of the dowager *Lady Watkin Williams-Wynn* who is 95. "Guessing, I'd say that our patent pudding dates from the late seventeen hundreds," he told me. "Probably from the time of the Jacobite Sir Watkin who was killed out hunting in 1749." A very tough administrator, he once had a man imprisoned in his dog kennel. His death was seen as an act of Divine Providence by Welsh malefactors. The pudding, however, is still known and well liked on the Welsh border. "I daresay if you went into one of the local pubs they would make it for you," *Sir Watkin* said.

The Watkin Williams-Wynn family pudding is unique in being made, not with suet, but with marrow — that delicious beef marrow from the shin bones which you can still get for about 5p from any good butcher. Baked marrow bones with hot toast and a glass of brandy were considered a delicacy in Georgian England and are still served hot in a napkin at City dinners and a few old-fashioned public houses.

For the pudding, mix 4 ozs. of finely chopped or grated beef marrow, 4 ozs. of sugar, 4 ozs. of soft white breadcrumbs, the strained juice and finely grated rind of a lemon. Beat up the yolks of 2 eggs and stir them into the mixture then add the two egg whites so stiffly whipped that the basin may be turned upside down without them falling out. Tip the whole thing into a well buttered pudding basin to come about three-quarters of the way up. Cover the top closely with well buttered kitchen foil or buttered greaseproof paper. Place the basin in a pan of boiling water to come half-way up it and boil for about 2 hours, filling up the pan when necessary with boiling water.

Turn the pudding out on a hot dish and bring it to table with a pot of hot raspberry jam poured over the top.

Sir Watkin Williams-Wynn is as fond of a piece of Cheshire cheese with a boiled apple pudding as I am. Blue Cheshire, for

preference, only you can hardly ever get it now. And, of course, a good hot apple pudding with a jug of warm cream or a piece of crumbly farmhouse Cheshire cheese, or both, is a dish for epicures.

RHUBARB BETTY

Wipe 1 pint of rhubarb and cut into very small pieces, melt 2 ozs. of butter and mix it with 5 ozs. of breadcrumbs. Add 2 ozs. desiccated coconut to the grated rind and juice of one lemon and one orange and mix well. Place about one third of the breadcrumbs into a buttered dish, add half the rhubarb, sprinkle with $3\frac{1}{2}$ ozs. sugar. Then add half the coconut mixture, repeat this again. Cover the last of the breadcrumbs with a buttered piece of paper. Cook in a moderate oven (350 F., Mark 4) until the rhubarb is soft. Before serving, decorate the top with a few pieces of cooked rhubarb.

Mrs. Davies,
Llandeilo, Carmarthenshire.

BAKED SUNDAY PUDDING

This recipe is one of my mother's who was born in 1848. Mix 1 cup of flour, 1 cup of breadcrumbs, 1 cup of sugar, 1 cup of suet, 1 cup of dried fruit, 1 cup of grated carrot and 1 cup of mashed potato together. Dissolve 1 teaspoon of bicarbonate of soda in 2 table-spoons of hot milk and add this together with 4 eggs to the mixture. Bake in a moderate oven (350 F., Mark 4).

We had this pudding every Sunday until 1934 (less the potatoes and carrots) hence the name now.

Mrs. N. H. Cox,
Caerphilly, Glamorgan.

PEAR PUFF

What I remember as a little girl was delicious, and as I realised when I had a family, was also economical.

Peel, core and halve 1 lb. of pears, lay them in a saucepan with 1 tablespoon of brown sugar or golden syrup and a little nutmeg. Just cover with water, bring to the boil, then turn the heat down just to a simmer. Make a dough with 2 ozs. flour, 1 oz. suet and a pinch of salt and about 2 tablespoons of water. With floured hands shape it to the size of the saucepan, pop it straight on top of the simmering pears and cook, simmering for 30 minutes.

Serve hot, on its own, or with cream or custard. It really is delicious. My grown up family and also my small grandchildren enjoy it.

Mrs. Elizabeth Mary Carpenter,
Newport, Monmouthshire.

BAKING

BARA BRITH

Mix 1½ lbs. of self raising flour, 1 teaspoon spice, 8 ozs. sugar. Then rub in 4 ozs. butter and 8 ozs. lard, then add 8 ozs. currants, 8 ozs. sultanas, 8 ozs. stoned raisins, 2 ozs. mixed peel: 2 eggs and 1 pint of milk. Mix well. Pour into a well buttered loaf tin and bake in a moderate oven (350 F., Mark 4) for 2 hours.

Mrs. Davies,
Llandeilo, Carmarthenshire.

Bara Brith or "Speckled Bread", somewhat similar to the Selkirk Bannock of Scotland, is traditionally made for New Year's Eve. In Wales and the Border Counties to ensure luck during the coming year a dark haired man should go out of the back door before midnight and return in the first few minutes of the New Year, coming in through the front door and carrying a piece of coal in his pocket "to let the New Year in". This custom is known in some places as "first footing" and the "first footer" is given a piece of Bara Brith.

TEISEN LAP

Traditionally the cake was beaten in a bowl on the cook's lap and cooked on a bakestone or a heavy frying pan. Nowadays a shallow well greased tin in a moderate oven will do.

Mix 1 lb. flour with ½ teaspoon mixed spice, 1 teaspoon baking powder, a pinch of salt. Rub in 4 ozs. butter. Add 4 ozs. sugar, 4 ozs. dried fruit, mix it with 2 well beaten eggs and gradually beat in ½ pint milk with a wooden spoon, beating until the batter just drops from the spoon. Use sour milk if preferred. Put it in a well greased tin, bake in a moderate oven (350 F., Mark 4) for 35–40 minutes.

Mrs. S. P. Barrett,
Cardiff, Glamorgan.

BARA CEIRCH (Oatmeal Bread)

All my childhood holidays were spent in Pembrokeshire. My sisters and I tended to make our way towards a certain farm in the evening in the hope that the lady of the house would be cooking one of our favourites — a simple mixture of peas and broad beans — but they were being cooked in a hanging pot over a large open fire!

Oatmeal bread, which can be eaten hot and spread with butter, also brings back the old kitchen and old friends very clearly and pleasantly.

Rub 1 tablespoon of lard into 1 medium breakfast cup of flour and 1 cup of medium oatmeal. Add ½ cup of brown sugar, ½ teaspoon salt, a good pinch of nutmeg and ground cinnamon and ½ teaspoon bicarbonate of soda. Mix it all to a stiff dough with a little water and

236

roll it out on a board sprinkled with oatmeal. Stamp it into rounds and bake them on a greased tin in a good oven (375 F., Mark 5) until brown. These cookies can be sandwiched together before cooking with a little paste made by standing stoned dates in a very little water for 10 minutes and allowing it to cool. Sugar and spices may be omitted if the hot cakes are to be eaten spread with butter.

Miss Myfi Jones,
Daily Express.

WELSH MACAROONS

Line some patty tins with a short crust pastry. Put a teaspoon of jam or marmalade into each. Mix together 4 ozs. butter, 4 ozs. sugar and then add 2 eggs. Fold in 5 ozs. self raising flour. Place a generous heaped teaspoon of this mixture on top of the jam in the patty tins. Sprinkle with sugar and bake for 30 minutes in a preheated medium oven (350 F., Mark 4). **Mrs. Vera Griffiths,**
Llanelli, Carmarthenshire.

ABERFRAW CAKES OR WELSH SHORTBREAD

This is a small fishing village in Anglesey along an estuary which used to be full of scallops and the local cooks used the scallop shells as moulds or patty pans for baking little cakes — a sort of Welsh shortbread. Mix 6 ozs. of flour and 2 ozs. of sugar. Rub in 4 ozs. of butter, add no liquid. Flatten the pastry and pat it into the well buttered scallop shells and bake the cakes in a moderate oven (350 F., Mark 4) until lightly brown.

BAKESTONES

The bakestone is a round piece of iron about an inch thick and similar to the griddle or girdle, it is traditional to the cooking of all the Celtic peoples whether Welsh, Breton, Scots or Irish.

In Scotland they use it to make bannocks and drop scones and so on, and in Ireland amongst other things for making soda bread. In Brittany a very similar large iron plate heated over an open fire (or more usually nowadays over a gas or electric heater) is used for making the big buckwheat pancakes which are a feature of their cooking. The name for them in the Breton language is very similar to the Welsh name for pancakes — *crempogs*.

When Alfred the Great, King of Wessex (871-901) took refuge in the legendary peasant's hut near Athelnay, he was asked to watch some cakes cooking on hot stones before the fire, absent-mindedly let them burn and had his face slapped for it by the angry housewife. The cakes must have been cooking on an early type of bakestone, and may well have been some kind of Welsh light cake.

SLAPAN SIR FON (Anglesey Cakes)

Rub 1 tablespoon of butter into 8 ozs. self raising flour with 1 table-spoon of sugar. Add a handful of cleaned currants and make it into a thick batter with a little milk in which is dissolved a pinch of bicarbonate of soda. Lightly grease a thick frying pan or girdle iron and make it hot on the stove. Cook the mixture in spoonfuls turning them when brown on the underside. Split open and butter.

Miss Myfi Jones,
Daily Express.

BLACKBERRY BAKESTONE TART

You can make it with rhubarb, gooseberries or apples in winter, when the blackberries are not in season.

Roll out 8 ozs. short crust pastry into a circle and cover half of it with what fruit you think. Then fold your pastry over it and seal the edges. Lift it onto a warmed greased bakestone with a wooden pastry slice. Cook it on one side then turn it over and cook it until the fruit is soft. Take it off the bakestone then lift the top off your pastry so you can sprinkle the fruit well with bits of butter and some brown sugar.

Miss R. Roberts,
Brecon.

INDEX TO RECIPES

PIES

POULTRY

PRESERVES

PUDDING

SOUP

VARIOUS

Space for your own
Family Favourites